# 世博会——国际经验与运作

## World's Fairs——International Experience and Operation

谢工曲　杨豪中　吴采薇　编著

中国建筑工业出版社

图书在版编目（CIP）数据

世博会——国际经验与运作/谢工曲等编著. —北京：
中国建筑工业出版社，2008
ISBN 978-7-112-10151-1

Ⅰ. 世… Ⅱ. 谢… Ⅲ. 博览会-经验-世界-汉、英
Ⅳ. G245

中国版本图书馆 CIP 数据核字（2008）第 079890 号

世界博览会是一项由主办国政府组织或政府委托有关部门或地区举办的有较大影响和历史意义的国际活动。它分为综合性博览会和专业性博览会两大类。专业性博览会又分为 A1、A2、B1、B2 四个级别。本书以博览会的主题构思和设计策划为主线，内容涉及博览会的规划设计、宣传策划、经营运作、场馆改造利用等诸多方面。全书以阐释案例的形式展现历届世博会的魅力和创新成果，它将对北京奥运会、上海世博会以及正在中国蓬勃发展的会展业有相当的借鉴作用。

本书图文并茂，中英文对照，它不仅可以作为广大会展设计与管理、建筑学与城市规划专业师生员工的良师益友，而且也为大型会展活动的翻译人员提供生动的语言素材。本书还可作为普及公众会展知识、提高公众对会展精神需求和鉴赏能力的学习指南。

* * *

责任编辑：吴宇江
责任设计：董建平
责任校对：兰曼利 陈晶晶

世博会——国际经验与运作
World's Fairs——International Experience and Operation
谢工曲 杨豪中 吴采薇 编著

*

中国建筑工业出版社出版、发行（北京西郊百万庄）
各地新华书店、建筑书店经销
北京嘉泰利德公司制版
北京市密东印刷有限公司印刷

*

开本：787×1092 毫米 1/16 印张：12½ 字数：312 千字
2008 年 12 月第一版 2008 年 12 月第一次印刷
定价：32.00 元
ISBN 978-7-112-10151-1
(16954)

自然瑰宝，文化遗产，民俗风情，物质资源，学术交流，信息互通，良好媒体

---

注释：中国风景园林学会原副理事长、北京林业大学教授孙筱祥先生为《世博会——国际经验与运作》一书题词：“自然瑰宝，文化遗产，民俗风情，物质资源，学术交流，信息互通，良好媒体。”

# 目录/Contents

# 第一章
# 国际博览会的历史背景

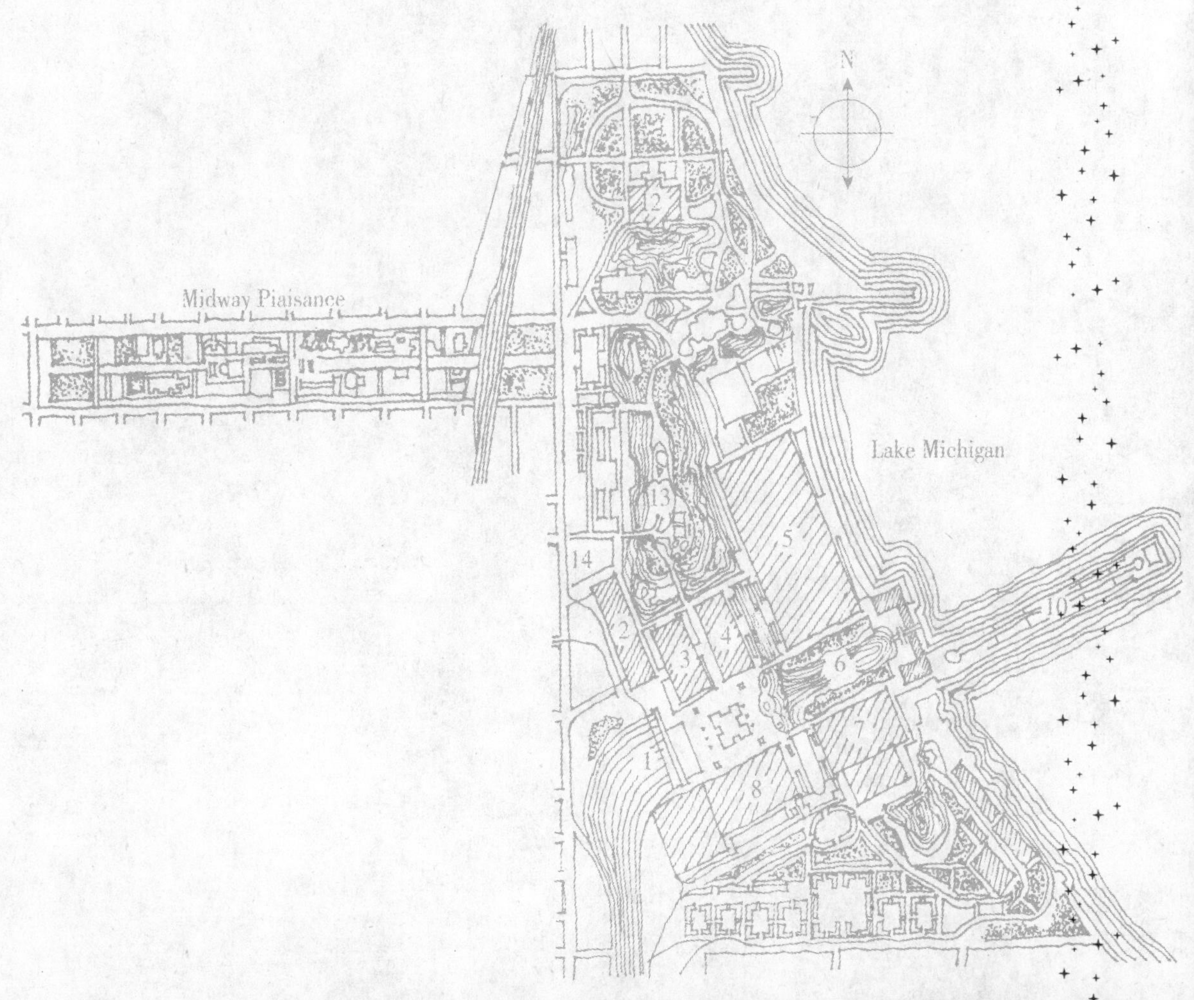

博览会的传统可以追溯到早期位于主要交通干道交会处的城市中定期举办的大型集市，大批人流涌向这些集市，有些人甚至长途跋涉，来这里从事各种商品交易。这些集市为人们表达与评价思想理念，展示与比较技艺技巧提供了平台。

这样的集会在来自不同国家，甚至是文化背景相互冲突的人们之间建立起一种相互理解、高度互利的氛围和伙伴关系，买家与卖家从中世纪的欧洲各地汇集里昂、法兰克福、莱比锡等集贸城市，这种早期的商品交易为今天的国际博览会铺平了道路。

全国性的博览会并不是英国人的发明，而是法国人的创举，早在 1798 年法国就举办了第一届全国性的工业产品博览会，并且从 19 世纪开始每五年举办一次这样的博览会。

然而，第一届现代意义上的万国博览会却是 1851 年在伦敦举办的，并且取得了巨大成功。巴黎紧随其后，分别在 1855 年、1867 年、1878 年、1889 年和 1900 年举办了辉煌灿烂的世界博览会。很快，其他大城市也都渴望举办世博会，维也纳、阿姆斯特丹、布鲁塞尔、巴塞罗那、圣路易斯、都灵和费城等城市都成功地举办了世博会。

美国也效仿伦敦，举办了自己的世博会。伦敦水晶宫世博会属于政府行为，欧洲其他城市随后举办的世博会也是如此，虽然，1853 年纽约世博会仿照 1851 年伦敦世博会的模式运作，但是在美国开创了非政府筹办世博会的模式。因此，美国举办的世博会都是由民间发起、政府任命的委员会负责筹办的。

自从 1851 年水晶宫博览会以后，西方国家纷纷效仿，举办自己的世博会，随着每一届世博会都试图超越前者，各种展示本国工业与艺术成就的创意和尝试层出不穷。然而，众多的世博会不可避免地造成多种利益之间的冲突，其主要表现通常是组织运作混乱，这种混乱状况给参展国政府带来严重问题，因此有必要建立规章制度，避免世博会过多过滥，为参展国家提供必要保障。显然，解决问题的办法是将各种利益集团召集在一起，充分表达他们的意见，为解决共同面临的问题而努力，有必要达成一项国际协议，巴黎自 1907 年以来一直在为形成这样的协议而呼吁。

1912 年，德国政府首先发起倡议，号召有关国家共同为达成一个国际协议而努力。各国政府迅速响应，表达了他们希望建立规范，改善举办方与参与方、举办国与参与国官方参展和企业参展之间关系的愿望。

正是这次柏林外交大会为形成国际展览公约奠定了基础。然而，由于 1914 年爆发的第一次世界大战，这次国际会议形成的决议未能正式生效。

直到 1928 年 11 月 22 日，在巴黎举行的另一次国际会议上，来自 31 个国家的代表签署了第一个国际公约，以建设性的方式规范了国际博览会的组织运作。

1928 年的国际展览公约规定了举办世博会的频率、参展国与举办国的权利和义务，规范了世博会的次序。1939 年，为了确保国际公约各条款的实施，国际展览局（BIE）成立。此后，该公约分别在 1948 年、1966 年和 1972 年经过 3 次修订。

根据国际展览局的规定，世博会分为两类：注册类（或综合类）世博会，主题广博，每五年举办一次，持续时间 6 个月（例如：汉诺威世博会 2000. 6. 1 ~ 10. 31——人类—自然一技术)；认可类（或专业类）世博会，主题专业性强，在两次综合类世博会之间举办，时间不超过3个月（例如：德国罗斯托克2003.4.25～10.12——海滨绿色世博会)。

自从1851年第一届世博会以来，世博会鼓舞激励了世界各国人民，使世界各地的人们可以跨越日常生活经历，探索外部世界——异域文化、科学进步和新发明。时代在变，世博会也在变，为了适应新形势，世博会不仅要继续反映时代的商业需求，而且要反映人们的理想、希望和抱负，为他们提供信息，带来思想启迪。

世博会与奥运会和联合国有许多相似之处，但是，世博会的独特之处在于让普通人，而不仅仅是运动员和政客，亲身经历体验世博会，任何人可以进入会场，感受新事物，成为国际社会的一部分，亲眼见证人类在这个世界上发挥的巨大潜力。

# Chapter 1

# Historical Background of International Exhibition

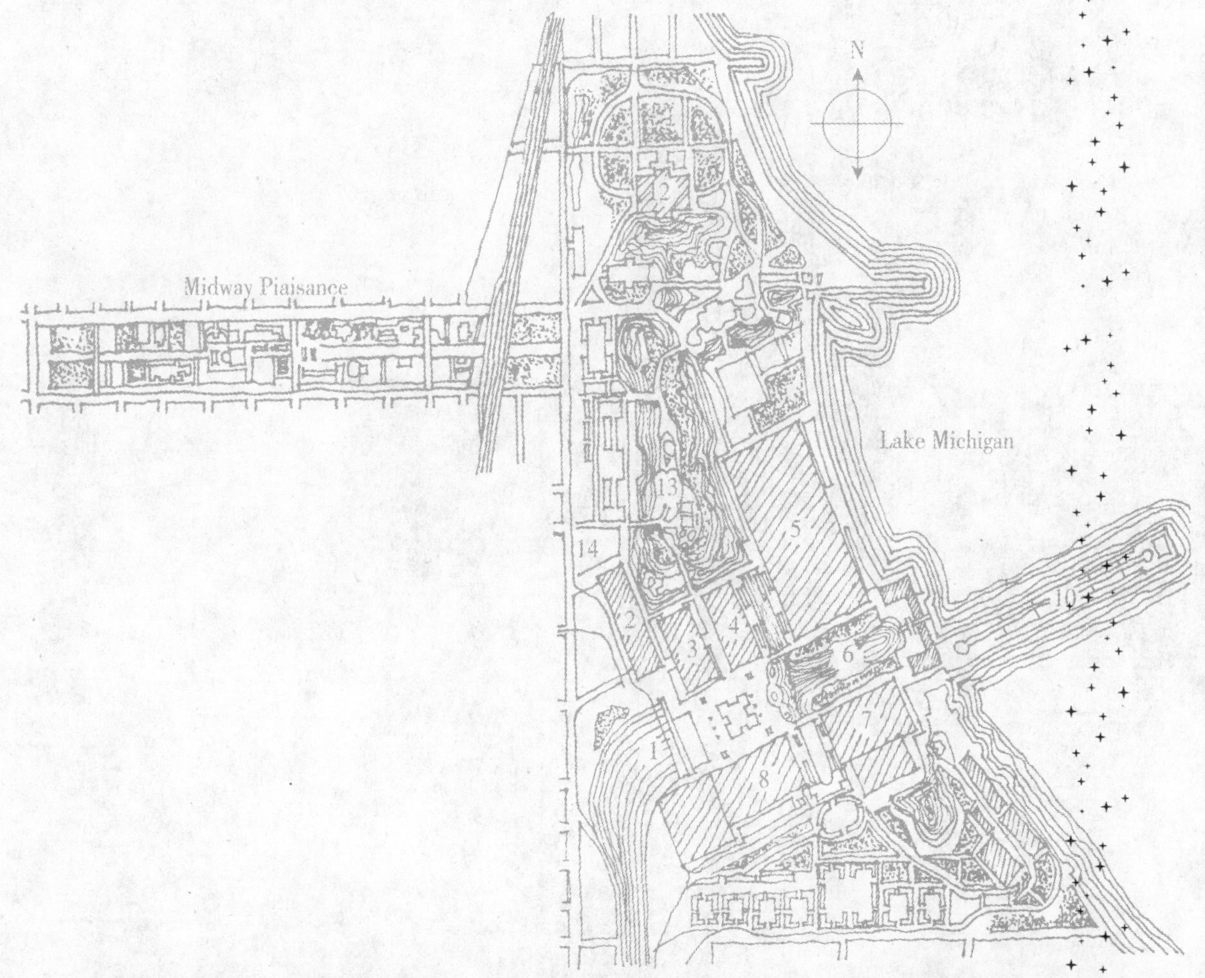

The tradition of exhibition can date back to the times when large-scale markets were regularly held in cities located at major route intersections. Crowds of people, some of whom had traveled great distances, would visit these markets, stay at the site and exchange a wide variety of articles. These events thus provided a forum for expressing and evaluating ideas and for demonstrating and comparing skills.

Through these gatherings, a highly beneficial atmosphere of mutual understanding and fellowship developed between people of different nations and often of conflicting cultures. Buyers and sellers would flock to the cities of Lyons, Frankfurt and Leipzig in particular from all over medieval Europe. The commercial transactions of long ago thus paved the way for the international exhibitions of today.

The idea of a national exhibition did not originate with the British, but with French, who had organized the first exhibition of national products as early as 1798 and had held an exhibition every five years since the beginning of the century.

However, the first universal and international exhibition in the modern sense took place in 1851 in London, which was an overwhelming success. Paris took over and organized brilliant exhibitions in 1855, 1867, 1878, 1889 and 1900. Soon other large centers were also eager to hold world fairs, and among the most successful international exhibitions were those held in Vienna, Amsterdam, Brussels, Barcelona, St. Louis, Turin and Philadelphia.

The United States was quick to follow London with its own fair. While London's Crystal Palace had been a government venture, as were most subsequent European fairs, the New York Fair in 1853 was modeled after the 1851 London Fair, but established a non-government approach to fair planning in the United States. Therefore, fairs in the United States are produced by private, government-appointed commissions.

Since the 1851 Crystal Palace Exhibition in London, western nations tried to emulate the accomplishment with fairs of their own. As each successive fair strove to outdo its predecessors, the western world was inundated with creative attempts at exhibiting industrial and artistic progress in each nation. However, these events inevitably gave rise to numerous conflicts of interest and were often characterized by very poor organization. This state of confusion caused the participating governments serious problems and, as a result they felt the need to establish regulations to prevent the proliferation of exhibitions and provide participants with certain guarantees. It became apparent that the various parties had to be brought together and their differences aired in an attempt to solve common problems. An international agreement seemed necessary. Paris had been calling for one since 1907.

In 1912 the German government took the initiative and called interested governments together in order to work out the basis for an agreement. The governments were quick to respond and they expressed the desire to establish regulations to improve relations between organizers and participants and between inviting governments and official or private exhibitors.

It was the Berlin Diplomatic Conference that established the basis for an international convention governing international exhibitions. However, the diplomatic decision that resulted could not be ratified because of the War of 1914.

It was not until November 22, 1928, at another conference in Paris, that delegates of thirty-one countries signed the first convention governing, in a constructive manner, the organization of international exhibitions.

The International Convention of 1928 brought order to the world exhibitions' situation by regulating their frequency and outlining the rights and obligations of the exhibitors and organizers. In 1939, the International Exhibitions Bureau (Bureau International des Exhibitions——BIE) was created in order to ensure compliance with the provisions of the Convention. Thereafter the Convention went through three revisions in 1948, 1966 and 1972 respectively.

As regulated and defined, international exhibitions are divided into two categories: the registered/universal exhibitions, having a theme of a general nature, subject to a five-year separation, last up to six months (for example, Hanover 2000. 6. 1—10. 31——Humankind, Nature, Technology); the recognized / specialized exhibitions with a specialized theme occur in the intervening years between these large events, and have a duration not exceeding three months (for example, Rostock, Germany, 2003. 4. 25—10. 12——The Green Exposition by the Seaside).

Ever since the first world fair in 1851, world expositions have excited and inspired millions of people around the world. They allow people to explore the world outside of their everyday experience——outside cultures, new scientific advancements, and new inventions. As times change, world expositions have changed to fit those times. They continue to reflect both the commercial needs of their times while presenting the ideals, hopes and aspirations of people, and providing information and inspiration.

Related to both the Olympics and the United Nations in many ways, world's fairs are unique in that an ordinary person can experience them firsthand, not just athletes or politicians. Anyone can enter the expo site and feel a part of something new, be a part of the world community, and witness what potential human beings have achieved in this world.

# 第二章

# 1851 年伦敦万国工业产品大博览会

冠名为“万国工业产品大博览会”的 1851 年世博会于 5 月 1 日至 10 月 15 日在伦敦海德公园的水晶宫举行，这是第一届国际工业产品博览会，对社会发展的许多方面都产生了重要影响，包括艺术和设计教育、国际贸易和国际关系，甚至促进了旅游。这届博览会也为以后百年来的众多国际博览会开创了先例。

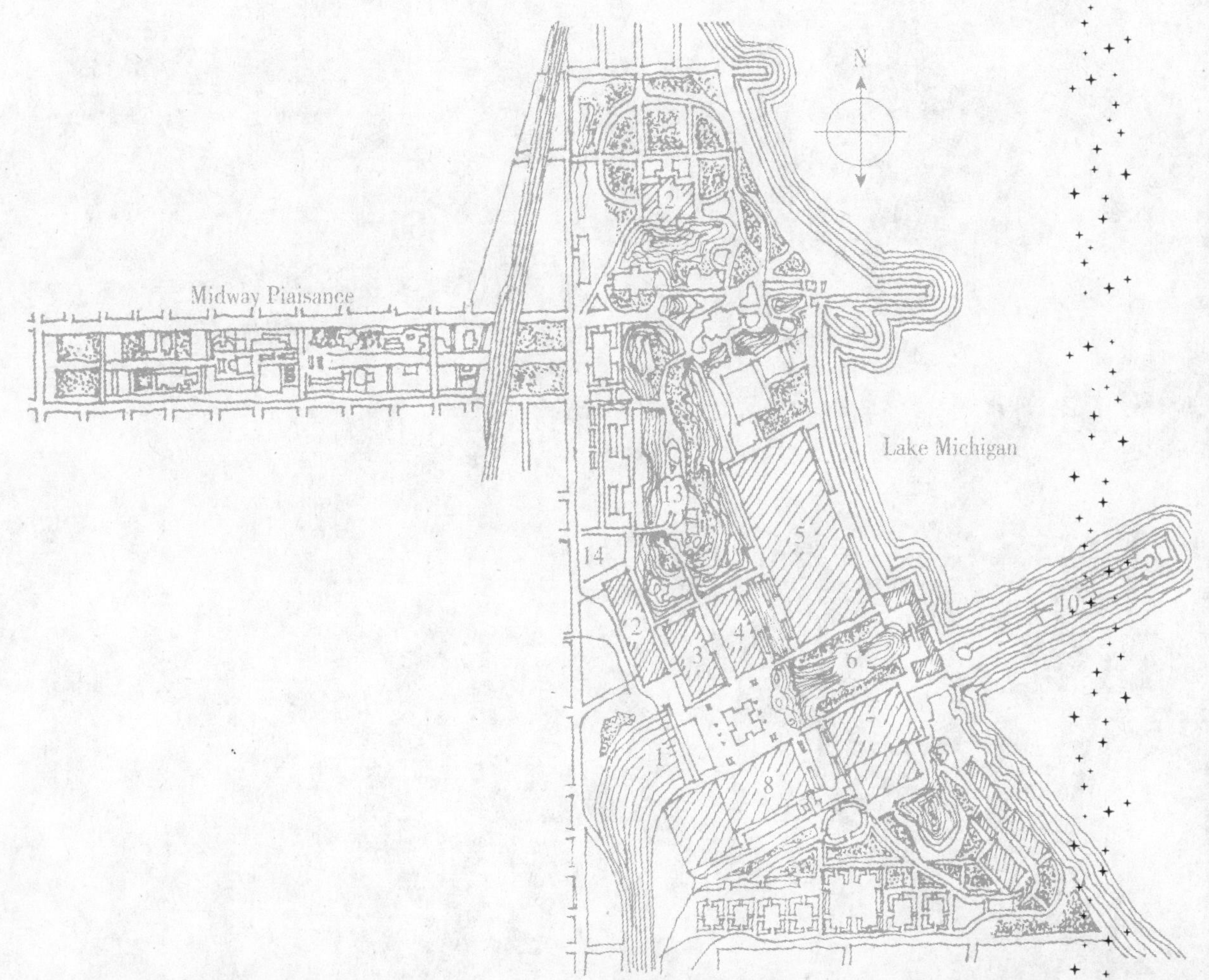

## 国际博览会理念的形成

1844 年法国工业博览会的成功对 1851 年万国博览会的诞生产生了直接影响。半个世纪以来，法国人已经建立了一个展览传统，完全致力于展示法国艺术与工业的成就，这些展览使法国工业受益匪浅。然而在英国，艺术与工业品展览只不过是地区性的活动，第一座完全用于工业产品展览的建筑于 1849 年在伯明翰建成。

万国博览会的发起组织是由英国一个权威机构召集组建的，它就是今天的皇家艺术协会。这个协会成立于 1754 年，一些贵族绅士、宗教和商界人士在一家咖啡馆里成立了这个“以促进艺术与工业产品和贸易发展为宗旨”的协会，其目标是奖励可能为英国带来巨大利益的发明创造和工业产品。艺术协会在鼓励艺术与工业进步方面取得的成功促使其他独立的艺术和专业组织成立。随之，艺术协会发现其作用已被后来成立的皇家艺术学会所取代，不得不调整方向，另谋生路。渐渐地，举办讲座传播新技术、出版专业杂志、举办工业成果展览成为艺术协会的工作重点，其重要性超过了奖励发明创造。艺术协会于 1848 年和 1849 年举办的展览越来越成功，因此，协会满怀信心地宣布要在 1851 年举办一个全国性的展览。

虽然，艺术协会提出举办全国性的工业产品展览对英国工业大有好处，但英国政府对这个建议毫无兴趣，公众漠不关心，制造商也无动于衷，一些名人甚至对这个建议充满了敌意，只有艾伯特亲王对此饶有兴致。

艾伯特亲王是维多利亚女王的德国丈夫，他作为君主之夫的角色并不轻松，尽管在幕后起着重要作用，但在很大程度上仍被排斥于君主的职权之外。艾伯特亲王一直公开倡导工业和科学进步，非常支持举办一个独自融资的万国博览会，他说这样的博览会“是对全人类所取得成就的一个真实检验，也是所有国家今后努力的新起点”。艾伯特计划在伦敦举办一个艺术与工业产品大博览会，并且要超越以往任何一届博览会。过去的博览会场地拥挤，对公众的吸引力很有限，而且缺乏国际影响力。

第一次博览会筹备会议于 1849 年 6 月 30 日在白金汉宫举行，博览会面临的大多数难题都得到了实质性的“落实”。博览会展品分为四个大类：原材料、机械与发明创造、工业制品、雕刻与雕塑艺术。会议就博览会的举办场地进行了讨论，艾伯特亲王建议在海德公园南部的空地建造展览场馆。艺术协会委派了一个特使团到全国各地争取支持。

会议还决定这届博览会不局限于英国工业界，“让英国工业与外国工业进行公平竞争对英国工业很有好处”；提供大额奖金鼓励制造商开发提升产品，此举虽然不会立即获利，但是会带来长远的好处。奖励采取“奖牌加奖金的形式，要以高额的奖金消除即便是最大最富有的制造商的顾虑和偏见，确保他们在该领域的最大投入”。一等奖奖金 5000 英镑。

实施这些计划的最好方式是成立皇家委员会，艾伯特亲王任主席，负责决定博览会的性质、实施方案和颁发奖牌奖金。艺术协会负责筹集颁奖和展馆建设所需的资金。

艾伯特亲王一直认为政府应当参与这个博览会，他写道，全国性乃至国际性的大型博览会“极具重要性，应该在政府的协作和指导下进行”。因此，政府接受了这个建议，成立了以艾伯特亲王为首的皇家委员会。与此同时，艾伯特亲王一直在与外国政府联系，宣传他的国际工业博览会计划。

## 寻找一座合适的建筑

博览会的运作大约需要5万英镑建设展馆，2万英镑颁发奖金，艺术协会无力支付这笔费用，英国财政部也无意拨款。但是，艺术协会的项目融资还在进行，包括寻找建筑承包商建造展馆，条件是承包商预先垫付2万英镑的奖金和筹备工作所需的其他费用，例如，代理、广告和印刷等费用，所有这些费用由博览会门票收入偿还。根据双方的约定，艺术协会将获得1/3的剩余利润，作为未来举办展览的资金，承包商将获得利润余额的2/3。承包商愿意出资7.5万英镑投资一个前所未有的项目，这种冒险精神使艺术协会得以继续实施这个项目。

然而，皇家委员会1850年1月召开第一次会议时，委员们就意识到如此规模的博览会盈利丰厚，他们的第一个反应就是撤销与承包商签订的合同，开展全国性的募捐。皇家委员会的首要任务是募集资金，返还承包商垫付的资金，然后征集设计方案，开工建设，并且向国内外招展。

为了争取广泛支持，全国的市长应邀到伦敦市长官邸聆听艾伯特亲王论证博览会的意义，其他重要人物也到场支持，会议取得了巨大成功，这个以募捐的方式融资，由皇家委员会管理运作的博览会方案得到了热烈响应，工商界巨头大力支持，他们知道国际博览会对英国这样一个在保护主义盛行的欧洲倡导自由贸易的国家十分重要。融资总额达到23万英镑，博览会的规模也已确定——要超过法国人举办的所有博览会。政府也同意将博览会作为保税仓库对待，这样参加博览会的进口货物可以免征进口税。

由于建造博览会展馆成为亟待解决的问题，世博会建筑委员会成立。1850年3月13日，建筑委员会举办了一个国际竞赛，征集展馆总体布局方案，并且提供了现场平面图，标示出需要保留的林木。建筑委员会制定了一整套设计规范和要求：采用单层建筑形式，顶部采光，采用防火材料建造；占地面积不得超过90万平方英尺（约8.36万$m^2$），最大限度地创造70万平方英尺（约6.5万$m^2$）的室内空间；参赛方案要求提交一张比例尺为1:1000的设计图，一张设计说明书。

显然，建筑委员会的意图是征集相关信息和建议，包括建筑造型、功能布局、出入方式以及展馆室内布置和设施等。建筑委员会认为他们不会局限于选择任何一个参赛方案，但是会从众多征集的方案中汲取有益的构思。

设计竞赛征集到大约 233 个方案，其中，38 个来自国外，51 个来自英格兰其他地区，128 个来自伦敦。然而，根据建筑委员会的报告，没有一个方案符合要求，虽然许多方案很有参考价值，“有的方案提供了应当避免的教训，有的方案提供了大量信息，因为这些方案预测到许多基本需求，而且在不同程度上提供了巧妙的解决方案”。

此时，建筑委员会面临着建造临时展馆的难题，从经济方面考虑，展馆要能重复利用，建造时间要短（已剩下不到 12 个月的时间），不仅要造价便宜，而且便于产品展示和游客流通。为了方便监管和灵活布置，展馆必须采用单一空间的形式，放射形布局不能满足要求，并列式布置展台又会使空间显得单调，缺少变化和美丽壮观的视觉效果。但是，若采用典型的建筑布局，形式太庄重，空间分隔过多，造价高昂。

建筑委员会只能自己综合一个设计方案，尽管这个方案遭到了参赛建筑师和公众的批评，认为这是一个造型丑陋且造价不菲的方案，建筑委员会继续为其设计方案招标，结果投标的报价比建筑委员会预计的还要高。

这时，承包商 Fox and Henderson 提交了一个修改方案的工程报价，这个方案改动很大，与建筑委员会原来的设计方案大相径庭，但是具有绝对的价格优势。这个方案来自于园艺师约瑟夫·帕克斯顿（Joseph Paxton）的设计，帕克斯顿突发奇想，构思了一个不断重复某个结构片段的方案，通过反复地复制这个立面，构成一个完整的建筑实体。帕克斯顿将自己的原创性设计绘制在一张图纸上，并在九天内赶制了一整套详细的设计图，于 1850 年 6 月 22 日提交给承包商 Fox and Henderson。7 月 2 日，《伦敦新闻画报》刊登了这个方案的雕版画。皇家委员会接受了这个方案，并且指出，如果在展馆内安装展示廊，这个方案还可以另外增加 1/4 的展览面积，但是委员会也作了局部修改，在设计中增加一个筒状拱形屋顶，这样公园里一些高大的树木可以罩在屋顶下得以保护，不必修剪。Fox and Henderson 根据帕克斯顿的设计方案提出了一个 79800 英镑的工程报价，另外附加保护树木免遭伤害的筒状拱形屋顶的造价 6000 英镑，皇家委员会接受了这个报价。

## 使用海德公园的难题

然而，对于在海德公园举办世博会有许多反对意见。海德公园在当时不仅是伦敦各界人士的氧吧，也是这个大都会时尚的聚会场所，附近居民对博览会对当地可能造成的干扰感到担忧。而且，正如《威斯敏斯特评论》所指出的那样，虽然选定的博览会场与贝尔格莱维亚广场和白金汉宫相距很近，步行就可到达，而且对从英格兰银行乘公交车到达博览会的游客十分方便，但是距火车站甚远，运送重型机械的费用很高，再加上装卸货物的费用，货物穿过伦敦街区的运输和看管费用，会让许多潜在的参展商望而却步。这个提醒并没有引起主办方的注意，这说明大都市的游客才是博览会主办方的真正目标。

另外，海德公园的主管上级林业部的许可授权必不可少。最初的方案受到许多限制：承包商只能使用公园的一个入口，其他入口在博览会之前或期间不得受到任何干扰和影响；公园内的排污系统不能改动；未经许可不得砍伐树木；皇家委员会要确定拆除展馆恢复场地的具体时间，如不能按时履行承诺，林业部有权拆除展馆，恢复场地原貌，并且要求皇家委员会承担相关费用。

皇家委员会正式通告林业部，博览会计划在1851年11月1日或之前结束，在此之后的七个月内拆除展馆，恢复场地原貌。经过一系列的谈判磋商，皇家委员会于1850年7月30日获得了场地的使用权和更加现实的使用条件：公园又增加了4个入口，其中3个是花岗石铺设的临时入口。两项皇家伐树许可获得批准，一项是1850年7月砍伐9棵树，另一项是1851年1月砍伐1棵树。9月26日，第一根支柱在现场竖立。

## 水晶宫的形成

最终，皇家委员会于1850年10月31日与Fox and Henderson签订合同。Fox and Henderson未等合同签订就开始施工，生产建筑构件，他们不仅甘愿冒险开工，而且具有丰富的运用玻璃和铁结构建造的经验。1851年2月1日，《伦敦新闻画报》向读者披露，建筑工程已基本竣工，展馆布置即将开始，展台、展位和陈列架上将要布置精美奇妙的展品。

帕克斯顿的方案切实可行，包含一些创新性的施工方式。这座由玻璃和铁制构件构成的革命性展馆设计方案最初让许多人担忧——包括城市规划师和科学家，他们对建筑的稳定性和安全性表示怀疑。虽然计算证明铁梁的承重能力不成问题，铁梁的设计承载力是预计压力的好几倍，但是共振似乎还是个问题——担心众人在建筑内有规律的活动会导致建筑晃动，最终坍塌，这类灾难曾经发生在桥梁结构上。

设计者用一个结构做试验，让300名工人在测试结构上有规律或无规律地来回走动，然后一跃而起，最大限度地引发位移，铁梁的最大位移是1/4英寸。展馆工程继续进行。

帕克斯顿的设计方案是一个标准化的杰作。主体结构由轻巧的铁质构件不断复制构成，墙壁和屋顶完全采用玻璃，铁柱、铁梁和玻璃板，组合尺度合理（图1），并在3个月内预制完毕，然后用3个月时间装配成一座巨大的建筑。这座建筑开创了铁和玻璃建筑的时代。

这座建筑与其说是一座水晶宫不如说是一座玻璃大教堂，中殿长1848英尺，宽408英尺，东西走向，中殿采用平屋顶，高64英尺，两侧有侧廊。出于结构稳定的考虑，中殿在中部与耳堂十字形相交（图2）。耳堂宽72英尺，高104英尺。宽阔的大道和两旁跃层式的

图 1　主体结构采用铁质构件，通过不断复制一个结构立面，构成一个完整的建筑实体，墙壁和屋顶完全采用玻璃板材。在顶层增加一个桶状拱形屋顶，高大的树木得以保护，不必修剪。宽阔的大道和两旁跃层式的展示廊贯穿于整个建筑之中，增加了展览面积

展示廊贯穿于整个建筑之中，创造出 $72700m^2$（18 英亩）的展览面积，是罗马圣彼得教堂面积的 4 倍。

随着博览会展品数量和种类的增加，需要对原设计进行进一步的深化和改进，加强建筑的稳定性，提供必要的展览空间，多方人士参与了项目的全过程，对展馆的建筑艺术形式、工程监理、合同执行和月付款方式——也就是今天所谓的项目管理等过程作出了不可估量的贡献。用帕克斯顿本人的话来说，就是“更确切地说，博览会展馆的设计和建造是一个由帕克斯顿、Fox 和 Henderson 组成的团队加上机遇共同努力的结果。”

---

注：本书中的钢笔画插图由西安建筑科技大学艺术学院樊敏、张骁、李妍超、张涵同学绘制。

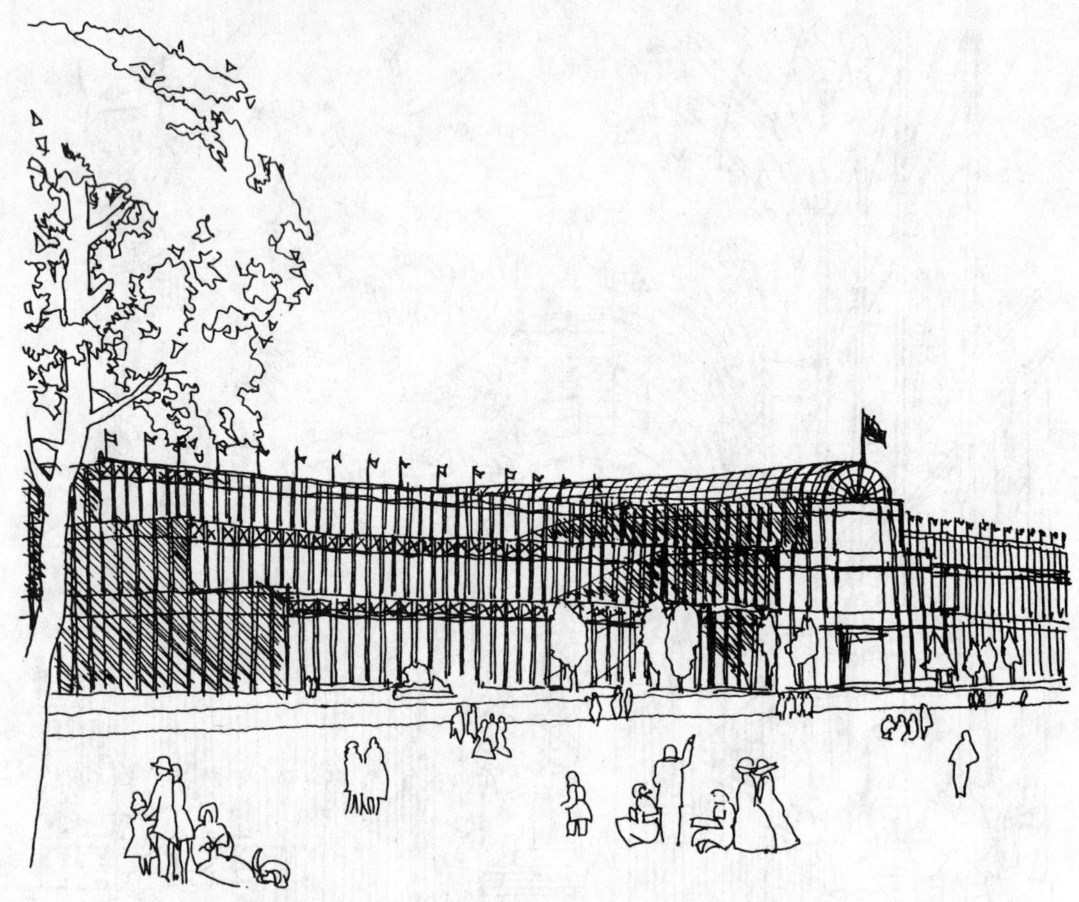

图2 水晶宫像是一座玻璃大教堂，采用十字平面。中殿长1848英尺，宽408英尺，高64英尺，平屋顶，东西走向，两侧有侧廊。出于结构稳定的考虑，中殿在中部与耳堂十字形相交，耳堂宽72英尺，高104英尺，耳堂采用桶状拱形屋顶

随着工程的进展和不断试验与验证，许多细节问题得到解决。由于事先明确了博览会结束后展馆拆除的原则，建筑结构基本采用标准化铁构件、木构件和玻璃板组装而成，这些构件可以重复使用。结构采用铸铁柱式体系和皇家委员会推荐的24英尺框架结构形式，地面层的空心铁柱高19英尺，二至三层的铁柱高17英尺，各层铁柱之间由一个3英尺长的构件纵向连接，这些构件同时与横向承载展示廊的铸铁梁连接，保持横向的稳定性，铸铁梁长24英尺。空心柱还担负着排水管的作用，将玻璃屋顶上的雨水和冷凝水引入公园内专门设置的排水系统，然后排入原有的市政排污系统。这种排水模式由屋顶上设计巧妙的木梁构成，也就是著名的帕克斯顿水槽，这种水槽不仅可以起着固定玻璃板的作用，还可以聚集冷凝水并将其排出，避免水滴落入展馆。

底层的外墙大部分用木板覆盖，二至三层的外墙安装玻璃。在底层高出地面部分和每一层的顶部安装金属百叶窗，改善通风。采光和隔热这个参展商和观众共同关注的重要问题也得到了解决，即用巨大的棉布材质镶板遮盖建筑外表的一半，使之免受阳光直射。展

馆内的温度受到严格监控，夏季可以将 90 多块高 20 英尺、宽 8 英尺的窗框打开，增加通风。尽管展馆内人流众多，又是夏季，还是可以保持室内温度比室外低 2～3℃。

展馆的原设计方案经过了多方扩充改进，扩大了面积，延长了展示廊，增加了饮食部、办公室和楼梯间，改善了设备，如：汽灯照明，加强通风，喷水池以及机械展区的锅炉房等。所有这些补充项目将造价由原来 79800 英镑的合同价增加到 107780 英镑。尽管如此，博览会结束后，Fox and Henderson 发现，他们加快工程进度所增加的额外费用可能使其遭受严重损失。在这种情况下，考虑到承包商为整个项目作出的巨大贡献，皇家委员会又另外支付了 3.5 万英镑。

## 从开幕日到闭幕日

1851 年 5 月 1 日，这座宏伟建筑奇迹般地竣工并准备就绪，维多利亚女王出席了开幕式。特别是，所有与工程造价相关的担忧都已不复存在——工程竣工时，日常的门票销售还未开始，皇家委员会已收到超过 10 万英镑的钱款，其中：64344 英镑来自公众捐款，40000 英镑来自季票销售，3200 英镑来自世博会的目录特许印制商 Messrs. Spicer and Clowes 的赞助，5500 英镑来自世博会饮食特许经营商 Messrs. Schweppes 的赞助。世博会的盈利为公共建设提供了基金，例如：阿伯特宫、科学馆、国家历史博物馆和维多利亚·阿伯特博物馆。

《艺术》杂志在其展览专栏中煽情地写道：

“第一次步入展馆，你的眼睛立刻被四周闪耀着的五光十色所迷惑，直到这种迷失状态渐渐褪去你才得以赞叹博览会的魅力，因为它无愧于其自身真正的绚丽与和谐之美，这种丽质是宏伟简洁的金属结构放射出的绚丽色彩经过艺术化处理，动感变幻的结果。”

展馆中央升起一座巨大的喷泉，从展馆的各个角落观赏，它都是最辉煌的景观。展馆的北端保留了翠绿的热带植物和高大茂密的树林，调剂人们的视觉。首先吸引游客目光的展品是布置在各处的雕塑作品，有些雕塑尺度巨大，具有无与伦比之美。

在这里，我们可以看到美术展区、英国雕塑展区、中世纪展区、家具展区……羊毛织品、混纺织品、丝绸、地毯、瓷器、珠宝、香水、钟表、厨房用具、彩色玻璃、五金制品、工具、仪器、机械、矿产、化学品、农产品、建筑材料、船只等，超过 10 万件展品。所有展品来自世界各地——从英国到法国、美国、瑞典、俄国、丹麦、西班牙、奥地利、澳大利亚和新西兰等。从获奖数量来看，法国产品最具竞争力。超过 620 万观众参观了世博会，人们惊奇地看到工业革命正在使英国成为当代最强盛的国家。整个博览会获得了巨大成功，可以肯定地说，博览会圆满地完成了自己的目标——“展览、竞争和鼓舞”。博览会进行得非常有序，正像一本当代杂志描述的那样：

“和普通观众一样，17000 多参展商来自世界各国，同属一个天下，他们将其财富和技能、其工业和企业最宝贵的见证物托付给50多名除了棍棒没有其他装备的警察看管。日复一日，昼夜轮回，无需增加任何警力去看管这些玻璃墙内存放着的数不清的财富。这样的工业与艺术博览会在世界任何其他国家都不可能举办。”

博览会在五个半月的展览期间吸引了600万观众参观，盈利186000英镑，博览会于1851年10月结束后，水晶宫搬迁至伦敦郊区的Sydenham，成为展览和娱乐中心，直至1936年毁于大火。

Chapter 2

# The Great Exhibition of 1851, London

Officially known as the "Great Exhibition of the Works of Industry of All Nations", the fair was held in the Crystal Palace in Hyde Park, London, from 1st May to 15th October 1851. It was the first international exhibition of manufactured products and was enormously influential on the development of many aspects of society including art and design education, international trade and relations, and even tourism. The exhibition also set the precedent for the many international exhibitions followed during the next hundred years.

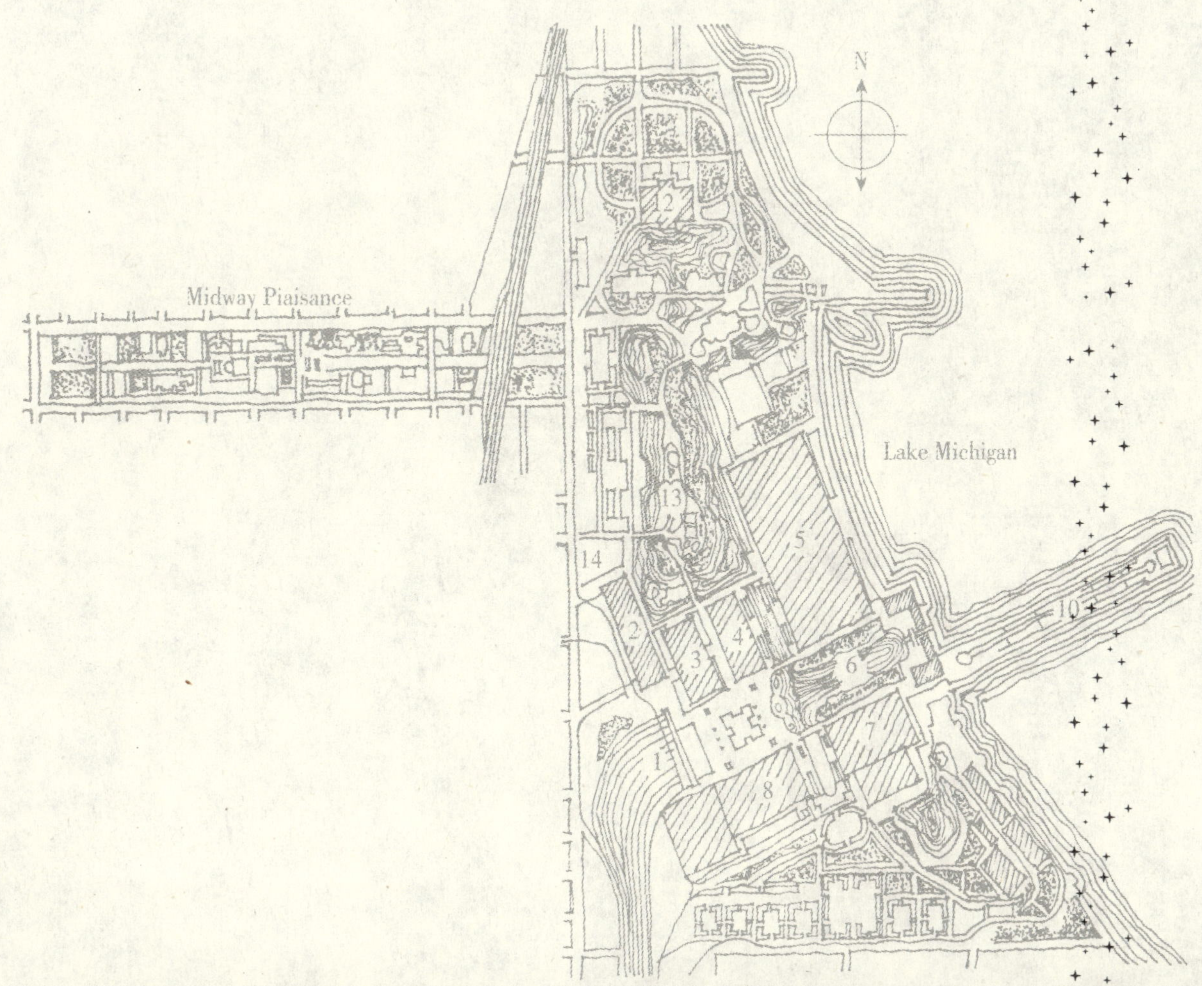

## The Idea of An Exhibition

The events leading up to the Great Exhibition of 1851 were prompted by the success of the French Industrial Exposition of 1844. For half a century, the French had already established a tradition of exhibitions, all devoted to the glory of the art and industry of France, which had proved so beneficial to French industry. However in England, few art-industry exhibitions were more than local affairs. The first building to be put up solely for the exhibition of manufactured goods was built in Birmingham in 1849.

The group who promoted the Exhibition was brought together by a well-established British organization, known today as the Royal Society of Arts. The Society was founded in 1754, when a group of noblemen, gentlemen, clergymen and merchants met in a coffeehouse to found the "Society for the encouragement of arts, manufactures and commerce". Its objective was to give prizes for inventions and manufactures which were likely to produce great advantages to the nation. The very success of the Society in stimulating arts and industry had led to the foundation of independent artistic and professional organizations, thus the Society found itself superseded in that role after the foundation of the Royal Academy, and needed to change direction to survive. Gradually, the holding of lectures to communicate advances in technology, its publication in a journal and the exhibition of successful manufactures became a greater concern of the Society than the giving of premiums for inventions. The Society's exhibitions of 1848 and 1849 were increasingly successful, so that the Society felt confident in announcing a national exhibition for the year 1851.

When it was suggested to the English government that it would be most advantageous to British industry to have a similar exhibition in London, the government showed no interest, the public were indifferent, manufacturers lukewarm, and some of the most eminent even hostile to the proposal. However, Prince Albert got really involved in the fair when approached.

Prince Albert, Victoria's German husband, did not find his role as consort an easy one as he was largely excluded from formal participation in the work of the sovereign, though he had considerable influence behind the scenes. Prince Albert, who had publicly advocated the advancement of industry and science, was very much in favor of a self-financing exhibition of all nations. Such an exhibition, he said, "would afford a true test of the point of development at which the whole of mankind has arrived in this great task, and a new starting point from which all nations would be able to direct their further exertions." Albert's plan was a great collection of works in art and industry to be held in London that would move far beyond the previous exhibitions, which often were held in crowded places, attracted relatively little public notice, and had few international dimensions.

The first meeting in the development of the Exhibition project was held at Buckingham Palace on June 30, 1849. Most of the difficult questions concerning the Exhibition were in essence 'settled'. The exhibits would be divided into four major divisions: raw materials of manufactures, machinery and mechanical inventions, manufactures, and sculpture and plastic art. The site was discussed and Prince Albert himself suggested the vacant ground on the south side of Hyde Park for the construction of a building. The Society sent a deputation around the country to gather support.

The decision was made not to limit the Exhibition exclusively to British industry. "It was considered that particular advantage to British industry might be derived from placing it in fair competition with that of other nations". Very large premiums in money, it was thought, would induce manufacturers to develop products, which though not immediately profitable, would be of long-term benefit. It was also decided that the prizes should take the form of "medals, with money prizes so large as to overcome the scruples and prejudices even of the largest and richest manufacturers, and ensure the greatest amount of exertion". The first prize would be £5000.

The best mode of carrying out the execution of these plans was thought to be a Royal Commission, with the Prince as the president, responsible for defining the nature of the Exhibition, and the way it was to be conducted, and finally the awarding of the prizes. The Society of Arts would undertake the raising of funds to finance the prizes and the provision of a building.

The Prince had always taken the view that government should be involved. He wrote that a great national and even international exhibition is "of the highest importance and ought not to be approached except in harmony with and under the guidance of the government". Thereafter, the government was persuaded to set up a Royal Commission headed by the Prince. Meanwhile, Prince Albert had been writing to foreign contacts about his plan for a world industrial exhibition.

## Finding An Appropriate Building

As the outlay for the Exhibition seemed to be about £50000 for the building and a further £20000 to provide attractive prizes, which the Society of Arts could not meet from its own resources. And the exchequer would have to pay no money. The Society of Arts pressed ahead at this point, negotiating with a building contractor to erect a suitable building, advance prize money of £20000, and pay preliminary expenses, such as the costs of agents, advertising and printing, all to be repaid from receipts at the gate of the Exhibition. They made it clear that one third of the surplus profits would go to the Society for funding future exhibitions, and the contractor would receive the balance of four-sixths of the profits. The contractor's readiness to take a very considerable risk by investing upwards of £75000 in an entirely novel and untested enterprise alone made it possible for the Society to proceed.

However, when the Royal Commission met for the first time in January 1850, and after digesting the concept that such an exhibition could make a profit, one of its first acts was to cancel the contract with the building contractor, and call for voluntary contributions nationwide. The

Commission's first concerns were to raise money to replace the "contractor's funds", to obtain a design, and to start the construction of the building on a suitable site, and then to solicit suitable objects from home and abroad to fill it.

In an attempt to whip up support, all the mayors from the whole country were invited to Mansion House, to listen to Prince Albert argue the case for an Exhibition. Other big names were present to give support. The meeting was a great success. The idea of an exhibition, funded by subscription, but under the management of a Royal Commission was enthusiastically received. Salvation came from leading businessmen, aware of the potential value of an international exhibition to a nation dedicated to free trade in a protectionist Europe. A total fund of 230,000 pounds was raised and the size of the exhibition was decided——bigger than anything the French had ever managed. The government was persuaded to treat it as a bonded warehouse, so that goods imported for the exhibition need not have import duties paid.

As the matter of the building was the most urgent, a Building Committee was appointed. On March 13, 1850, the Committee set up an international competition asking for suggestions for the general arrangement of the building. They provided a plan of the site and a set of rules and conditions to guide the design, setting out which trees had to be preserved, and suggesting a single story building, top-lit and built of fireproof materials. It was not to occupy more than 900,000 square feet or 65,000 square meters, of which a maximum area of 700,000 square feet or 50,000 square meters could be roofed. Contributors were instructed to confine themselves to a single sheet of drawings, with buildings drawn to the scale of 1:1000, with a single sheet of explanation.

The Committee made its intentions clear: seeking information and suggestions involving the general form of the building, the distribution of its parts, the mode of access and internal arrangements and contrivances, and etc. The Committee thought it probable that when the plans were received they might not be limited to the selection of any one plan, but they might derive useful ideas from many.

Some 233 designs were received: 38 from abroad, 51 from around England, and 128 from London. However, as the Building Committee reported, none of the plans actually suited, though it was admitted that they were very useful: "from some designs the lesson was thus learned of what to avoid, from others much information was gained, since many indispensable requisites had been foreseen, and more or less ingeniously provided for".

The Committee was faced with the problem of a temporary building, which economy demanded should be as reusable as possible, which had to be constructed in a very short time, by then under twelve months. It had not only to be cheap, but also to provide for the display of goods, and the convenient circulation of visitors. A single space would be required to make supervision easy and to give flexibility, and a radiating plan would not work, while schemes with rows of parallel counters would be monotonous and devoid of variety or grandeur. Plans of an architectural character were generally too monumental, too much divided, and far too expensive.

Now, the Building Committee set out to provide its own plan. In spite of much condemnation from the competing architects and others on the grounds of ugliness and vast expense of their schemes, the Committee proceeded to ask for building contractors to tender for their own designs, which arrived at a cost somewhat more expensive than the Commission had envisaged.

However, one contractor, Fox and Henderson, presented an amended design, one amended so much that it bore no resemblance to the Building Committee's original proposal, but with the compelling advantage of a better price. It was based on a design by Joseph Paxton, a gardener, who had struck on the idea of a simple repeating structure so that one cross-section could be repeated indefinitely to make a whole building. Paxton drew his original design on a sheet of paper and managed to have a complete set of plans within nine days. He presented it to the contractor Fox and Henderson on 22 June 1850, and the Illustrated London News published an engraving of it on 6 July. The plan was accepted by the commissioners, which, as they pointed out, could provide an additional one-fourth of space if equipped with galleries, but modified to include a domed roof so that some rather large trees on the site in Hyde Park could be accommodated without trimming them. Fox & Henderson tendered £79800 for Paxton's scheme, with an additional cost of £6000 for the barrel vault, to save some of the threatened trees, which the Commission accepted.

## The Problem of Using Hyde Park

However, there was opposition to the use of Hyde Park, at the time not only a lung for Londoners of all classes, but also the fashionable parade for metropolitan society. And the local anxiety about the prospect of the disruption in the neighborhood was obvious. In addition, as the Westminster Review pointed out, though the proposed site was sufficiently convenient for omnibus passengers coming from the Bank, and within an easy lounging distance of Belgrave-Square and Buckingham Palace, it was a long way from any railway station. The expense of transporting heavy machinery would be sufficiently serious. When the further expense of loading, unloading, conveyance and superintendence through the streets of London is added, many possible exhibitors would be deterred. This warning was ignored by the promoters, indicating perhaps that the metropolitan visitors were the real target of the exhibition organizers.

There was also an authority in charge of the park, the Department of Woods and Forests, whose agreement was essential. The initial proposals were very restrictive. The contractors were only to use one gate, the other gates were not to be interfered with in any way, either before or during the Exhibition, no drains within the Park were to be interrupted, and no trees were to be cut down without consent. The Royal Commission was to name the date on which they would remove the building and reinstate the ground, and on failure to do so, the Department of Woods and Forests would be entitled to remove it and reinstate the ground, and consequently charge the Royal Commission for the costs.

The Royal Commission formally gave notice that it was intended to close the Exhibition on or before November 1st 1851, and it was agreed that the building should be removed and the ground reinstated within seven months of the closing. After all its negotiations the Commission obtained possession of the site on July 30, 1850, and more realistic conditions were provided: some four entrances into the Park were added, of which three were temporary granite-paved entrances. Two royal warrants for the felling of trees were granted, one for nine trees in July 1850, and one for a single tree in January 1851. The first column was erected on September 26.

## Development of The Crystal Palace

The contract with Fox and Henderson was finally signed on 31 October, 1850. Fortunately Fox and Henderson did not wait for the contract to begin work, or to set in motion the manufacture of the components for the building. They were not only prepared to start work at their own risk, but were also very experienced in constructing glass and iron buildings. On 1 February, 1851, the Illustrated London News could tell its readers that the task was nearly complete and the interior would be ready for the arrangement of counters, stands, shelves, etc, with the interesting and marvelous objects which would be stored upon them.

Paxton had produced a viable project involving some innovative construction methods. The building's revolutionary glass and iron design at first made many people nervous——including city planners and scientists. Doubts were raised about the stability and safety of the structure. The amount of strain on the iron girders was calculated not to be a problem, as they were designed to take several times the expected weight. What seemed to be a problem was resonance——the fear that a large crowd, moving regularly inside the structure, could cause it to vibrate more and more until it collapsed. This had happened before on structures such as bridges.

An experiment was set up, with a test structure, on which 300 workmen walked backwards and forwards, regularly, irregularly, and then jumping simultaneously in the air, to induce the most regular oscillations possible. The maximum girder movement was 1/4 inch. The building work was continued.

Paxton's scheme was a masterpiece of standardization. It was based on a recurrent iron skeleton of extreme lightness and delicacy. The walls and roofs were made entirely of glass. Iron columns, girders and glass panels were made with coordinated dimensions, and were prefabricated in three months. Afterwards it took another three months to erect the immense structure. The building gave rise to an era of iron-and-glass construction (Figure 1).

Essentially the building was a glass cathedral rather than a Crystal Palace, with the Nave running east and west, 1848 feet in length and 408 feet in width. The Nave with flat roof was 64 feet high, flanked with galleried aisles, intersected in the center by the Transept, for structural reasons. The transept was 72 feet wide and rose to a height of 104 feet. A grand avenue and upstairs galleries ran the whole length of the building. Altogether, an area of 72700 square meter (18 acres) was roofed over, four times that of St Peter in Rome (Figure 2).

As the number and variety of the exhibits grew, a great many modifications and improvements were necessary to ensure the building's stability, and to provide all the space needed. Various parties were involved in the process of the project, and made invaluable contribution to the improvement in the architectural beauty of the building, and supervision of the general building construction, fulfillment of the contract and the payment of monthly accounts——what today we might see as project management. "It would be more accurate to regard the design and the erection of the Exhibition Building as a piece of inspired teamwork by Paxton, Fox, Henderson and Chance," in Paxton's words.

A great many details were only solved as the building progressed and was put to test. Since it was understood from the beginning that the building would be removed after the Exhibition closed, it was essentially a modular building of iron, wood and glass, built of components which were meant to be recyclable. It was constructed on a system of cast-iron columns based on the Commissioners' 24-foot grid. The hollow columns were 19 feet high on the ground tier and 17 feet on the two upper tiers, connected vertically by 3-foot-long pieces. These also provided a horizontal connection with the girders which carried the galleries and provided lateral stability. These girders were 24-foot cast-iron girders. The hollow columns provided drainage, carrying both the rainwater and the condensation from the glass roof down into a system of specially constructed drainage channels through the park into the existing sewers. This drainage was made possible by the cleverly designed wooden beams, the famous Paxton gutters, in the roof, which not only carried the glass panes, but were channeled to catch the condensation and carried it away before it could drip into the building.

The outside walls were vertically boarded on much of the ground floor, but glazed in the upper stories. Metal louver panels provided ventilation, placed immediately above the floor at ground level, and at the top of each story elsewhere. The problem of light and heat, a serious consideration for both exhibitors and visitors, was addressed by the use of cotton cloth in great panels which shielded about half the building area from the direct light of the sun. The temperature was carefully monitored, and in the course of the summer it was decided to remove some ninety sashes 20 feet high by 8 feet wide, to increase ventilation. Despite the large number of people in the building, and the summer season, it was usually possible to keep the temperature inside 2 or 3 degrees below the outside temperature.

Considerable additions had been made to the original design in the form of increased space and extended galleries, refreshment rooms, increased offices and staircases, better amenities in gas-lighting and additional ventilation, water for the fountains, and a boiler-house for the Machinery in Motion section. All these had raised the price from the contract sum of £79800 to £107780. However, after the Exhibition closed, Fox and Henderson discovered that the additional costs incurred by their speedy work were likely to incur a heavy loss for them. Under the circumstances, and in view of the contractors' contribution to the success of the whole enterprise, the Commission paid a further £35,000.

## From Opening to Closing Day

Remarkably, the complete edifice was ready on time, on 1st May, 1851, for Queen Victoria to attend the opening ceremony. Best of all, worries about covering costs had been laid to rest——by the time the building was ready to open, without any day-by-day ticket sales at all, well over 100,000 pounds had been recovered: 64,344 pounds by public subscription, 40,000 pounds from sale of season tickets, 3,200 pounds from Messrs. Spicer and Clowes for the honor of printing the catalogues, and 5,500 pounds from Messrs. Schweppes for the privilege of supplying refreshments. The profits from the event allowed for the foundation of public works such as the Albert Hall, the Science Museum, the National History Museum and the Victoria and Albert Museum.

In its catalogue of the exhibition, the Art Journal glowingly wrote:

"On entering the building for the first time, the eye is completely dazzled by the rich variety of hues which burst upon it on every side, and it is not until this partial bewilderment has subsided, that we are in a condition to appreciate as it deserves its real magnificence and the harmonious beauty of effect produced by the artistic arrangement of the glowing and varied hues which blaze along its grand and simple lines."

From the center of the entire building rises the gigantic fountain, the culminating point of view from every quarter of the building, while at the northern end, the eye is relieved by the verdure of tropical plants and the lofty overshadowing branches of forest trees. The objects, which first attract the eye, are the sculptures arranged on every side, some of them of colossal size and of unrivalled beauty.

We have here fine arts court, English sculpture court, the medieval court, furniture court…… We see woolen and mixed fabrics, silks, carpets, china and pottery, jewelries, perfumes, clocks and watches, kitchen appliances, stained glass, hardware, tools, instruments, machinery, minerals, chemicals, agricultural products, building materials, boats and so on, up to more than 100,000 exhibits. All the exhibits came from all over the world——from Great Britain to France, United States, Sweden, Russia, Denmark, Spain, Austria, Australia, New Zealand and so on. The most successful competitors were the French, in terms of the number of medals won. Over 6,200,000 visitors to the Great Exhibition marveled at the industrial revolution that was propelling Britain into the greatest power of the time, and the whole event was a great success. It may fairly be described as having fulfilled its aims of "exhibition, competition and encouragement". It was remarkably peaceful. As noted in a contemporary magazine:

"Seventeen thousand exhibitors, who like the visitors were of almost every nation and kindred under heaven, entrusted the most valuable evidences of their wealth, their skill, their industry, and their enterprise to the guardianship of some fifty policemen, armed with no better weapon than a wooden baton. Day after day and night after night passed on, and no added force was requisite for the safety of the almost countless wealth deposited within these fragile walls. In no other country of the world could such an exhibition of the industrial arts have taken place."

The Great Exhibition attracted more than six million visitors during its five-and-a-half-month run and showed a profit of £186,000. After the exhibition closed in October 1851, the Crystal Palace was moved to Sydenham, a London suburb. There, it served as an exhibition and entertainment center until it was destroyed by fire in 1936.

# 第三章

# 1893 年哥伦布纪念世博会

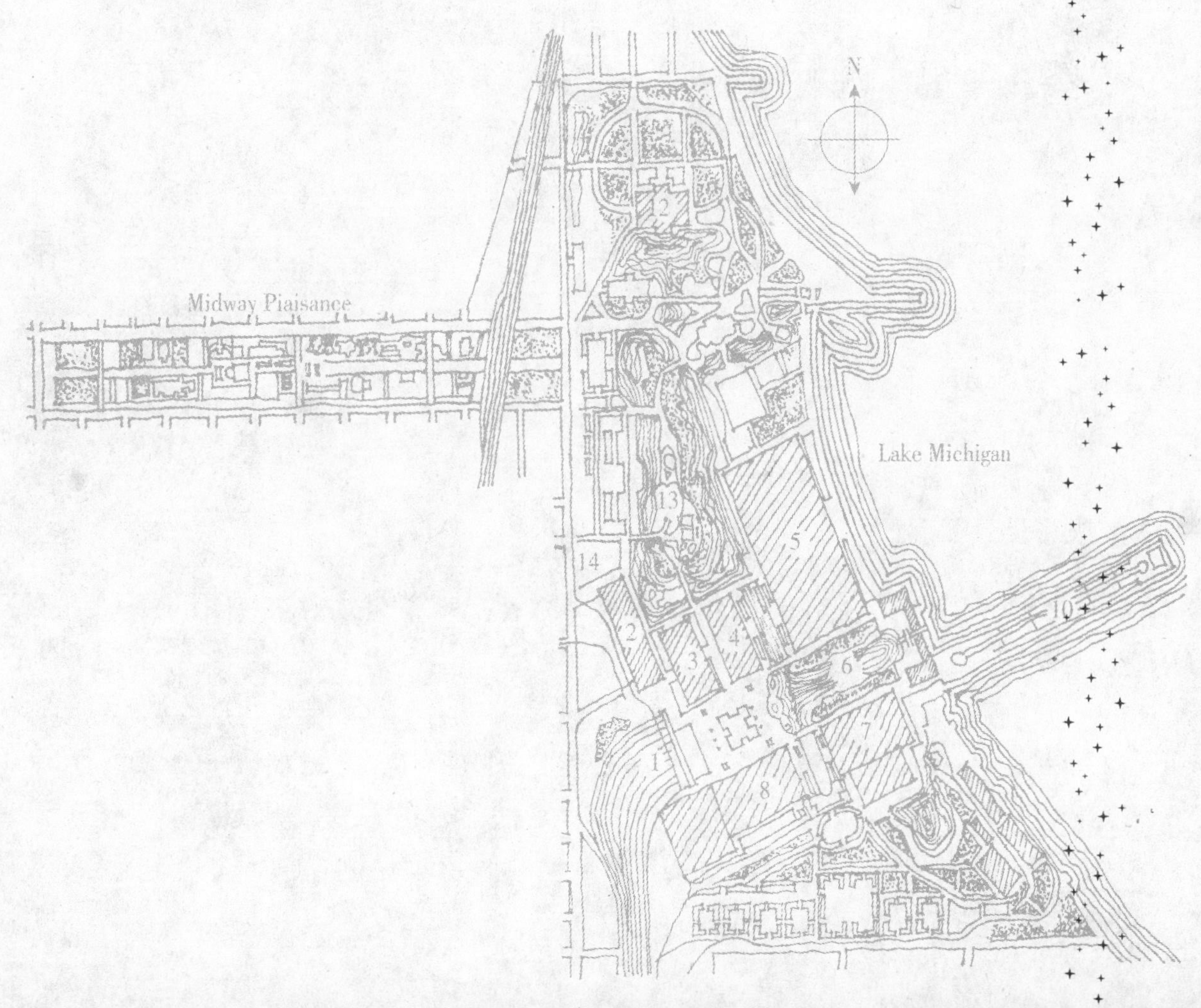

## 背景

美国中西部城市芝加哥于1893年和1933—1934年分别举办了两次世博会，哥伦布纪念世博会（The World's Columbian Exposition 和世纪的进步世博会（The Century of Progress Exposition），为世博会的发展作出了卓越贡献。这两次世博会在展览的形式和风格上反映了当时美国的物质和文化发展水平，稳固地确立了芝加哥的地位。

19世纪后半叶是一个博览会的时代，世界许多著名大都市都举办了国际博览会，如巴黎、伦敦、维也纳等。博览会是极具魅力的活动，1876年费城举办的美国独立百年博览会（The Centennial Exhibition in Philadelphia）吸引了1000万观众，1889年巴黎国际博览会（Exposition Universelle de Paris 1889）更加轰动，吸引了2800万观众。由于世博会集合了时代的体验和关注——从体育到娱乐，到高雅文化（high culture），是具有长远社会影响力的国际性文化娱乐活动的统一体。

当举办世博会庆祝哥伦布发现新大陆400周年的设想一提出，几座城市都想争夺世博会的主办权。芝加哥市议会于1889年7月22日启动了世博会申办工作，成立了当地的世博组委会，称之为芝加哥公司（Chicago Company），具体实施这个项目。为了证实芝加哥举办世博会的决心，世博组委会发行了500万美元的债券，截止1890年4月，这种10美元一份的债券被认购一空。众议院从1889年下半年开始受理来自芝加哥、圣路易斯、纽约和华盛顿的申请，经过几个月的考虑和争论，众议院于1890年2月24日将世博会的主办权授予芝加哥，但是附加一个条件，芝加哥要再筹集500万美元的资金。

芝加哥有理由争取这样的殊荣。芝加哥所处的中心位置（能够代表广大的中西部地区）、便利的交通网络和温和的夏季气候使芝加哥成为理想的世博会举办地。在这里举办世博会可以让欧洲观众更多地游历和了解美国。

## 历史回顾

或许是由于这里土地肥沃，气候适宜，而且传说要开挖一条运河（1836年开工）从水路连接芝加哥与新奥尔良的缘故，自1833年起（芝加哥1833年8月建镇，1837年建市），大批移民涌入。19世纪40年代末，芝加哥的发展速度加快，成为中西部的商业中心。1847年，这里举办的河流和港口大会（The River and Harbor Convention）吸引了全国的目光，来自美国各地3000名代表出席了会议，大会引起了主要媒体对联邦政府投资河流和港口改造项目的关注。河流和港口公约的发布给芝加哥带来了更多的商机和人口激增，加速了运河和铁路的建设速度，这两项工程于第二年竣工。特别是铁路的建成使芝加哥成为中西部最重要的城市。

到1870年，芝加哥成为美国最繁忙的铁路运输中心，不断涌入的移民为肉食加工、炼铁、木材加工和运输等新兴工业提供了充足的劳动力。不料，1871年10月8日，这座城市的巨大心脏，那些在城市急剧扩张时期建造起来的木结构建筑群，在不到24小时里被一场大火完全化为灰烬。

然而，这座城市迅速复苏。芝加哥的开拓者奔赴纽约等东部城市宣传芝加哥重建的投资潜力，获得了成功，新建筑在老城区的废墟上拔地而起。一切都需要从头开始，年轻的建筑师被这里大批的设计项目所吸引，纷纷投入芝加哥重建，使这里成为新一代建筑设计和工程技术创新的中心。

到1889年，芝加哥在工业实力和商业财富方面已经成为美国第二大城市，是西部（从芝加哥向西部延伸直至落基山脉的广大地区）的谷物、肉食和木材交易中心。大型集会在芝加哥的发展历史上起着重要作用，芝加哥每年都要举办州际博览会，美国的铁路交通也以芝加哥为中心。到1890年，芝加哥已成为美国第二大钢铁制造中心，在现代工业中发挥着重要作用。

在文化和社会领域，19世纪90年代的芝加哥也见证了一个博物馆、艺术馆、教育机构和图书馆蓬勃发展的历史时期，而且，一些富有创造力的建筑师已经赶超了纽约在高层商业建筑——摩天楼的雏形——发展方面的领先地位，为芝加哥的建筑增添了新的美学意义和纯净的结构形式，增强了城市作为旅游目的地的吸引力。哥伦布纪念世博会就成为这场文化大发展时期最令人瞩目的部分。

随着城市的持续扩张，成千上万的新移民不断涌入，芝加哥的人口从原来不到40万（19世纪80年代）发展到120多万（19世纪90年代），已经超出了城市的负荷。这样的人口剧增不可避免地带来许多问题：贫困潦倒、政治腐败、劳工骚乱、血腥的阶级对抗和犯罪率居高，这些都是人口增长过快带来的社会问题。工厂里进行的工业生产喷出滚滚黑烟，加剧了这座“黑色城市”（Black City）的浓重色调：浓烟加尘埃，还有大批悲凉沮丧的人们。

1889年的芝加哥对于纽约和其他东部地区的人来说只不过是一个过度发展的边远小镇。芝加哥企业界和政府采取了多种应对措施，治理整顿城市环境，改善穷人的生活条件，例如发起社区改良运动，在公立学校进行欧洲语言教学的同时，加强职业培训等。

## 世博规划

在世博会筹备过程中，芝加哥组委会派出了一个由执行委员 Edward T. Jeffrey 率领的代表团观摩1889年巴黎博览会，并起草了一份考察报告，这份报告对确定哥伦布纪念世博会的性质产生了重要影响。芝加哥企业界力图展示芝加哥工商业取得的成就，展示一座具有

60 年历史的城市，展示一个经历火灾毁灭性打击仅22年后又奇迹般再生的城市。哥伦布纪念世博会实际上是芝加哥作为宏伟建筑的诞生地和迅速崛起的经济实力在国际舞台上的第一次亮相，同时也把芝加哥的天才建筑师伯纳姆、奥姆斯特德、沙利文（Daniel Burnham, Frederick Law Olmsted, Louis Sullivan）推向国际舞台。

授予芝加哥主办权就是把大部分的具体规划和几乎所有的责任，无论是经济还是其他方面的责任，都交给了芝加哥。然而，国会认为有必要成立一个由各州和地区代表组成的全国委员会，监督世博会的组织、建设和管理工作。全国委员会称之为委员会，芝加哥组委会称之为董事会，委员会和董事会的成员由政界人士和商界领袖构成，包括参议员、铁路公司总裁、银行行长、百货公司总经理和地产业巨头，他们同时也是专业人士、建筑师和教授。这两个委员会由参议员 George Davis 领导，他曾经在国会帮助芝加哥申博成功。有了这两个政治和经营实体的参与，世博会规划于 1890 年启动。

**1. 世博理念的形成**

Jeffrey 的巴黎博览会考察报告对哥伦布纪念世博会的建设和运作产生了重大影响，通过研究这个报告，芝加哥组委会得以实现超越巴黎博览会的目标。报告详细描述了巴黎人策划组织的许多娱乐休闲活动，例如，剧院、音乐厅和带有异域风情表演的外国风情园等，所有这些项目都要向观众收取一定的费用。Jeffrey 还赞美了夜色中灯光与喷泉交相辉映的景观，窄轨火车载着游客游览塞纳河沿岸的情景，以及大量学术会议，许多权威人士在此参与了重大主题的讨论。博览会的综合性展览和专业性展览都给他留下了深刻印象，这些展览包括人们“想象到的一切和想象不到的一切，实用性的或装饰性的，可谓应有尽有”。

关于世博园的设计——世博园应该是什么样，这样的讨论从 1889 年开始一直在进行。讨论基于两个重点展开：首先，有必要精心打造一个世博会消除其他美国人对芝加哥人的成见，而且，许多美国人都感觉到了欧洲人对他们的不屑一顾，在打造世博会的过程中，设计要表现美国的团结统一和美国文明走向成熟；其次，设计要考虑的第二个重点是人们想要超越 1889 年巴黎博览会的愿望。这一点可以从早期《芝加哥论坛报》组织的一个活动得到证实，该报向读者征集埃菲尔铁塔式的世博会标志塔设计方案，然而经济困难使标志塔的建设搁浅，最终，位于 Midway 乐园中心的 Ferris 摩天轮成为世博会的标志。

展馆建设和世博会选址是世博规划议程中首先要考虑的问题。到 1891 年 2 月，世博会场址最终选在杰克逊（Jackson）公园尚未开发的沼泽区，多数建筑布置在公园内，少量建筑布置在湖滨区。这个会址可以满足组委会的所有要求：面积大，便于开发，交通条件便利，而且还可以根据早期规划完善公园建设。伯纳姆和鲁特（John W. Root）被任命为建筑顾问，这种组合也在情理之中，他们这对合作伙伴在芝加哥执业已长达 15 年之久，伯纳姆和鲁特事务所是芝加哥知名度最高的建筑事务所，1871 年火灾以后，在芝加哥市区拔地而起的几座最引人注目的摩天大楼就是这个事务所的杰作。

根据组委会的要求，伯纳姆提交了一个利用杰克逊公园景观地貌的世博园规划方案，这个规划是伯纳姆与鲁特和奥姆斯特德共同完成的。规划提出：主要展览建筑包括一个称之为“荣誉广场”的建筑群，环绕一片几何形水面布置；另一片水面——潟湖——按其自然形态布局，湖中心布置一个大型岛屿，其他建筑灵活地分布在潟湖周围和园区的其他地段（图3）。伯纳姆意识到世博会建设工程巨大非其事务所能独立承担，决定亲自挑选建筑师，组成一个设计团队。他拒绝了举办设计竞赛的建议，因为那样既耗时费力，也容易产生平庸的设计。伯纳姆的设计团队吸收了美国建筑界的大师，这些人大多来自东部，也许，他这样做是为了让芝加哥博览会成为美国全民的博览会。

伯纳姆的建筑师团队大都出自巴黎美术学院（Academie des Beaux-Arts in Paris），他们共同制定了一个独特的世博园设计方案。奥姆斯特德是一位资深的景观建筑设计师，曾经设计了纽约中央公园，他利用杰克逊公园的自然景观，设计了一个由潟湖和水路构成的水系，与密歇根湖相连。这个水系承担着多种功能：水面具有装饰作用，像镜面水池一样反射建筑景观，水路便于水上交通，绿树成荫的湖心岛为夏日疲惫的游客提供了一个歇息的去处。14座主要建筑环绕水路布置，采用新古典主义建筑风格，强调建筑的逻辑性、协调与统一。荣誉广场上的建筑环绕一个大水池布置，用白灰泥饰面，给主要建筑带来高贵典雅的白色，因此得名“白城”（White City）。

世博会工程建设从1891年7月开始，进展迅速。由于采用了钢铁框架结构——当时一种较先进的建筑技术，以及由灰泥、水泥和可塑纤维混合而成的材料，造价便宜，易于施工。为了节省时间，荣誉广场建筑群用白色粉饰，并且将这个建筑外部装饰方案推广到所有主要建筑，只有沙利文设计的运输大楼除外。为了更加省时，所有展览建筑不做内部装修，只有用于会议和博览会业务的行政管理大楼例外。

### 2. 世博宣传推介

到1892年2月，世博园区已有大量建筑竣工，国会议员应邀到现场视察。为了有效地宣传推介世博会，伯纳姆亲自陪同政府官员和其他显要人物参观世博园，聘请著名摄影师用图片纪录世博园建设的进程，这些图片刊登在多种世博会宣传材料中。

伯纳姆竭尽全力宣传推广世博会，他允许公众进入施工现场参观，尽管这样做会妨碍施工进程。公众对世博园建设兴趣十足，以致参观门票从原来的25美分增加到50美分，每天仍有数千观众参观世博会工地。Moses Handy，世博会的官方宣传机构，出版了一本世博园工地参观指南，为观众提供方便。这本售价10美分的指南向观众具体介绍了每座建筑的功能，描绘世博园蓝图。伯纳姆和董事会利用多种机会将这种世博会开幕之前的世博情结变成利润丰厚的商机。

世博会筹备工作取得的另一个成就是创造了历史上最高效的宣传机构——Moses Handy，不断推出大量文献资料向美国和世界介绍世博会筹备进展情况。自1890年开始运作以来，Moses Handy一直为国内外许多报刊杂志提供世博会信息和新闻，重点是宣传推介芝加哥和世博会商机，并且编制了“哥伦布纪念世博会指南”，“投入50美分，饱览万象世界”是一个成功的广告宣传，成人票价 50 美分在当时是很高的费用，但肯定物有所值。

因为急需联邦政府更多的资金支持，最终，财政部发行了面值 50 美分的哥伦布纪念币，总价值达到 250 万美元，组委会以面值两倍的价格作为纪念品发售。

由于世博园区面积巨大，633 英亩（包括 80 英亩带状形娱乐街区），工程进展缓慢，巨大的工程量迫使伯纳姆和委员会将世博会开幕日期从 1892 年下半年推迟到 1893 年 5 月，开幕日期的推迟更增加了公众对世博会的期盼。

经过 3 年的准备和 2800 万美元的投入，世博会于 1893 年 5 月 1 日开幕。46 个国家参加了本届世博会，其中 19 个国家政府建立了自己的独立展馆。从 1893 年 5 月 1 日到 10 月 31 日，世博会接待了 2700 万游客——接近当时美国人口的 1/4。

世博会令人鼓舞，大部分预期目标都已实现。世博园面积 633 英亩（约 256 公顷），展品 65000 多件，还有许多饭店、餐厅、茶馆、午餐部和饮食店，游客可以边吃边游，边看展览。世博园的卫生保洁维护工作受到了高度赞扬，成为现实生活中城市效仿的楷模。在这里，游客们惊喜地发现高架铁路上运行的火车清洁安全，电动汽艇在潟湖中穿梭航行。在许多方面，世博园实际上就是一个乌托邦——与游客居住的布满尘埃的城市大相径庭。游客们在通往游乐场和景点的道路上感到安全踏实，人群中混入了几百名世博保安和便衣侦探。人行道上聚集了数以千计的特许经销商，他们出售的商品从纪念品到爆米花，还有新发明的碳酸饮料，应有尽有。几乎每天都有一个特别的主题庆祝活动，每天举办的演说和报告主题广泛，从伦理道德到作家点评、经济学、劳工问题和宗教等。博览会规模巨大，影响力持续不减。

## 从开幕日到闭幕日及尾声

几乎是在世博会刚刚拉开序幕，1893 年经济恐慌爆发，股市崩溃导致了美国历史上最严重的一场经济大萧条，芝加哥的失业率飙升。1892—1893 年的冬天也特别寒冷，博览会前三个月的经营状况令人失望。随着天气转暖，世博园收尾工程结束，农民收获并销售了谷物，铁路也调低了运价，尽管调价来得太迟，世博会的人气开始逐渐上升。

世博会期间举办了许多以国家、州或组织机构等命名的特别庆祝日，这些日趋频繁的庆祝活动以游行、体育竞赛和其他娱乐活动为主要特征，都是为了增强主要展区吸引力的商业运作行为。10 月 9 日“芝加哥日”是芝加哥大火 22 周年纪念日，这天吸引的观众最多，超过 70 万观众参加了庆祝活动。8 月 25 日“有色人种日”举办了题为“美国的种族问题”的演讲，还有专为主题而作的诗歌朗诵，并且上演了“汤姆叔叔的小屋”歌剧选段。这一年，在芝加哥杰克逊公园和 Midway 乐园外周边的空地，游客还会发现大量的娱乐活动，像杂耍表演、喜剧和西大荒表演（Wild West Show）等，那里场地租金便宜，入场费较低，这些世博园外的晚间表演吸引了大批观众。

对于成千上万的游客来说，世博会就是Midway乐园，但对世博组委会，Midway是财富之源。Midway乐园是第一个完全独立于专业展区的世博娱乐区，多数Midway景观是异域建筑和景观的复制品，这种最早出现在1889年巴黎博览会上的外国风情村（foreign-village）式的展览在Midway乐园随处可见，最受欢迎的维也纳老街是仿照1750年Der Graben大街的风情建造的；开罗街是另一处有吸引力的景点，除了复制景观外，还有骑骆驼和骑驴的活动，并且有集市。

在Midway乐园中央，矗立着世博会的一项伟大的工程奇迹——巨型摩天轮，这是世博会的一个主要标志，也是奉献给人类娱乐活动的长久礼物。这座轴长45英尺的Ferris摩天轮是当时最大的钢结构，匹兹堡桥梁工程师Feorge W. Ferris设计建造。巨轮的实际直径是250英尺（约76m），但是总体高度达到264英尺，乘坐摩天轮可以纵览世博园景观和附近的芝加哥地区。摩天轮上安装了36个木镶板面吊箱，每箱可乘载60人。Ferris摩天轮为博览会创造了利润。

Midway乐园的其他亮点有：动物表演；“电力剧场”——一个将声光效果与景观画面相结合创造山区雷暴场景的展览；涡轮机驱动的雪茄形火车在位于水面上的高架铁路上驰骋——这样的铁路也出现在1889年巴黎博览会。

本届世博会在经济上取得了巨大成功。1893年10月31日世博会闭幕时，入场观众达到2750万人次，只有大约600万人次免票。世博会总支出3050万美元，总收入3275万美元，仅特许经营一项就创造了400万美元——大约是预计收入的4倍，不仅支付了世博会的所有运作费用，而且还向30000债权人返还了100万美元的红利，虽然这是他们最初投资的一部分，但是在全国性的经济萧条时期，这已是一个令人瞩目的成就。

随着世博会接近尾声，一些芝加哥人也在考虑世博建筑的未来用途，考虑是否能让荣誉广场成为“威尼斯似的风情美景”保留下来，虽然他们知道要使之成为永久性建筑需要花费大笔资金。

1894年1月1日，世博园移交公园管理处，公众可以免费入园观赏，一场大规模的肆意破坏随即开始。1月8日，一场大火焚毁了荣誉广场这片柱廊式建筑群，工业与文学艺术品展馆也遭到了破坏。公园随之变成流浪者和经济萧条时期落难者的庇护所，这种破坏进一步扩大。6月初一场更大的火灾摧毁了荣誉广场的残余部分和其他几座主要建筑，园区剩余的其他建筑，除美术馆外，都被拆除或搬迁。

## 世博园概览

总的来说，世博园区可划分为三个部分（图3）。

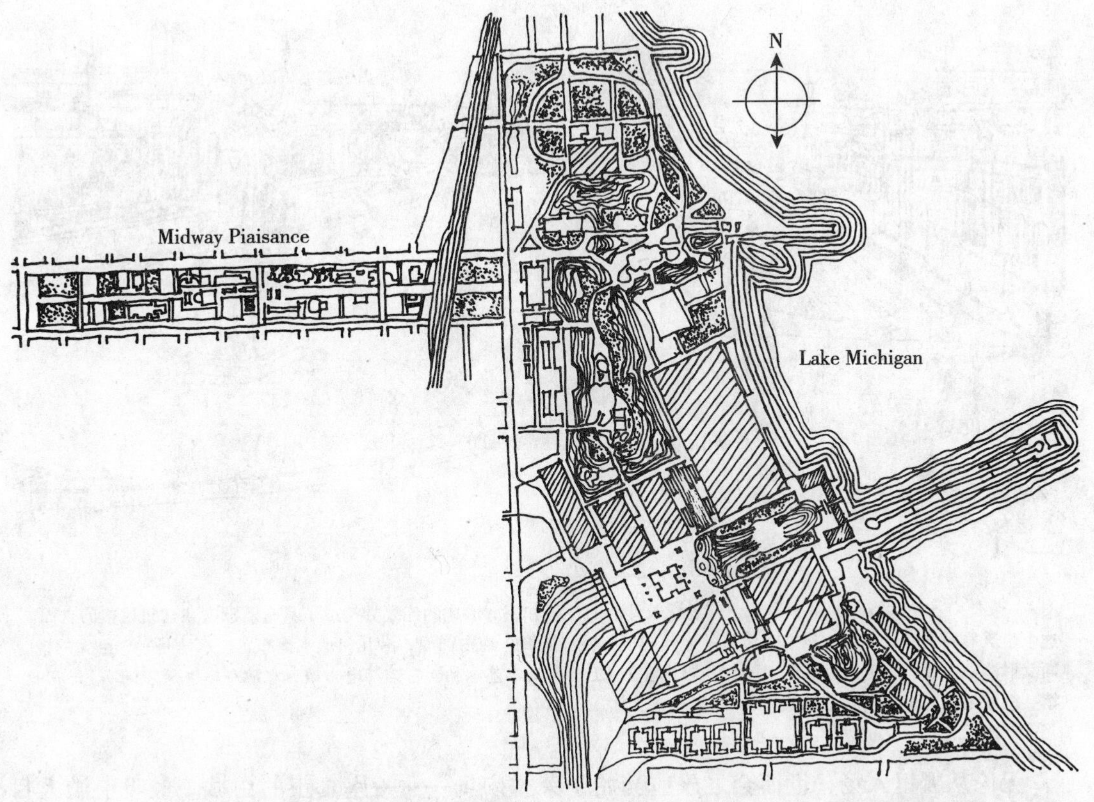


图3 世博园由三个部分组成。第一部分是荣誉广场，位于公园南端，包括几何形大水池（Basin）及两岸展馆：工业与文学艺术品展馆、电力馆、行政管理大楼、机械馆和农业馆；第二个部分位于公园北端，包括潟湖、绿荫岛、美术馆、运输馆、园艺馆等展馆；第三部分是 Midway plaisance，这是一条向西延伸一英里的大街，两侧布置了各种娱乐设施和展览

荣誉广场，位于公园南端，包括称之为大水池（Basin）的几何形水面及两岸的展馆：工业与文学艺术品展馆、电力馆、行政管理大楼、机械馆和农业馆。

从荣誉广场向北向西延伸是第二个部分，包括潟湖、绿荫岛、美术馆、运输馆、园艺馆、渔业馆、矿产与采矿馆、妇女馆以及美国各州展馆和外国馆。这部分占据了公园北端，建筑依自然景观形态布置，掩映在绿荫丛中。

第三部分是 Midway Plaisance，这是一条一英里长，从杰克逊公园的妇女馆附近向西延伸通向华盛顿公园的大街，沿着 Midway 大街两侧布置了各种娱乐设施和外国风情园似的展览，这些展览力图搭建起一座联系教育与娱乐的桥梁。

多数乘火车的游客从荣誉广场西面进入世博园，乘船的游客从东面进入，因此，荣誉广场是世博园的第一景观。这个建筑群由五座巨型新古典主义风格的建筑构成，檐口同高，纯白饰面，极尽装饰，沿几何形水池布置。水池是一个巨大的镜面反射池，东北西南走向，350 英尺宽，1100 英尺长，广场建筑外部的柱廊和拱廊形成的连续券构成了具有欧洲古典建筑风格的立面（图4）。水池东端矗立着 65 英尺高的镀金共和雕像，西端是哥伦布喷泉，这是世博会庆祝发现新大陆的标志。

图4　荣誉广场是世博园的第一景观，广场建筑外部的柱廊和拱廊形成的连续券构成了具有欧洲古典建筑风格的立面。这个建筑群由五座巨型新古典主义风格的建筑构成，檐口同高，纯白饰面，沿几何形水池布置。水池是一个巨大的镜面反射池，东北西南走向。水池右岸（从右向左）：工业与文学艺术品博物馆、电力馆；水池左岸（从左向右）：农业馆、机械馆；画面中央（水池西岸）：行政管理大楼

无论从哪里入场，世博会之旅应当始于荣誉广场——一座真正的白城。最吸引游人目光的两座建筑是行政管理大楼和工业与文学艺术品展馆。行政管理大楼位于广场西端，巨大的穹顶主导着西边的景观，这里不仅是世博会官员工作的总部，而且这里着重介绍14座主要展馆的建筑主题。

工业与文学艺术品展馆自称是当时世界上最庞大的建筑，规模显赫，其中布置了大量外国展厅，展示海外工业的最新产品。大量的展品包括供销售的商品和文学艺术品，如芝加哥大学提供的Yerkes望远镜，重70吨，还有乐器、林肯的就职演说手稿和莫扎特的古钢琴等。许多大学和出版社都在这里举办了重要展览。展览将美国社会生活中的两个重要方面——文化与消费——展示在同一屋檐下并不是一个巧合，它表明艺术为物质消费，无论是生产者还是消费者，带来文化品位，同时，艺术可以被消费，美国工业不是低品位的标志，而是高雅文化的组成部分。

机械馆不仅展示了Whitney轧棉机、缝纫机和世界上最大的传送带，而且还展出了为世博会提供动力的发电厂，包括43台蒸汽机和127台发电机。为了让白城在世博会期间保持白色，组委会颁布了在世博园区禁止使用煤作燃料的禁令。

电力馆致力于展示电力的神奇，这是一个历史性的时刻，是一场革命的开始，电力让世博会大放异彩，展览向公众宣传电力知识，让公众亲眼目睹交流电的特性和威力。

在大水池的东端有一条长830英尺（约253m）的柱廊连接水池两岸，形成环状广场（图5），柱廊的南北两端各有一座风格尺度完全相同的建筑，北楼是世博园的音乐厅，在

图5 在大水池的东端有一条长830英尺的柱廊连接水池两岸，形成环状广场，柱廊的南北两端各有一座风格尺度完全相同的建筑，北楼是世博园的音乐厅，南楼是乘船游客的候船大厅。水池东端矗立着65英尺高的镀金共和雕像，西端是哥伦布喷泉，这是世博会庆祝发现新大陆的标志

这里演出古典音乐；南楼是乘船游客的候船大厅，从这里一条250英尺宽2400英尺长的码头伸入湖面，码头上安装了一条“移动人行道”——一条安装有顶棚和长条座椅的电动传送带，从登船处一直传送到候船大厅。

虽然众多游人对荣誉广场的欧洲古典风格建筑赞叹不已，有些游人则认为美国人的自豪感不应来自对欧洲古典形式的模仿，而应表现在对美国精神的颂扬和对源自新大陆的本土文化的自信心。几年后，沙利文在他的自传中宣称世博会对欧洲古典形式的强调使美国的建筑思想倒退了40年。

从荣誉广场向北走，进入公园的北区，这里的建筑布局更加灵活多样，游人可以看到运输馆和美术馆。沙利文设计的运输馆由于其风格迥异的“金色”大门与周围的建筑不协调而独处一隅，独立于其他主要建筑之外（图6）。美术馆的总体设计风格与荣誉广场建筑群一致，其所处位置使之成为一个世博园建筑风格的转折点，从布局规整的大型建筑向美术馆周围布局灵活的小型州立展馆和外国展馆过渡。

州立展馆展示各州的发展历史及其显著特征，但是设计方案必须事先提交伯纳姆的办公室批准，同样，其他参展国也必须提交初步设计方案并获得批准。总的来说，外国展馆比州立展馆和荣誉广场建筑群更具个性和传统风格，多数外国展馆力图在设计中反映各自的本土文化。从一开始，国际参与对世博会主办方一直很重要，1891年夏季，组委会派代

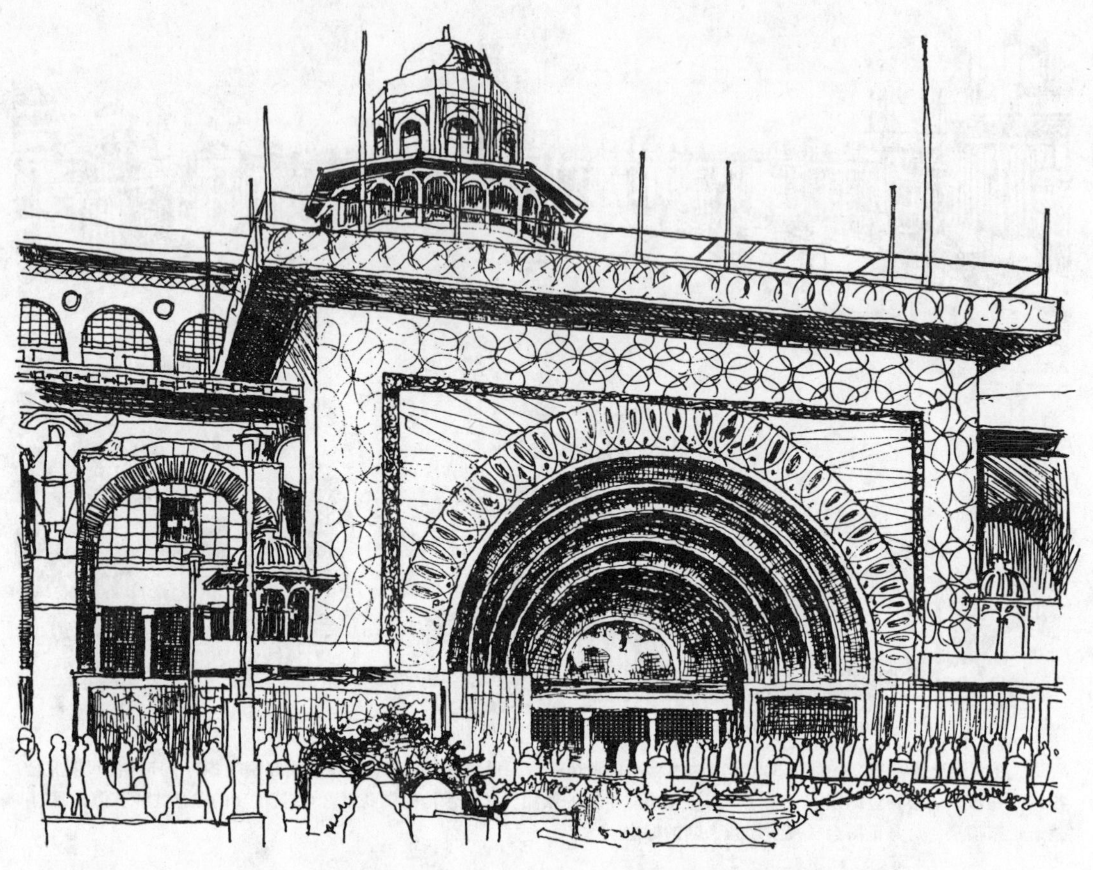

图6 Sullivan 设计的运输馆由于其风格迥异的“金色”大门与周围的建筑不协调而独处一隅，独立于其他主要建筑之外

表去欧洲和南美洲招展，邀请外国政府搭建各自的展馆。

相反，Midway 乐园的建筑没有什么个性可言，Ferris 摩天轮也许是个例外。Midway 乐园主要包括一些地方性的展览，有些展览由私人主办，外国政府也赞助了一些这类展览，这些展览有针对性地强调了世博会的文化层面。Midway 的这些项目很受欢迎，只是所有项目都要另外收费，这些收费的抽税为博览会提供了资金。

芝加哥世博会面积633 英亩（与 1889 年巴黎博览会的 160 英亩相比），是当时世界上最大的世博园，规模远远超过以往的世博会，包括十几座主要建筑及其附属建筑、19 座外国政府展馆和38 座州政府展馆，再加上服务设施和私人展馆，建筑总数约 200 座。据估计，观众要想匆匆看一遍展览需要三周时间，跨越 150 多英里的路程。

因此，一本题为《省时策略——本书标示了 5000 个世博会不可错过的展览》的世博指南发挥了重要作用，《省时策略》带领游客游遍世博会的所有展馆，直至 Midway 乐园。该书采用三步打分体系，给每个重要展览或项目打分：1 分代表有趣，2 分代表很有趣，3 分代表特别有趣，这样游客在有限的时间内可以集中参观标示 3 分的展览。

## 教育作用和文化影响

世博会的领导者同时也是工商业者，而且，他们都是 19 世纪 90 年代芝加哥的社会文化精英，对这座城市倾注了巨大心血，他们要创造符合理想城市理念的芝加哥城市形象和市民形象。

### 1. 强调教育作用

组委会在世博建筑设计中采用欧洲古典形式，在世博园区的各类展览中强调教育性，以此表现美国与欧洲在文化发展水平上已并驾齐驱，欧洲文化既是美国人效仿的榜样，同时也是美国文化自我肯定的参照。世博会是一所学习知识丰富阅历的大学校，是美国人拓展知识，提高文化层次的“实物课堂”，这已成为民众的共识。正像当年的一本文学杂志《大都会》（The Cosmopolitan，September 5，1893）所指出的那样：“世博会是最新版的内容最全面图解最详尽的百科巨著”。不仅世博会的官方指南和宣传，而且众多观众都强调了亲历世博会的教育作用。对大多数人来说，世博会的展示活动改变了他们的思维，使他们更易于接受新事物。在同一地点亲眼目睹如此大规模的展览，近距离了解不同种族和不同文化已不仅仅是一种教育活动，例如，向观众演示电话机、留声机，以及早期电影是一种教育形式，但是对于有些观众，这更是一种娱乐形式。世博会不仅仅是建筑景观和展品的静态展示，而且是一系列文化教育活动和娱乐休闲活动。

美国人的学习热情还体现在世博会的学术报告部（The World's Congress Auxiliary）每天举办的演讲和讲座中。学术报告部是世博组委会的一个分支机构，学术报告部将这些演讲活动视为改变芝加哥偏远城市形象的另一途径，因为单纯的展示活动不足以激发人类的智慧。这些邀请公众参与的演讲和讲座涉及的内容广泛，如：妇女进步、医学与外科、道德与社会改革、商业与金融、科学与哲学、教育、文学、音乐、工程、艺术、政府等，总共举办了 1283 场，来自 97 个国家和美国各州的讲演者宣读了 5978 篇讲稿和论文。

世博会举办的各种会议（国际会议或专题研讨会）总结了人类智慧的结晶，指明了未来的发展方向。在建筑专题会议上，奥姆斯特德、伯纳姆和沙利文宣读了世博会规划设计方面的重要论文，许多杰出女性在妇女代表大会上发表了演说，妇女展馆举办的女性作品展反映了妇女社会地位的改变。

### 2. 创造一个乌托邦

“规划”与“统一”这两个词是哥伦布纪念世博会给人留下的深刻记忆，特别给观众带来耳目一新的感觉是，世博会本身就是一座配套齐全的城市。游客一进入世博园，展现在他们眼前的便是系统的规划，大型建筑的和谐布局和前所未有的大型园林景观，此情此景与19世纪晚期混乱无序发展的城市形成鲜明对比。他们被世博园的清洁卫生，保安人员的彬彬有礼，饮水池和洗手间等公共设施所打动，所有这些世博会的典型特征也许只有在"理想"城市中才能找到，而现在，普通市民只需花费50美分入场便可享受。荣誉广场统一的建筑风格和古典形式，整齐划一的檐口线和细致的景观规划，从规则的几何形水池到形态自然的潟湖，从正统的古典建筑到灵活多变、别具一格的建筑，一切都显得那么自然有序，所有这些处理手法有助于世博会的成功。

**3. 创造新型都市娱乐方式**

Midway留给后人的重要影响是创造了一种新型的都市娱乐方式，这种没有多少文化内涵的纯粹的娱乐方式如雨后春笋在美国的许多城市和度假地涌现，是一种商业化运作的，集游戏、杂耍表演和多种娱乐活动为一体的娱乐公园，为逃避都市生活压力的人们提供了一个消遣的去处。纯粹的娱乐享受对当时的美国人来说并不是一个陌生的概念，正如1893年5月的《世纪》周刊所指出的那样："多数美国人参观世博会带着认真的学习目的，然而，不是所有美国人都渴望在此获取新知识，总是有许多人去芝加哥不是为了获益，而是为了娱乐身心，这些人也都如愿以偿。"Midway以其娱乐性大受欢迎，游客们似乎陶醉于Midway的异国情调之中，即便是仿制品，他们也乐在其中。当他们看完正规的展览感到疲惫时，就会在Midway大街上漫步，在这里他们发现了一种美国本土的表达方式，一种更准确地反映当代美国的景象。"Midway不可能取代世博会，但是，没有Midway，世博会的乐趣就会减少一半，这里比其他地方更有人情味。正如教皇所说，对人类的研究不只是研究人本身，同时也是寻求无与伦比的最大乐趣。"（引自1893.9《大都会》）

## 商业与技术

世博董事会主要由工商界领袖组成，因此，倡导消费型社会，提高公众对美国工业及其产品的信心也是本届世博会的一个目标。世博会正是一个展示消费品的大舞台，在世博会上展示产品有望在产品竞争中赢得世博会奖牌，这是赢得产品认知度的理想途径，广告部门也从中受益匪浅。世博会的商业化运作不仅仅局限在Midway乐园，同时也包括特许经营、纪念品销售以及工业与文学艺术品展馆的商品销售。世博会还向美国公众推广彩图名信片和20世纪晚期流行的两种主要食品——碳酸饮料和汉堡包。1893年的美国正在经历着由生产型社会向消费型社会的转变。

在商业与技术领域，美国已处于世界领先地位，这已成为人们的共识，美国的这两大优势在成千上万的展品中，在位于大水池畔的电力馆和工业与文学艺术品展馆中得到了充分展示，与之相呼应的是农业馆和机械馆，它们曾经是美国社会的基石。世博会的主题之一——技术，特别是电力——深入人心，它们对商业时代的到来也很重要。观众对电力馆展品的迷恋，对电动人行道、汽艇、高架铁路和成千上万盏闪亮的灯饰的痴迷溢于言表。世博会管理层的目的是使世博园及其展馆成为表现电力进步的盛大展会，电力是美国技术和商业进军20世纪的基础，对技术进步的赞颂弥漫在本届世博会的各个角落，这种赞颂肩负着多种作用：让美国人接触技术，打消他们对电力（技术进步）的恐惧，取而代之以情趣和愉悦；让美国人看到，从农业社会向技术社会的转变并不可怕，实际上是一种进步；技术和商业对美国社会转型起到了积极作用。

本届世博会的影响已超越世博范围，1893 年在芝加哥形成的发展趋势和理念塑造了现代美国的面貌，从通俗文化到高雅文化，从美国能源结构的改变到商业与技术的持续影响，世博会的影响广泛而深远。由于世博会对产品展示和教育意义的重视，公共科学和艺术博物馆在美国各地的人口聚居区大量涌现。

1893 年哥伦布纪念世博会是美国第一个在经济上取得成功的世博会。世博会传递的信息——团结统一的梦想，文化与教育主张，更重要的是美国在技术与商业方面取得的成就——产生了巨大反响。这届世博会成为未来许多博览会学习的榜样，也是40 年后“世纪的进步世博会”主办者必须赶超的时刻隐现着的目标。

## Chapter 3

# The World's Columbian Exposition of 1893

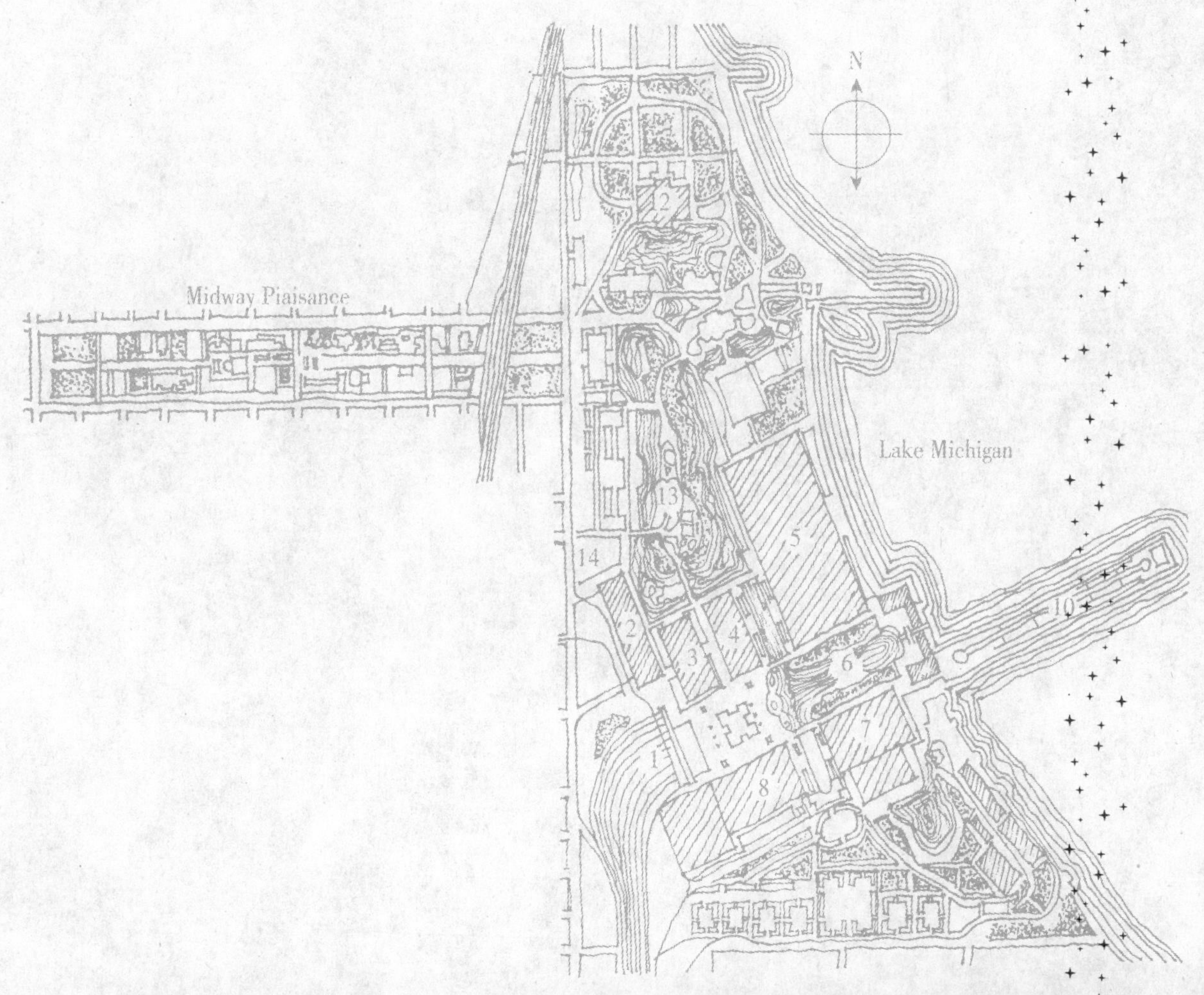

## Background

In 1893 and again in 1933—1934, the Midwestern city of Chicago hosted world's fairs, the World's Columbian Exposition and the Century of Progress Exposition, that contributed significantly to the history of exhibitions. These two fairs reflected in the manner and style of their exhibits the state of material and culture in the United States at the times they were staged, and permanently establishing the status of Chicago as well.

The second half of the 19th century was an age of fairs and expositions held in London, Paris, Vienna and other great cities throughout the world. Fairs were incredibly popular events. The Centennial Exhibition in Philadelphia drew over 10 million visitors in 1876 and Paris's extremely popular Exposition in 1889 drew over 28 million visitors. As fairs encompassed the spectrum of experience and the interest of the time——from sport to entertainment to high culture, they were seen as a combination of an international entertainment and cultural event with lasting social importance.

When the idea of celebrating the 400th anniversary of Columbus' discovery of the New World surfaced in 1880s, cities began to scramble for the opportunity to host the fair. Chicago's City Council began their campaign for the fair on July 22, 1889, when a local committee was appointed, known as the Chicago Company, to carry out the project. It issued five million dollars' worth of bonds, to establish Chicago's determination that they would have the fair. The ten-dollar shares were fully subscribed by April 1890. The House of Representatives took up the issue in late 1889 and considered petitions from Chicago, St. Louis, New York, and Washington, D. C. After months of consideration and conflict, the House gave the award to Chicago on February 24, 1890——but with a catch. The city was required to raise an additional $5 million.

Chicago had special reasons to pursue the honor. The city's central location (its ability to represent the large Midwestern region), transportation network, and moderate summer weather would make it an ideal location for a world's fair. Having the fair in Chicago would allow European visitors to see much more of the United States.

## A Glimpse of the Past

Lured, perhaps, by stories of the rich land and agreeable climate as well as by talk of a canal (the construction began in 1836) that eventually linked the city by water to New Orleans, settlers came in significant numbers after 1833 (incorporated as a town in August 1833 and as a city in 1837). Later in the 1840s, the city's development as a regional commercial center sped up, attracting national attention in 1847 by hosting the River and Harbor Convention. This convention attracted 3000 delegates and national press attention over the issue of federal-sponsored river and harbor improvements. The publicity generated by this convention was important in bringing more business and people to Chicago and hastening the completion of the canal and the arrival of the railroad, both of which occurred the following year. More than anything else, the railroad keyed Chicago's development into the most important city of the Midwest.

By 1870, Chicago was the busiest railroad center in the country. Immigrants provided a ready labor supply for new enterprises in meatpacking, iron, lumber, and transportation. No one could have foreseen that on 8 October 1871 the great heart of the city, its buildings hastily built of wood during the years of rapid expansion, would be utterly destroyed by fire in less than twenty-four hours.

However, the city recovered quickly. Chicago promoters went to eastern cities like New York and successfully touted the investment potential of rebuilding their city, and new buildings soon began to rise from the ashes of the old. Young architects, attracted by the opportunity to design a city practically from scratch, came to Chicago and made it into the center of architectural and engineering innovation for the next generation.

By 1889 Chicago was already the second city in terms of industrial and commercial wealth and power, the economic center of the grain, meat and lumber trades of the west——a region stretching all the way to the Rocky Mountains. Large-scale gatherings had always been important in Chicago's history and the Chicago Interstate Industrial Exposition had been holding annual exhibitions. The nation's railroads had centered on Chicago, and by 1890 Chicago was the nation's second steel-making center and was a major player in modern industry.

In the cultural and social areas, the 1890s witnessed a flowering of museums, art galleries, educational institutions and libraries. In addition, a handful of inventive architects had overtaken and surpassed New York's lead in the development of the tall commercial building, or proto-skyscraper, adding fundamental new esthetic and structural refinements and thereby contributing to the city's tourist attractions. The World Columbian Exposition became the centerpiece of this cultural expansion.

As the city expanded through annexation and attracted more than its share of the thousands of immigrants, its population grew from well under 400000 (1870s) to over 1.2 million (1890s). This growth was not without its problems. Poverty, political corruption, radical labor agitation, bloody class confrontations, and a high level of crime were social consequences of the rapid growth. Industrial activity, carried on in factories that spewed thick black smoke, contributed to the darkness of the 'Black City': smoke, clouds dirt, and an extraordinary number of sad and grieved persons.

To many New Yorkers and other easterners, Chicago of 1889 was little more than an overgrown frontier town. Chicago business and government responded in many ways, such as the development of the social settlement movement, designed to deal with urban disorder and improve life for the poor. Increasing emphasis on job training, along with European languages, in public schools was a part of the same response.

## Planning the Fair

In creating the World's Fair, the committee sent a delegation headed by Edward T. Jeffrey, an executive committee member, to visit the Paris exposition of 1889 and prepare a report on its major features, which was influential in determining the nature of the World's Columbian Exposition. Chicago's business community sought to display the triumphs of commerce and industry, to showcase a city just 60 years old, a city magnificently reborn just 22 years after the Chicago Fire. In effect, the Columbian Exposition was Chicago's debut on a world stage as a locus of great architecture and burgeoning economic power. It also placed before the world the genius of Chicago architects Daniel Burnham, Frederick Law Olmsted, and Louis Sullivan.

The award to Chicago placed most of the detailed planning as well as almost all of the responsibility, financial and otherwise, in local hands. However, the Congress decided that a national committee, consisting of representatives from each state and territory, to superintend the organization, construction, and management of the exposition, would also be required. The national organization came to be known as the Commission and the local group was the Directory. The Commission and Directory were made up of both politicians and business leaders——U. S. Senators, presidents of railroads, banks, and department stores, and heads of real estate empires. They were also professional men, architects and professors. The two bodies were directed by one man, George Davis, a senator who helped plead Chicago's case in Congress. With this political / corporate body in place, the work of planning the Exposition began in 1890.

### 1. Conception of the Fair

Jeffrey's report on Paris fair was of great importance in the building and staging of the World's Columbian Exposition. And through it, the Chicago Company was able to meet its objective of outdoing the Paris fair. The report described in detail how the Parisians made ample provision for entertainment and recreation, with theaters and concert halls, foreign 'villages,' featuring exotic dancers, all available at a reasonable cost to visitors. Jeffrey also praised the effect of electric lighting at night and in conjunction with fountains, the narrow gauge railroad that took visitors along the Seine River, and the multiplicity of intellectual conferences that featured discussion of important themes by leading authorities. He was impressed with the comprehensive and well-organized exhibits, which included 'everything conceivable and inconceivable, useful and ornamental'.

Discussion of the design of the fair——what it should look like——had been going on since 1889 and was predicated on two important points. First, it was necessary to create a fair that would do away with the lack of respect that Chicagoans felt they received from the rest of the nation, and indeed, the lack of respect that many Americans felt on the part of Europeans. In doing this, the design had to show the unity of the United States and the full-fledged development of its civilization. The second point of design consideration was the perceived necessity to outshine the Paris exposition of 1889. This was seen early in the Chicago Tribune's request that its readers send in designs for an Eiffel-like tower to be constructed for the fair. However, financial problems prevented the construction of the tower, and the signature structure for the fair became the Ferris wheel, located at the center of the Midway.

The construction of buildings and the choice of a site were the first items on the agenda. By February 1891 a firm decision was reached to have a single site for the fair, the little-used and marshy Jackson Park, with the majority of the buildings to be located in the Jackson Park area and a few on the lakefront. This site seemed to meet all the requirements of the company: it was large enough, available for development, and in a location convenient to visitors. In addition, the park could get improved according to the design made many ears earlier. Daniel H. Burnham and John W. Root were selected as consulting architects. This was a natural choice, as they had been partners in Chicago for fifteen years and were the city's best-known architectural firm. Specializing in commercial building, Burnham & Root was responsible for a number of downtown Chicago's most highly regarded skyscrapers, which had arisen after the devastating 1871 fire.

At the request of the Chicago Company, Burnham presented a site plan utilizing Jackson Park. Burnham's plan, worked out in conjunction with Root and Olmsted, proposed that the major exhibition buildings comprise a 'Court of Honor', grouped around a formal body of water. Another body of water, a lagoon, would be situated in more natural surroundings and have a large island in its center. Other buildings would be arranged more informally around the lagoon and in other areas of the large site (Figure 3). Burnham knew that there was more architectural work than his office could possibly handle, so he decided to bring in a team of architects of his own choice, rejecting the idea of a competition as too time-consuming and too likely to result in mediocrity. Burnham's choices were some of the great names in American architecture, most of whom were from the east. It is probable that his motivation was based on a desire to make the fair a national effort.

Burnham and the team of architects, generally trained at the Academie des Beaux-Arts in Paris, decided on an unusual fair plan. Utilizing the natural landscape of Jackson Park, Frederick Law Olmsted, a venerable landscape architect who had designed New York's Central Park, created a system of lagoons and waterways fed by Lake Michigan. These bodies of water served as decorative reflecting pools, waterways for transportation, and provided a place of respite necessary for weary summer visitors——the shady wooded island. The 14 main buildings surrounding the waterways were in a neo-classical architectural style, with its emphasis on logic, harmony, and uniformity. The Court of Honor buildings——surrounding a Grand Basin——were covered with stucco, giving the main buildings a magnificent whiteness, hence called "White City".

Actual construction began in July 1891, and proceeded rather rapidly because of iron and steel framing techniques, relatively new in construction, and the use of stuff, a substance made of plaster, cement, and fiber that were malleable, and relatively cheap and easy to work with. As a time-saving device, the decision to paint the buildings in the Court of Honor white was extended to all the other major buildings, except Louis Sullivan's Transportation building. Even more time was saved by leaving the interiors of the exhibition buildings unfinished, except for the Administration building, which was used for meetings and fair business rather than the display of exhibits.

### 2. Fair Promotion

By February 1892, there was enough standing on the grounds to impress a large group of Congressmen who had been invited to inspect the site. Burnham insured good publicity for the fair by personally escorting groups of visiting public officials and other dignitaries around the site and by employing a well-known photographer to make the official photographic record of the fair's construction, which found their way into various forms of promotional material.

Burnham was also generating as much publicity as possible for the event by allowing visitors on the site under construction, despite the fact that they often got in the way of the work. The interest surrounding the construction of the fair became so great that even after admission to the unfinished fair had been raised from 25 to 50 cents, several thousand people a day came to the site. Moses Handy, the official public relations agent for the exposition, published a guidebook for the benefit of people visiting the site during the construction period. For a cost of ten cents, visitors could use the book to tell which building was which and to get a notion of the layout of the fair. Burnham and the Directory had plenty of opportunity to make this pre-fair interest a profitable venture.

Another Exposition development was the creation of the most high-powered publicity department in history, Moses Handy, which ceaselessly produced large quantities of literature to familiarize the country and the world with the progress of the fair preparation. In operation since 1890, the department was the source for information and news about the progress of the Fair for many national and international newspapers and journals. Its focus was on the promotion of Chicago and the commercial opportunities of the Fair, and was the basis for the Official Guidebooks of the Columbian Exposition. "Providing the world for 50 cents" was a successful promotion campaign. Adult admission to the fairgrounds was 50 cents, very high at the time but surely well worth it.

As more money was urgently needed from the federal government, eventually, a Columbian 50-cent piece was coined by the Treasury, and two and a half million dollars' worth of the coins was presented to the Exposition Corporation, which sold them as souvenirs at a total of about twice their face value.

With a total area of 633 acres (including 80 acres for the Midway Plaisance, an entertainment strip), the construction process was slow. In fact, the enormity of the task at hand forced Burnham and the Commission to push the opening day back from late 1892 to May, 1893. The change of opening date only served to increase public anticipation of the Fair.

After three years of preparation and $28 million, the Fair opened on May 1, 1893. 46 foreign nations participated in the fair, 19 of which erected separate government buildings on the fair grounds. From May 1 to October 31, 1893, the exposition was the host to 27 million visitors——nearly one quarter of the country's population at the time.

The Fair was inspiring, and in large part achieved its goal. Visitors were greeted with 633 acres of fairgrounds, 65000 exhibits and a large number of restaurants, cafes, teahouses, lunch counters, and refreshment stands on the grounds for those who eat their way through the shows. The sanitation and the general maintenance were highly praised and held up as a model for real cities to follow. They were amazed by the clean and safe elevated railway and the electric launches plying the canals and lagoons. In many respects, the Fair in fact was a utopia——so unlike the gray and dusty cities many of the visitors had come from. Guests, on the way to the entertainment and the spectacle of the Midway felt quite safe with the hundreds of Columbian guards and plainclothes detectives on the grounds. Hundreds of concessionaires, selling everything from souvenirs to popcorn and the newly invented carbonated soda, crowded the walkways. Nearly every day had a special theme for visitors to celebrate, and presentations and lectures were held daily, covering subjects like ethics, authors, economics, labor and religions. The event was massive, and its popularity sustained.

## From Opening to Closing Day, and Beyond

Almost immediately after the fair opened, the Panic of 1893 broke out. This stock-market crash led to one of the worst depressions in American history. In Chicago, unemployment soared during 1893. The winter of 1892—1893 was extremely severe. The fair's business was unsatisfactory for the first three months, picking up only gradually after the weather improved, unfinished areas were completed, the farmers had gathered and sold their crops, and the railroads had belatedly reduced fares.

During the fair, many specific days were set aside for special celebrations in honor of nations, states, organizations and so on. Parades, athletic contests and other amusements characterized these increasingly frequent occasions, a commercial scheme to bring attractions onto the main part of the fair grounds. Chicago Day, October 9, the twenty-second anniversary of the devastating fire, brought the biggest crowd of any single day——well over 700,000 visitors. On Colored People's Day, August 25, an address on "The Race Problem in America" was given, a poem written for the occasion read, and selections from the opera Uncle Tom's Cabin were presented. In addition, Exposition visitors found plenty of entertainment in Chicago that year just outside Jackson Park and the Midway, where rent was cheaper and admission prices were low. Vaudevilles, comic operas and the great Wild West Show appealed to the audience of the Fair, offering nightly shows just outside the Exposition gates.

For thousands of visitors, the fair meant the Midway. For the fair corporation, the Midway meant moneymaker. Midway was the first amusement area in a world's fair, strictly separated from the exhibition halls. Most of the Midway exhibits were the imitations of buildings and places elsewhere. The foreign-village type of show, introduced at the Paris 1889 fair, was present in Chicago. The very popular Old Vienna exhibit was largely a reconstruction of the Viennese street Der Graben as it was supposed to have looked about 1750. A Street in Cairo was another notable attraction. Besides the topographical reconstructions, there were camel and donkey rides, and bazaars there.

In the center of the Midway Plaisance, stood one of the Exposition's great engineering marvels——one of its great emblems and one of its lasting gifts to the amusement of mankind: the giant wheel invented and constructed by the Pittsburgh engineer Feorge W. Ferris, a bridge builder. The 45-foot-long axle of the Ferris wheel was the largest single piece of steel that had yet been forged. The actual wheel was 250 feet in diameter, but the full height at the top was 264 feet, and riders had a remarkable view of the fair and nearby parts of Chicago. There were 36 wood-veneered cars with room for 60 people in each. The Ferris wheel turned a profit.

Other Midway highlights were: animal show; a so-called "electric theater" in which light and sound effects, used together with landscape paintings, created the sensation of a mountain storm; elevated railway with speedy cigar-shaped cars on runners propelled by turbine motors over a film of water——this type of railway had been shown in Paris in 1889.

The World's Columbian Exposition was an immense financial success. When the Fair closed on October 31, 1893, it was disclosed that there had been about 27 1/2 million admissions, only about 6 million being free. Total expenses amounted to 30 1/2 million dollars, total receipts to about $32, 750, 000. The concessions had provided about four million dollars of these receipts——about four times what had been expected. It paid off all of its operating expenses, even returning $1 million of dividend to its 30, 000 stockholders, a portion of their initial investments. This was a noteworthy achievement during a national depression.

As the fair drew to a close, some Chicagoans mused about the future of the fair buildings, wondering if it might be nice to keep the Court of Honor intact as 'a sort of Venice of pleasure and beauty,' although it was realized that a great deal of expense would be necessary to make the buildings into permanent structure.

On 1 January 1894, the grounds were turned over to the park board, and the public was given free access to the site. A wave of vandalism immediately ensued, and on 8 January a fire destroyed the Peristyle complex and damaged the Manufactures and Liberal Arts building. Further damage occurred as the park became a refuge for vagrants and others suffering in the national depression, and much larger fire in early July destroyed the rest of the Court of Honor and several other major buildings. The remaining buildings on the site, except for the Fine Arts building, were demolished or moved to other locations.

## Tour the Fair

In general, the fairgrounds can be divided into three areas (Figure 3). The Court of Honor, located at the south end of the park, included the formal body of water known as the Basin and the major exhibition halls flanking it; the Manufactures and Liberal Arts building, the Electricity building, the Administration building, the Machinery building, and the Agricultural building.

Stretching north and west of the Court of Honor, the second area of the site encompassed the lagoon and Wooded Island, the Fine Arts building, the Transportation building, the Horticultural building, the Fisheries building, the Mines and Mining building, the Women's building, and all the state and foreign nation buildings. This area took in the north end of the park and featured many of the buildings in a natural, wooded setting.

The third area of the exposition was Midway Plaisance, a mile-long street that ran west from Jackson Park near the Women's building to Washington Park. Along the Midway were all the entertainment venues, as well as exhibits like foreign villages, which strove to bridge the gap between entertainment and education.

Most visitors entered the fairgrounds at the west end of the Court of Honor, if they came by train, or at the east end, if they arrived by boat. Thus, the spectacle of the Court of Honor was the first sight most people saw. Five massive neo-classical buildings, with cornices at a uniform height, painted a dazzling white, and supremely ornamented, surrounded the formal Basin. The Basin is a large reflecting pool, with a northeast-southwest orientation, 350 feet wide and 1100 feet long. A continuous stoa made of the porticos and arcades of the court buildings formed the classical European facades of the Court of Honor (Figure 4). At the east end of the Basin stood a 65-foot tall, gilded Statue of the Republic, and at the west end was Columbian Fountain, a presentation of the discovery that the fair was celebrating.

Any tour of the Fair should begin with the Court of Honor, the real White City. The two most remarkable buildings were Administration building and Manufactures and Liberal Arts building. The Administration building at the west end of the court dominated the vista by virtue of its large dome. It served as the headquarters for the chief officers of the Exposition as well as the chief introduction to the main architectural theme of the 14 great buildings of the Fair.

The Manufactures and Liberal Arts Building, advertised as the largest building in the world at the time of its construction, was noteworthy for its size. It contained pavilions from many nations displaying the latest in their industrial production. The vast collection of exhibits combined goods for sale with items of liberal arts, including University of Chicago's 70-ton Yerkes telescope, musical instruments, as well as the manuscript of Lincoln's Inaugural address and Mozart's spinet. Many universities and publishing houses had important exhibits here. It was no accident that these two aspects of American life were brought together under one roof. The arts gave cultural cache to the consumption of goods, their producers, and their consumers, while art could be consumed. American business was not low-class, but a necessary component of high culture.

The Machinery Building not only contained exhibits such as Whitney's cotton gin, sewing machines, and the world's largest conveyor belt, but also the Fair's power plant, with 43 steam engines and 127 dynamos providing electricity for the Fair. A ban on coal as an energy source was enacted on the fairgrounds, so that the White City could remain white for the duration of the Exhibition.

The Electricity Building was devoted to electrical exhibits. It was a historical moment and the beginning of a revolution. It introduced the public to electric power by illuminating the Exposition. The general public observed firsthand the qualities and abilities of alternating current power.

A 830-feet-long Peristyle complex, flanked by two identical pavilions at the north and south ends, closed the ring of the court at the east end of the Basin (Figure 5). The north pavilion, the Music Hall, was the Exposition's concert hall for classical music. The south pavilion served as a waiting hall for boat passengers, with a 250-foot-wide and 2400-foot-long Pier extending into the lake. The Pier featured a "movable sidewalk", a covered, electrically driven moving belt with passenger benches that ran from the boat landing out in the lake all the way to the pavilion.

While many were impressed by the beauty of the classical European facades of the Court of Honor, some visitors believed that a sense of pride in America would not come from aping European forms, but in celebrating an American spirit, feeling confidence in the vernacular culture that had grown in the New World. Sullivan, in his autobiography years later, asserted that the Fair's emphasis on the European Beaux-Arts form set back American architectural thought for the next 40 years.

Moving away from the Court of Honor into the northern part of the park, where the arrangement of buildings was more informal, visitors would notice the Transportation building and the Fine Arts building. The Transportation building, designed by Sullivan, stood apart from the other major exhibition buildings because of its imposing 'golden' doorway (Figure 6). The overall design of the Fine Arts building was compatible with the buildings of the Court of Honor, however, its location served as a kind of transition point between the formal arrangement of most of the largest exhibition buildings and the smaller state and foreign buildings, situated informally around the Fine Arts building.

State pavilions were supposed to be representative of some aspect of the state's history or character, but designs had to be submitted to Burnham's office for advance approval. As with the states, foreign nations were required to send a preliminary design to Chicago for approval. On the whole, foreign pavilions tended to be more distinctive and traditionally-styled than either the state pavilions or the buildings on the Court of Honor, and most foreign nations attempted in their design to reflect something of their culture. From the beginning, international participation had been important to the organizers of the fair. The fair sent representatives to Europe and South America during the summer of 1891 looking for exhibits and inviting foreign governments to construct pavilions.

By contrast, the Midway contained no architecture of distinction, with the possible exception of the Ferris wheel. In addition, the Midway contained native exhibits that were in some cases privately organized, and in others sponsored by foreign governments. There was a purposeful effort to emphasize the cultural aspects of the fair. The Midway attractions were very popular, and since they all involved an extra charge, the royalty payments helped finance the exposition.

The area of the Exposition was 633 acres (as compared to 160 for Paris 1889), far and away the largest up to that time. Added to the dozen or so major buildings and their dependencies, and to the 19 foreign-government and 38 state-government buildings, the service structures and individual exhibitors' pavilions brought the total of separate buildings to about 200. It was estimated that to see everything in the fair once quickly, a visitor would need about three weeks and would have to walk over 150 miles.

Therefore, one of the guidebooks for the exposition, named The Time-Saver, whose sub-title, "A Book Which Names and Locates 5000 Things at the World's Fair that Visitors Should Not Fail to See", spelled out the purpose of the book. The Time-Saver took the visitors through the entire fair, building by building and down the Midway, and using a three step rating system, gave every significant exhibit or attraction a '1' (Interesting), '2' (Very Interesting), or '3' (Remarkably Interesting). Thus, visitors with only a limited amount of time could confine themselves to those exhibits awarded a '3' rating.

## The Educational and Cultural Impact

The leaders of the Exposition were businesspeople as well, but more than that, they were the social and cultural elite of 1890s Chicago, men who had a great stake in their city and wanted to create an image of Chicago and its people that suited their notion of what an ideal city should be.

### 1. Emphasis on Education

It was asserted that America had reached cultural parity with Europe, through its adoption of the European Beaux-Arts form in the Exposition's architecture, and through its emphasis on education throughout the Fairgrounds. Europe was the standard to which the United States had to aspire, and to whom the country must prove itself. The idea that the Fair was a great University, a place for learning and enrichment, a certain kind of "object-lesson" by which Americans could become more knowledgeable and cultured, was taken in wholeheartedly by the public. As a literary journal, Cosmopolitan, pointed out: " The World's Fair, in short, is another edition, the latest and most complete, and by far the best illustrated, of an Encyclopedia, published in one enormous volume (5, September 1893). The official guidebooks and publicity, and many visitors as well, emphasized the educational potential of simply being at the Fair. For the majority, the displays of the Fair changed their minds and left them open to new advances. Witnessing such an overwhelming grouping of items, peoples, and cultures together in one place would be more than education. The introduction of the telephone to a wide audience, the phonograph, even an early motion picture, was an education, and for some, even a form of amusement. The Exposition was not just static groups of buildings and exhibits, it was also a series of cultural and educational events, and entertainment.

The American desire for learning was also expressed in the daily presentations and lectures held by the World's Congress Auxiliary, a separate organization from the Chicago Company. The World's Congress Auxiliary saw it as another way to dispel the frontier image of the city, as the exhibits alone would not be intellectually stimulating. These presentations and lectures, to which the public was invited, covered a great variety of topics like Woman's Progress, Medicine and Surgery, Moral and Social Reform, Commerce and Finance, Science and Philosophy, Education, Literature, Music, Engineering, Art, Government and so on. A total of 1283 sessions were held, with 5978 addresses or papers read by speakers from 97 foreign nations as well as every state and territory in the United States.

The various Congresses (international conferences or symposiums) associated with the Exposition sum up the achievements of the intellect, and indicate the lines of future progress. In the Congress on architecture, important papers by Olmsted, Burnham and Sullivan explained many aspects of the fair. Many distinguished women spoke at the Congress of Representative Women. The exhibition of women's work in the Woman's Building displayed women's new place in society.

## 2. Creating an Utopia

Planning and unity stand as the two words in remembering the World's Columbian Exposition. It was the notion of the fair as a self-contained city that was particularly attractive to the visitors. In contrast to the wild growth of actual cities in the late 19$^{th}$ century, the systematic planning, the harmonious distribution of the enormous buildings, the display of landscape gardening on a scale never before attempted were what visitors noticed immediately upon entering the fairgrounds. They were impressed with the cleanliness of the site, the courtesy of the security staff, and the public drinking fountains and restrooms. All of these features might be found in an 'ideal' city, and all were accessible to the average citizen once he or she had paid the fifty cents to enter the fairgrounds. The architectural unity of the Court of Honor, the use of classical forms and a uniform cornice line, the landscape plan, the smooth transitions from the formal Basin to the irregular lagoon and from the setting of the formal classical buildings to the more picturesque structures, all contribute to the success of the fair.

## 3. Creating A New Kind of Urban Entertainment

The Midway left a significant legacy in the form of a new kind of urban entertainment devoid of cultural value that sprung up at American cities and resorts. This was the commercialized amusement park, featuring a mélange of rides, sideshow attractions, and other opportunities for visitors to escape the stresses of city life. The enjoyment of pure amusement was not a foreign concept to America of the time. As **The Century** (May 1893) put it: "Most Americans will go to the Exposition with some serious purpose before them. Nevertheless, not all Americans have minds that are eager for new knowledge. There must be many who do not intend to visit Chicago because of any profit they may gain. They are going because they hope to amuse themselves. They, too, will have their reward." It was the entertainment aspect of the Midway that was the most popular. The visitors seemed to revel in the outlandishness, the foreignness, and even the fakery of the Midway. When they grew tired of formal sightseeing, they would stroll down to the Midway, where they found a vernacular expression, a more accurate vision of contemporary America. "The Midway could not take the place of the Fair, but the Fair would not be half as delightful as it is without the Midway. There is more of the human here than elsewhere; and the study of mankind is not only, as Pope says, the proper study of man, but it is likewise incomparably the most entertaining." (The Cosmopolitan, September 1893)

## Commerce and Technology

As a large part of the Exposition Directory was made up of business leaders, the importance of promoting a consumer society, and encouraging American confidence in business and its products was also a goal of the Fair. The exposition was the venue for the debut of consumer products. To debut at the fair, and possibly win a Columbian medal in product competitions, was a perfect way to win product recognition and a boon for the advertising department. The commercial aspect of the Fair was not limited to the Midway but included concessionaires, souvenirs, and the goods for sale in the Manufactures and Liberal Arts building. The fair also introduced picture postcards to the American public, as well as two staples of the late-twentieth century diet——carbonated soda and hamburgers. The United States in 1893 was already well on its way to completing the transition from a producer to a consumer society.

The two areas in which America was already considered an international leader, commerce and technology, were celebrated extensively in the thousands of exhibits and the placement of the Electricity Building and the Manufactures and Liberal Arts building directly on the Grand Basin, counterparts to the former bedrocks of American society, the Agriculture and Machinery Buildings. One theme——so important to the coming of commerce——was quite well received by visitors: technology, especially electricity. Their fascination with the exhibits of the Electricity Building, the electric moving sidewalk, launches, elevated trains, and thousands upon thousands of incandescent lights was undeniable. It was the intention of the management to make the World's Fair site and the buildings one grand exemplification of the progress that had been made in electricity. Electricity was to be the basis for America's technological and commercial advances into the twentieth century, and the Fair celebrated it throughout the grounds. This celebration served a number of purposes: it introduced Americans to the technology, and attempted to remove the element of fear associated with electricity (technology progress), replacing it with fascination and amusement; it showed Americans that their transition from an agricultural to a technological society was not frightening, but was in fact progress; and finally, along with the celebration of commerce, it had a positive effect on the changes in American society.

The influence of the Exposition extended beyond the confines of the World's Fairs. Trends originating in Chicago in 1893 and many of the ideas advanced there have shaped the very landscape of modern America. Its legacy is wide-ranging, from movements in popular and high culture to changes in the nation's power structure and the lasting influence of commerce and technology. Thanks to the emphasis on exhibits and education at the exposition, public science and art museums can be found in every population center in the country.

The World's Columbian Exposition of 1893 was the first economically successful U. S. world fair. The message of the fair——the dream of unity, the assertion of culture and education, and most importantly the achievement in American technology and commerce——were well received. The fair was a model for many subsequent fairs, and a looming presence with which the organizers of the Century of Progress Exposition had to contend some forty years later.

# 第四章

## 1933 年芝加哥世博会

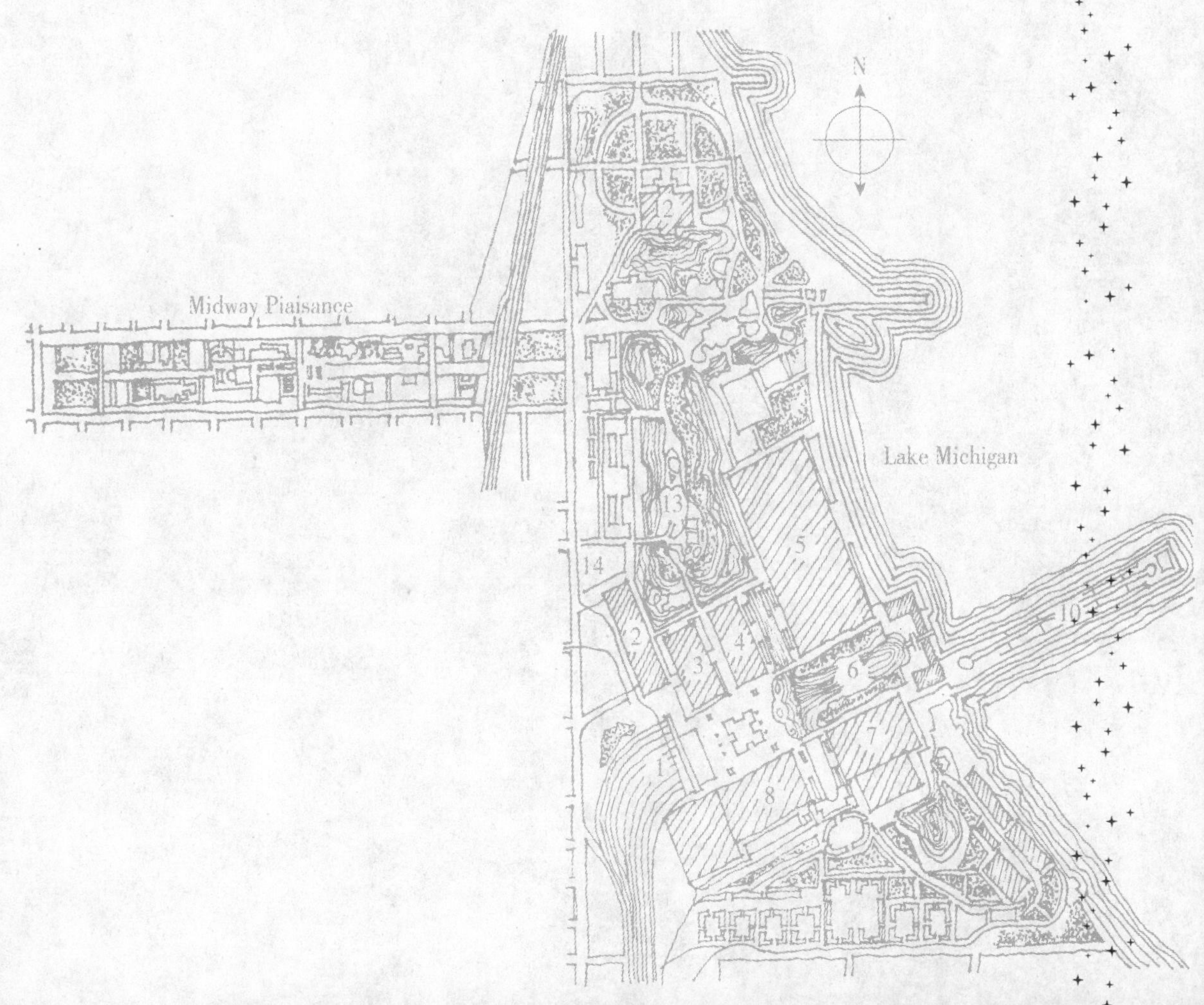

## 策划第二届世博会

20 世纪 20 年代，美国的博览会时代已经过去，在那个现代主义蓬勃发展的时期，博览会已显得过时。哥伦布纪念世博会的影响到了 20 世纪仅有间接体现，那便是城市规划运动，也就是伯纳姆的 1909 年芝加哥规划，芝加哥这座商业与文化相融合的城市依然在稳步发展。

受到哥伦布纪念世博会的启发，人们认识到了治理芝加哥迅速重建造成的混乱无序发展的必要性，探讨以世博会为样板重建城市的可能性，哥伦布纪念世博会的统一规划布局使人们相信世博经验可以用于改造城市生活——城市可以像世博会一样进行规划布局。

1909 年芝加哥规划通过强化市区内外及其周边的交通，确定了芝加哥的重要商业地位，规划还考虑到劳动阶层的休闲需求和保持城市品位的重要性，预留了公园和公共建设用地，并进行了艺术化的布局设计。这个规划被采纳，是芝加哥未来 50 年城市发展的指南。然而，该规划在经济和法律方面遇到的主要障碍从多方面影响了其近期目标和远期目标的实施。

到了 1923 年和 1925 年，一些芝加哥人建议举办世博会庆祝芝加哥（1833 年）建城 100 周年，他们相信借助这次世博会可以最终实现伯纳姆的城市美化计划。这个建议得到了公众的积极支持和市议会的批准。1927 年，世博组委会成立，决定将市政建设与 1933 年的庆典准备工作相结合，芝加哥规划所涉及的公共建筑、文化场馆和娱乐休闲空间在世博会开幕前得以完全实施，为世博会的举办起到了重要作用。从芝加哥规划到世纪的进步世博会这段时间，芝加哥经历了一段商业建筑的繁荣时期，直至 1929 年 10 月股市崩溃，经济萧条随之到来。

从 1928 年开始，世博组委会高速运作，新成立的世博董事会在以后的 6 年里成为世博组委会的中枢系统，一系列与世博会有关的活动迅速展开。

美国国家研究委员会（the National Research Council）是一个由科学家组成的，在第一次世界大战期间为美国政府出谋划策的庞大机构，1916 年成立。由这个委员会领导的科学咨询委员会（the Science Advisory Committee）应邀为世博会策划展览思路，构思世博主题，聚焦百年科技进步。

通过新闻发布引起公众对世博会的关注是十分重要的，因为组委会不想把有限的资金投入广告宣传，这个宣传策略对哥伦布纪念世博会和 1915 年旧金山巴拿马世博会的宣传很奏效。1928 年 4 月成立的公共信息委员会为报刊杂志提供了充足的世博新闻和特别报道。该委员会从 1931 年 4 月 1 日起开始发行名为《进步》的周报，世博会开幕时更名为《世博会周报》，专门向游客提供世博信息。

鉴于 1893 年哥伦布纪念世博会选在 5 月 1 日开幕，时值天气阴冷多雨，学校还未放假，观众的数量令人失望。1928 年 5 月，世博董事会决定 1933 年 6 月 1 日为世博会开幕日。

1929 年 6 月，世博董事会采纳了一些芝加哥市民的建议，将 1933 年世博会的名称由

"芝加哥第二届世博会"更名为"世纪的进步世博会"，这个名称既反映了主办城市的百年庆典，也反映了科学进步的主题。

## 融资方式

世博会项目融资是从发起销售"世博会员券"活动开始的，公众花5美元购买一张世博会员券，世博会开幕后可兑换10张入场券，这是一个类似战争时期发售自由债券式的挨家挨户上门销售债券的活动。虽然这项活动开始进展缓慢，但几年中一共销售了118773份会员券，连本带利为董事会筹措了$637754美元的资金。更重要的是，这项活动通过让公众入股参与即将举办的盛事提高了人们对这个百年庆典活动的热情。紧接着，另一个"发起人会员券"活动开始了，这是一种向芝加哥富裕阶层出售的1000美元一份的债券。

然而，这种融资方式远不能满足世博会对资金的需求，因此，一种新的融资方式应运而生，这就是1929年10月发行的1000万美元债券，称之为金券，用世博会门票收入的40%偿还。这些资金的注入对世博项目建设十分重要，例如，建设行政办公楼很有必要，这样，世博官员可以进入现场办公，每年可节省4万美元的市内办公场地租金。

此外，董事会要在世博会开幕前举办一些公众喜爱的展览，增强世博会的吸引力，同时也增加收入。为了达到预定目标，一座代表芝加哥1833年建城的Fort Dearborn城堡复制品建成，还举办了一个运输展览。为了筹措足够的资金实施世博规划方案，董事会要让这笔1000万美元的资金产生更多的经济效益。

1929年4月，董事会聘请《军事工程》杂志的前任主编，军事工程师Major Lenox Lohr担任世博总经理，以高效的组织和商业运作模式负责世博会的日常经营。当股市崩溃，经济萧条到来时，正是这位总经理毫不动摇的资本运营理念和一切以人为本的办事能力为世博会另辟蹊径，节支增收。

1933年世博会要与1893年世博会比高低是不可避免的，世博经理们花费大量精力潜心研究从1904年到20世纪30年代早期在北美和欧洲国家举办的博览会，从每天的观众数量、气象报告、经济状况、参观景点到娱乐项目，从色彩、照明到夜景等诸多方面进行比较和研究。

虽然20世纪30年代初的经济萧条放慢了债券认购的速度，但还是筹措到了相当数量的资金，这笔资金使世博经理们得以建造科学馆、旅游与运输馆和电力馆组团，并将这些设施出租给工业界举办展览。让企业、政府和其他机构有偿使用展览设施的想法最初是在1928年向组委会提出的，因为，工业展览一般是由行业协会共同举办的，行业协会为每年的贸易展览支付展馆租金已成为惯例。虽然，像以往的世博会一样，哥伦布纪念世博会提供免费展位，但是，从此以后，免费展位已不再是惯例。世博董事会采纳了这个建议，用一个展馆的租金收入建造另一个展馆，董事会在展馆租金创收方面取得了成功，为按计划建设世博园提供了重要的资金支持。

此外，经济萧条也确实给世博会带来了一定好处。因为承包商急于寻找工作机会，无论利润空间大小，随时都有大量的廉价劳动力、便宜的物资设备和低价的服务提供。董事会还常常以世博金券或入场券等形式支付部分商品和服务。经济萧条也降低了公众对大型国际博览会可能会产生的过高期望，因此，世博会开幕时，盛况超过了公众的期盼，令人震撼。

与此同时，董事会还制定了一系列其他措施，使世博会在经济困难时期从出让特许经营中获得了相当可观的经济收入。在某些情况下，世博会允许特许经营者在收回大部分投资后再支付特许经营费；在另一些情况下，企业可以赞助其产品在世博会上销售以换取世博会的广告宣传和独家经营某种产品的特许。例如，发行名信片是世博宣传的一个常规手段，同时也是企业广告宣传的媒介，名信片上印有企业的标志性建筑和醒目标识。通过发行这种印有企业形象的明信片，企业得以将其形象与世博现代建筑象征的进步主题联系在一起。企业赞助成为1933 年芝加哥世博会的重要收入来源，组委会常常用企业赞助的方式推出代表美国科技进步的某种产品。1933 年展期，世博会获得了 302 万美元的特许经营收入，1934 年展期，获得 380 万美元。

多种商业经营和娱乐项目对世博经济产生了重要影响，1933 年世博会使芝加哥受益匪浅。截至 11 月 1 日原定的闭幕日，购票入场的观众大约 2300 万人次，门票、特许经营（包括食品和饮料）和特别展览的收入合计 3500 万美元。在 1933 年展季的高峰期，世博会雇用的员工达到 22000 人，世博会直接或间接地创造了 10 万个就业机会，给芝加哥带来 4 亿美元的商机，使银行储蓄增长 17%（全国平均增长 7%），百货零售业增长 19%，扭转了 1932 年同期零售业下降近 25% 的局面。

根据世博新闻发布的数据，1933 年在芝加哥举办的会议和展览达到 1478 个，接待游客 160 万，这个数据超过了上一年在芝加哥举办的会展和游客数量的一倍还多，大约 90% 的会议和展览在世博会期间举办。从此，芝加哥成为一座著名的“会展”城市。

## 建设世纪的进步世博会

从一开始，世博组委会就清醒地认识到世博建筑既要风格独特，又要反映科学进步的主题。鉴于 1893 年世博建筑由美国著名建筑师组成的设计团队创造并大获成功，1933 年世博董事会决定采用同样的方式，挑选芝加哥和美国其他地方的建筑师组成建筑委员会。

1928 年 5 月，在第一次建筑委员会上，委员们决定构思一个组合方案，设计原则要反映 1893 年以来世界建筑在设计风格、建造模式、发明创造和人工照明方面取得的新进展，强调建筑工程的经济效益和防火性能。因为世博园位于密歇根湖畔，委员们决定突出水面景观设计（图 7）。此时此刻，美国还处在经济繁荣和高速发展时期，建筑师们构想了一个华丽的世博会，决定将世博园划分为若干片区，每个委员负责一个片区的建筑设计。很显然，这样的设计与 1893 年世博会的主体建筑设计无法比拟，毫无鲜明的“风格”可言。

考虑到以往的世博会占地面积过大，增加了游客的疲劳，委员们认为设计多层建筑集中展览很重要。这些讨论还涉及世博会的交通、多层展厅中游客的流向、景观设计和建筑的色彩运用等方面。

直到1930年10月，主办方才意识到即将到来的全球性经济危机对世博会构成了严重威胁，随之对原规划设计作了一些调整和修改，例如，取消了建造世博会标志性建筑的计划。

**1. 现代风格的形成**

经济萧条也有一定的积极作用，建筑师不得不重视他们原先制定的一个设计原则——建造经济实用的建筑，同时，世博建筑还要有自身的新意和美的形式，不再重复1893年的古典建筑形式，要为使用新材料新技术创造机会，例如旅游与运输馆采用的悬索屋顶，行政办公楼采用的预制构件等新技术。

从1931—1932年，主要展馆的建设正在进行，工程中应用的经济节俭原则包括两个方面：一是提高劳动力的工作效率；二是运用轻质材料，减少结构中钢材的用量和地基处理的工程量。采用预制构件，如桁架、墙板等，可以大大减少现场施工人员的数量。其他一些因素也为降低造价创造了条件。像多数展览建筑一样，世博建筑是临时性建筑，采用非对称性的规划方案为降低造价和尝试新设计提供了自由创作的空间。结果，主要展馆的造价只相当于普通商业建筑造价的1/6。这些1933年世博会采用的建筑技术将会对未来的建筑技术产生巨大影响，甚至未来采用轻质无装饰的预制构件建造的摩天大楼也可以从中受益。

由于考虑到控制建筑造价和使用新型建筑材料，按照临时性建筑功能要求建造，1933年世博建筑是一种朴实无华的现代建筑，没有复杂的几何造型和随处可见的具有古典风格的浅浮雕装饰。在这里，建筑的目的是根据实际需要提供高效快速的展览设施。

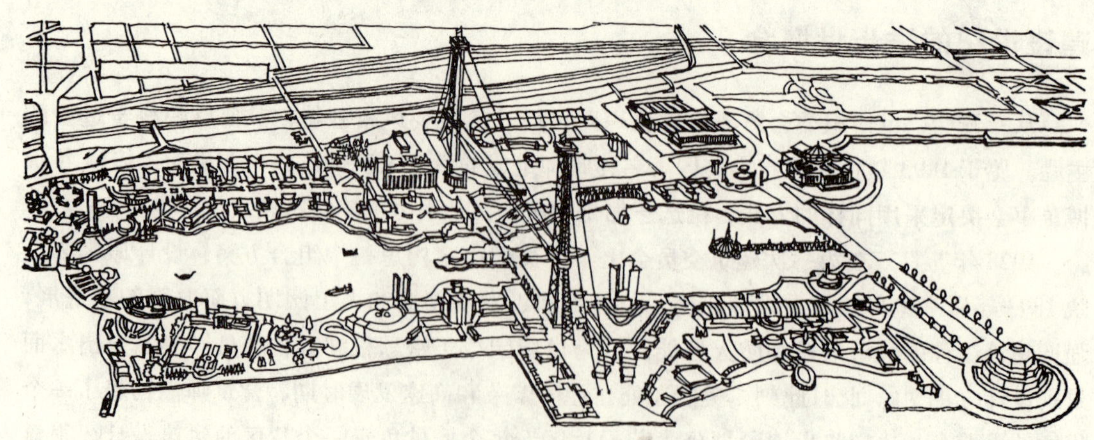

图7 位于 Michigan 湖畔的世博园

这种建筑风格也加速了工业设计师向流线型设计和新材料应用方向转变，例如采用无装饰的酚醛塑料、玻璃砖和贴面塑料。同时，这种发展趋势为好莱坞著名舞台设计师 Joseph Urban 发挥作用创造了条件，Joseph Urban 运用鲜艳而富于变化的彩色系列，并且将照明灯管排列组合形成大面积绚丽的光谱替代传统的建筑装饰，为 1933 年世博会增添了独特魅力，深受观众喜爱，但是，这种装饰手法也时常被某些建筑评论家斥之为艳俗或微不足道的雕虫小技。

### 2. 色彩成为重要的装饰元素

由于经济萧条削减了建设资金，建造豪华气派的展馆已不可能，建筑师不得不寻找其他方式装饰建筑，因此，色彩作为主要装饰元素的作用显得更加重要。1932 年 1 月，Joseph Urban 应邀为世博会设计了一整套色彩装饰方案，将色彩与灯光以及世博园景观协调搭配。

1933 年 5 月 27 日世博会开幕，展现在游客面前的是与 1893 年世博会大相径庭的建筑景观，虽然没有统一的建筑尺度、檐口高度和统一的色彩，但总体建筑风格基本相似，采用“现代”建筑形式。这种建筑风格以装饰艺术或现代艺术原则为基础，这类艺术风格主要出现在 20 世纪 20 年代的欧洲，在 1925 年巴黎装饰艺术博览会，在德国包豪斯风格和荷兰风格派建筑师的作品中，在 1930 年瑞典哥德堡博览会和 1931 年巴黎殖民地博览会均有突出表现和展示。

或许“世纪的进步世博会”给观众留下印象最深的是其建筑外墙上喷涂的鲜艳色彩形成的彩虹和闪现在世博园各处新颖别致的装饰构件。这类尺度小巧的装置的确为世博会增光添彩，最突出的例子是那个巨大的温度计，一座 240 英尺（约 73m）高的塔形结构，标有刻度，安装了一只装有类似红色液体的管子，可以准确标示温度。然而，真正的温度装置设置在塔基中。

运用色彩装饰建筑在世博会的历史上绝无仅有，哥伦布纪念世博会以典雅的“白城”而闻名于世，受到广泛称赞，主广场荣誉广场（Court of Honor）上洁白闪亮的古典风格建筑成为这届世博会的重要形象。虽然，1901 年泛美博览会和 1915 年旧金山巴拿马太平洋博览会都曾采用过柔和的淡彩，但是色彩并不是这两次博览会的主要装饰特征。20 世纪 20 年代末和 30 年代初在欧洲举办的一些博览会比以前更多地运用了色彩，特别是 1931 年巴黎殖民地博览会上的色彩运用美丽动人，因此，世纪的进步世博董事会决定调整预算，在世博会上更多地运用色彩。

色彩的运用涉及两个方面的问题：选择什么颜色和如何协调多种颜色之间的相互关系；考虑到天气变化和建筑外表材质的不同，选择什么样的涂料。

Urban 的设计方案包括 23 种鲜艳的色彩：白、灰、黑、银、金和 6 个层次的橘黄色、3 个层次的红色以及 9 个层次的蓝和绿色。Urban 要求多数建筑采用 3～4 种颜色，色彩的运用不仅要突出单体建筑的个性，还要与其周围的建筑和谐，绚丽的色彩对营造博览会的节庆氛围很重要。

一般情况下，冷色调（蓝、绿、紫）用于建筑的北立面，中性色调（白、灰、金、银、黑）用于东西立面，暖色调（红、橙、黄）用于南立面。这种布置既考虑到阳光下的色彩效果，同时也考虑到色彩的持久性，冷色调最经不起强烈的阳光照射。

天气状况也是要考虑的重要因素，采用的涂料不仅要经得起各种天气的考验——无论是芝加哥晚春或早秋阴冷的雨天还是七、八月份的烈日炎炎，还要保证在不同材质的表面上至少保持8个月。

除了色彩，人工照明也是世纪的进步世博会的一个主要装饰元素，世博园夜景更是需要考虑的因素。灯光装饰是1893年世博会的一个重要特征，绚丽的灯饰勾勒出主体建筑的轮廓。1893年以后的博览会都运用灿烂的灯饰达到了预期的装饰效果。1933年世博会的经理们决定要突出灯光的奇特装饰效果。利用不同材料形成的色屏或滤光作用，将彩光喷洒在墙面，让灿烂的灯光变得更加耀眼夺目，更加聚焦；霓虹灯管照明利用惰性气体氖可以在灯管中形成艳丽的彩光，这种灯管可以任意组合，形成多种图案。

室内照明也很重要，出于经济方面的考虑，也是为了在任何时间任何天气情况下保持同样的采光效果，展馆没有布置窗孔。

1933年世博会的灯光工程达到了预期目标，灯光的运用强化了世博建筑的整体感和统一性，有助于增加建筑的视觉高度，表现高贵典雅的气质。灯光的运用使世博园在晚间别有一番景致，各种灯饰大放异彩让世博园在夜间充满活力。射灯的运用将世博园夜景与芝加哥城的灯火区分开来。

科学馆和旅游与运输馆是最具特色的展馆建筑。科学馆是世博会最重要的“主题”展馆；旅游与运输馆是世博会最富有创意的建筑，虽然许多建筑评论家对其古怪的外形感到失望。得到最多赞誉的是克莱斯勒馆（Chrysler，图8），其开阔舒展的设计，以及与其相邻的旅游与运输馆协调的处理手法给人留下深刻印象。

图8 克莱斯勒馆以其开阔舒展的设计，以及与其相邻的旅游与运输馆协调的处理手法给人留下深刻印象

从某种意义上说，1933年世博建筑是一种转型时期的建筑，现代建筑的雏形及其色彩鲜艳的外表与世博会节庆般的氛围相结合，创造出一种自股市崩盘以来久违了的轻松愉悦

的心境。与此同时，世博建筑对现代建筑在美国的普及也起了重要作用，对于具有装饰艺术风格的居住建筑和商业建筑的发展，对于后来的国际风格的流行，以及对于工业领域的流线型设计趋势，大到火车机车，小到烤面包器，都起到了积极作用。尽管某些建筑评论家对此颇有微词，1933 年世博建筑对新型建筑材料的运用和对预制构件技术的重视都对美国建筑技术的发展产生了相当大的作用。1939—1940 年纽约世博会也采用了类似的建筑风格，这是对 1933 年世博建筑成就的充分验证。

## 科学：走向进步的关键

20 世纪 20 年代中期，人们开始谈论举办世博会庆祝芝加哥建城 100 周年的议题，多数人把举办这届世博会看作是展示芝加哥自 1893 年世博会以来所取得的成就，炫耀 1933 年世博会将给芝加哥带来丰厚利益的契机。然而，主办方知道，世博会的成功需要一个更加广泛的主题，不能仅仅局限于主办城市的过去、现在和未来。因此，美国国家研究委员会应邀参与，为世博会策划“主题”，组织相关的科学活动。

**1. 聚焦科技进步，创造富有新意的展览**

1928 年 8 月，董事会正式请求国家研究委员会提供咨询和帮助，为此，国家研究委员会成立了一个科学咨询委员会参与世博会的工作。根据科学咨询委员会的意见，科学馆应当是一座标新立异的建筑，是世博会的中心标志，在这里，观众会不知不觉地受到“潜移默化的教育”，领悟基础科学与人们日常生活的联系；展览应当重点展示科学如何为人类服务，展示现代工业产品的生产过程，而不是像以往的博览会那样仅仅展示现成的产品；不同学科的展品要尽可能地组合展示，例如：生物学与动物学可以是一个恰当的组合。

同样，1930 年 8 月，董事会决定邀请社会科学研究委员会为世博会组建一个咨询委员会负责社会科学方面的展览。一个以人类学为主题的展览方案形成，涉及多个种族，从爱斯基摩人到西南部的印第安人，并且复制玛雅建筑，展示美洲土著民族在欧洲人到来之前达到的文明水平。

为了贯彻展示百年科技进步的主题，世博会的展览都赋有教育意义，世博官员努力使所有展览贴近主题。1932 年，世博会设计部成立，负责策划展览理念，确保展览达到管理部门制定的设计标准。所有租用主题展馆的参展商，如电力馆组团或综合展览馆，都要向设计部提交最终的设计方案和色彩方案，便于同相关参展商协调方案，避免设计雷同的展览。有的时候，世博组委会先设计若干展览理念，然后再寻找赞助商举办展览。

**2. 实现主题创意，策划新的展览运作模式**

世纪的进步世博会或许是第一个自主举办大量展览的世博会。为了紧扣主题，董事会组建了基础科学部，专门负责世博会出资举办的纯科学领域的展览；成立应用科学和工业部，与基础科学部协调合作，专门负责吸引工业界参与世博会，此举得到了美国工业界的积极响应。有众多的个人和机构参与展览策划，世博会从中受益，许多展品来自大学和企业的捐助或租赁。

如上所述，展览的重点是过程而不是最终产品，许多大企业都各自建造了规模宏大的展馆。造价160万美元的通用汽车展馆展示了一个完整的雪佛兰汽车生产线。克莱斯勒馆更胜一筹，展示了一个1/4英里长的试车场，观众可以乘坐著名电影特技替身演员或赛车手驾驶的汽车在车道上驰骋。

住宅展览几乎完美地体现了世博主题，由世博管理层策划与合作开发，建筑商具体实施。在展出的11座不同建筑商承建的样板住宅中，在与之相邻的家庭与工业艺术展馆中，观众可以看到科学技术如何影响到美国人的家庭生活。

住宅展览是一个重要的展览，因为家庭影响到每一个人，因此，住宅展览与其他工业展览不同，应当区别对待。住宅展览吸收了欧洲建筑师参与，因为住宅也是欧洲国家关注的重要话题，这样有助于确保欧洲国家参与世博会。

在11座样板住宅中，8座是舒适小巧的经济型住宅，设计从多方面展示了运用预制单元和新型建筑材料的可能性，同时又保持了各自的风格和个人品位。另外两座住宅显然属于高档住宅，一座强调现代风格，另一座采用古典风格。最后一座是“明天的住宅”，这是一幢玻璃和钢材构筑的两层住宅，布置了许多不打开的窗户，因为要使用中央空调。一个中心支柱作为结构支撑，同时也是布线、上下水管线和煤气管道的管槽。房屋里的一切设施都具有防水防火性能。该住宅的宣传是“设想大胆，从里到外”。

虽然，世纪的科技进步是本届世博会的主题，主办方知道过去每一届体面的世博会都包括美术展览，但是随着经济萧条的到来，考虑到防火和安全的需要，美术馆造价昂贵，建造美术馆的设想只能悄然放弃。1932年6月，世博董事会与芝加哥美术学院达成正式协议，授权美术学院以世博会的名义举办艺术展览，美术学院负责举办展览的所有费用，董事会同意不再赞助其他重要的艺术展览，并且在世博会结束后将20%的剩余资金支付给美术学院。美术学院距世博园一英里之遥，往返有穿梭巴士服务。

1933年美术学院举办的艺术展览在5个月的展期中吸引了70多万观众，票价25美分。展览以“世纪的进步——美国的艺术收藏”为主题，汇集了从25个艺术馆和200多个美国私人收藏者那儿借来的艺术品。

重视过程的展示使原本枯燥乏味的展览变得颇具娱乐性。

## 世博会的乐趣

到了1933年，Midway的理念，也就是游乐园，已经成为世博会的一个主要特征。Midway 乐园最初在 1893 年世博会上大受欢迎，是人们参观了正统的工农业展览之后疲惫不堪时的娱乐休闲场所，汇集了各种纯粹的娱乐项目，像驾骑、游戏、古怪秀和夜总会表演等，这些活动常常是对时代道德底线的挑战。

对世博会主办方来说，保持 Midway 乐园的传统是个两难的问题。一方面，主办方要全力打造以科学进步为主题的高品位教育性的博览会，而粗俗的 Midway 娱乐节目肯定会削弱这个目标的实现。另一方面，主办方也很清楚只有广泛吸引公众参与，世博会才能成功，粗俗的 Midway 娱乐节目有助于实现这个目标。最终，主办方采取了最明智的解决办法，这就是由世博会出资建设与世博会教育目标一致的娱乐项目。与此同时，主办方出租场地，以商业运作的模式经营纯粹的娱乐项目，这些商业性娱乐项目为白天参观科技展览的观众提供了晚间活动的去处，对世博会的晚间经营尤为重要。

在主办方赞助的娱乐项目中，Fort Dearborn 城堡和中国式的喇嘛庙在 1932 年夏季向公众开放，入场费 10 美分，约 60 万人参观了正在建设中的世博园，部分展馆和项目已经完工。Fort Dearborn 是一座芝加哥建城时期的城堡建筑的复制品；喇嘛庙是一座中国式宗教建筑的复制品，在中国建造，由 28000 个构件组装而成，拆卸后运到芝加哥重新组装。这两座建筑是 1932 年的著名景点。主办方赞助的其他受欢迎的项目还有以运输发展历程为主题的户外盛装大游行和一个名为“一万年前的地球”的展览等。

在世博园的最南端有一个航空展，称之为“世纪的进步之三”，在这里参展的多架飞机展示了自莱特兄弟 1903 年第一次飞行以来航空技术的发展历程。美国空军也展示了他们的最新机型。有些更大胆的游客还在世博园上空飞行，他们中 70% 的人都是有生以来第一次体验飞行。然而，1933 年 6 月 11 日发生了世博会最惨重的灾难，一架飞机坠毁，机上 9 人全部遇难。

大多数商业娱乐项目都集中在两个娱乐区经营，一个是 Midway 乐园，另一个是彩虹乐园（Rainbow Area)。巴黎街在 1933 年展季非常成功，这里有巴黎典型的建筑、街道和广场，商店和咖啡馆，是由一群芝加哥投资商建造的。

对孩子们来说，主要的娱乐区是梦幻岛，面积 5 英亩，是个很有吸引力的地方，1933 年展季的游客访问量达到 300 多万人，受到报纸杂志的好评。尽管梦幻岛为儿童活动而建，几乎 70% 的游客都是成年人。

梦幻岛上有一个艺术馆展示儿童艺术和手工艺品，还有一座称之为“健康之舟”的咨询中心，在这里职业医师向儿童及其家长提供健康咨询。除了娱乐场，儿童剧院也很成功，儿童剧院推出业余团体的表演，降低成本吸引观众。

从一开始，世博会主办方就很清楚投资体育项目会提升世博会的知名度，主办方在举办重大的足球、棒球赛事上作了大量投入，许多较小的体育项目也在计划之列，例如周六下午在潟湖上举办的划船比赛很出名，主办方要让体育活动成为世博会的一部分。

为了能在 1933 年展季更多获利，特许经营者要求世博会在 11 月 1 日闭幕日之后再延续一段时间，董事会满足了这个要求，确定 11 月 12 日为新的闭幕日，结果证明这是一个错误的决定，由于天气阴冷多雨，世博会 1934 年重新办展的信息已经发布，观众数量锐减。

董事会和世博特许经营部想尽一切办法增加观众访问量，设计安排了一系列特别活动。11月8日，为了庆祝禁酒令结束，世博会免费供应啤酒，颇具讽刺意味的是，这一天被命名为“个人负责日”，有5万观众到场，是平时观众数量的2倍，他们消耗掉了所有啤酒和近20万份免费的三明治，60人因醉酒被撵出世博园。11月10日，所有享受社会救济的人凭身份证免费入场。尽管有这样的特别活动，延长展期并没有为多数特许经营者招徕足够的观众，未能平衡经营支出。

## 第二展季：1934年

接近1933年展季的尾声，特别是富兰克林·罗斯福总统10月2日亲临世博会后，观众的数量依然众多，人们的世博热情高涨，对重新办展，举办第二个展季的兴趣和讨论大增。

10月下旬，主办方对展商重返世博会参加第二展季的意愿作了调查，重新办展的计划已经完成，董事会对第二年重新办展进行了投票表决，正在等待伊利诺伊州立法机关的支持和当地工商业的积极参与。《芝加哥论坛报》道出了举办第二个展季的重要原因：世博会还有500万美元的债务未偿还，价值2100万美元的设施已经就位，举办第二个展季会抹平所有剩余债务。

对于世博董事会的决定，公众没有什么异议，虽然有人认为如果举办第二个展季纯粹是出于经济方面的考虑，重新办展就像是“热剩饭”，索然无味。然而，董事会认为1933年展季让芝加哥大为受益，而且世博会还欠债权人的钱未偿还，再者，公众大力支持，展馆建筑完好无恙，1933年展季的成功强化了民族精神。

为了增强1934年展季的吸引力，主办方在1933—1934年冬季将世博会的一些重要展览运送到许多地方巡回展览，约有53个展览被运到其他城市展出，像匹兹堡、费城、克利尔沃特等城市。

### 1. 创造新意

新展季没有对世博会进行重大调整改造的意愿，也没有这个财力，观众看到的许多展览和表演与1933年相同，但是，有些变化还是显而易见的。首先，新的色彩方案令人赏心悦目。夏日的阳光使许多建筑退色，约75%的外墙需要重新粉饰。新的色彩方案只采用了10种颜色，每座建筑选用的颜色不超过3种，包括白色在内。新的色彩方案具有明确的“分区”导向作用，每一座主要建筑或每一个片区都有一个主色调，帮助游客以色彩为导向辨别方位。新的色彩系列使世博园变得更加紧凑有序。

灯光的运用得到了加强，特别是在湖区及其周边地段。1933年展季没有在潟湖上布置夜间灯景，但是1934年，潟湖北端设置了一排射灯，模拟创造出一种极光效果，还新建了一座喷泉，75英尺高的水柱在五彩灯的映照下大放异彩，号称世界第一。与此同时，陆地上又增添了 300 棵树和 51000 株新的花卉植物，与新的色彩系列搭配成趣。沿着湖边还增加了多种新的经营项目，包括饭店和一个露天剧场。

### 2. 福特汽车的加入——新的亮点

1934 年展季最大的惊喜莫过于福特汽车公司展馆的出现。亨利·福特原打算在 1933 年展季举办展览，展示一条自动生产线，但是，1931 年 7 月通用汽车公司宣布要在其展馆展出一条自动生产线，恼怒的福特说他要避开芝加哥另行举办展览，也就是称之为“福特的进步”的展览，这是一个纯粹的汽车展览，1933 年下半年在底特律和纽约市分别举办。在三周半的展期中，大约 350 万观众蜂拥而至前往参观。但是，超过 1000 万观众在 1933 年展季参观了通用汽车和克莱斯勒展馆，因此福特决定加入 1934 年展季。世博管理层对福特的加入兴奋不已，为他在其他运输展馆附近划出了一块 11 英亩的场地，福特在这里建造了一座造价 200 万美元的展馆。展馆中央的圆形大厅里布置了一个 20 英尺高的地球仪，展示福特在全球的经营业绩，还有一个历史车型展览，包括 67 辆车。工业展厅展示了自动化机械工具的最新技术革新成果，这里的机器飞转声和撞击声与其旁边布置的一个展览的宁静氛围形成鲜明对比，这是早期福特生产车间的复制品，就在这个车间里福特手工制造出他的第一辆汽车。另外，福特展馆前设计了一个露天壳体结构音乐台，底特律交响乐团在这里做了为期 13 周的常规演出，福特公司赞助。福特还修建了一条 2000 英尺长的走道，从福特馆穿过 5 英亩见方的绿地通向湖滨，走道分为 19 段，分别代表了不同历史时期的道路。

福特本人对这个展览很感兴趣，对办展过程中的细节问题他都要亲自一一过问，比如游客休息用的座椅采用什么风格等，尽管通用汽车公司在 1933 年世博会上取得了销售汽车 3000 多辆的业绩，福特禁止在展览中向观众施加任何销售压力。第二展季开始后，福特 13 次亲临展馆，经常亲自向年轻观众介绍展品，特别是当有新闻媒体和摄影师在场时更是如此，他认为世博会有助于教育人民，减少无知。福特馆赢得了报纸和专业杂志的高度赞扬。数据显示，1934 年展季，超过 75% 的世博会观众参观了福特馆，而 1933 年展季参观通用汽车展馆的观众大约是 45%。

### 3. 加强展览的娱乐性

1934 年展季还有一些更细微的变化。大约 75% 的 1933 年展季的参展商报名参加 1934 年展季，随着像福特这样的新展商的加入，实际的参展商数量超过 1933 年展季。从展览内容来看，1934 年展季更注重轻松的娱乐项目和电影展播。

这种新的娱乐倾向甚至出现在正统的科学馆，科学馆依然是最有吸引力的展馆之一，虽然展览主题还是基础科学理论和数学定理，但是展示方式发生了戏剧性的变化，许多展览都降低了难度。新的展览要符合三个指导原则：1）展览是否简单明了？2）展览是否与观众的共同经历相关？3）是否采用动态展示？有些展览强调了不同学科之间的相互依赖关系，例如，一个称之为“世纪之钟”的巨型元素周期表在 42 秒钟内展示了地球的地质发展演变过程，又如，一个巨大的展示食用盐分子结构的模型等。

商业性展览也作了调整改进，保持了1933年展季的优点，弥补了一些不足之处。例如，克莱斯勒充分利用其展览区1/4英里长的试车场，在场内增加了一个大型看台，赞助汽车赛。标准石油公司停止播放与石油工业相关的影片，以野生动物节目取而代之，但在节目上打出公司标识。Hupmobile引进了一部模拟真实驾车环境的驾驶测试影片，通过驾驶测试的游客可以得到一个证书。安全玻璃公司让游客用石块击打玻璃窗，测试玻璃强度。Armour是一家肉制品包装公司，展示了常规的熏肉切片包装程序，并且雇用"红褐色头发的美女"操作机器。观众对观赏动态的工作情形更感兴趣。

在住宅展览中，George Fred Keck用"水晶住宅"取代了他的"明天的住宅"。这座玻璃和钢材构筑的试验型住宅是一座超现代、低造价的独立户型住宅，便于快速建造，采用预制玻璃墙板和钢框架构件，安装在现浇的混凝土板基础上，机械设备都集中在中央设备间，滑动布帘提供私密空间。由于采用玻璃墙板，需要采用复杂的供热和制冷系统，加之住宅的特殊造型和外观，该住宅更多地体现出它的现代主义象征意义，而非实用的住宅模式。

7月，世博会主办了一个"世纪的进步——更好的住宅论坛"，就当地政府、州政府和联邦政府的住宅计划进行讨论。10月24日，也就是"住宅现代化日"，工人志愿者在一天之内将一座从市区搬迁至住宅展览区的世纪老宅重新建造，材料造价在预计的750～1000美元之间。

1934年展季，世博会与芝加哥艺术学院续签了艺术展览合同，展览的主题是世界艺术背景下的"美国艺术"，展出了350多件从欧洲借来的艺术精品，据说价值7500万美元，同样数量的美国绘画也同时展出，包括了从殖民时期到20世纪30年代的作品。

经济萧条的影响减少了官方和半官方参与1934年展季的数量，只有6个外国政府和11个美国州政府参展，为了吸引更多的外国政府参展，主办方将美国州展馆变成国际展馆，在此为外国政府提供展位，但是这些努力并未奏效。国际参展数量减少的部分原因是受到1928年巴黎公约的限制，世纪的进步世博会延长展期被视为违反公约。有些国家将官方参展变成半官方参展。

1934年5月31日，第二展季开幕几天后，超过50万观众在"儿童日"光临世博会，儿童入场券5美分，并在入口处得到一瓶赠送牛奶，观众的数量比1933年展季的任何一天都多，世博管理层大受鼓舞，宣布每周四儿童入场费只需5美分。接近1934年展季的尾声，世博管理层安排两天让享受社会救济的家庭免费参观。

1934年展季的观众接近1650万人次，第二展季结束时，管理层还有近69万美元的剩余资金支付撤展费、组织费和其他可能发生的费用。世纪的进步世博会是唯一全部返还债权人债务的世博会。许多特许经营者都表达了愿意继续参加第三个展季的愿望，还有一些人打算参与未来的世博会或经营其他娱乐场所。

世博会闭幕不久，撤展工作迅速展开，主要涉及三个方面。第一步，通过一系列竞标拍卖程序处置世博会的家具、设施和其他可移动财产；第二步，拆除世博会的多数展馆和其他设施，恢复场地原貌；第三步，世博会最终结算，包括结清遗留债务，根据预定方案分配剩余资金。

芝加哥在 1934 年展季继续受益。世博会为芝加哥带来了价值 5000 万美元的施工和维护工程，外地游客给芝加哥商界带来了 7 亿美元的财富，这部分钱增加了当地和州政府的税收。与此同时，世博会使芝加哥的文化品位有了明显的提高。

## 两次世博会的显著特征

虽然，世纪的进步世博会继承了哥伦布纪念世博会的某些风格，但依然独具特色。

首先，在融资方面，世纪的进步世博会主要依靠大企业和芝加哥富裕阶层的投资赞助，而哥伦布纪念世博会主要依靠政府部门的支持。世纪的进步世博会是一个成功的实业项目，在世博会的策划、运作和后期收尾过程中，世博管理层始终准确把握世博会的经济状况，在没有政府补贴的情况下，不仅度过了全球性的经济危机，而且还全部返还了投资人的投资。

更重要的是，这两次世博会的目标有着显著区别。哥伦布纪念世博会创造了一个乌托邦，从多方面赞颂了传统和理想化了的过去，具有强烈的怀旧情感。与之形成鲜明对比的是，1933 年世纪的进步世博会把人们的思绪和想象力带到了未来，它是对未来的展望，而不是对过去的回顾。1933 年世博会创造了一个人间仙境，展示美国在艺术、文学、建筑、科学和工业方面取得的伟大成就，不仅让人自豪，而且也从中得到了急需的心理慰藉，那就是，尽管目前困难重重，但是美国的未来充满了希望。

在建筑风格上，与 1893 年世博会力图以其古典建筑风格和布局形式回顾过去的光荣与辉煌不同，1933 年世博会以光感、升腾和色彩为设计理念，努力创造一个梦幻般的未来城市。设计采用了众多建筑造型，但是有一点是共同的，那就是设计中所强调的轻盈和动态倾向，每一座建筑都展示了这种向上而舒展，伸向天穹的线条。在教堂曾经是城市最高大最宏伟的建筑的地方，表现进步的殿堂——科学馆、工业馆和艺术馆——已经取而代之。建筑委员会将进步诠释为渴望和动态，这种诠释体现在每一座建筑的设计中。建筑采用流线型、高科技的现代风格，特别强调造型简洁，其目的是要创造一个崭新的世博会，不断强调 1933 年世博会不是对 1893 年世博会的复制与再现。

在展览方式与运作模式上，世纪的进步世博会与以往世博会也有显著的区别。首先，世纪的进步世博会承办了大量的展览——基础科学方面的展览，并且创新了展览方式，包括展示模型，播放幻灯片和电影短片等，用普通人的语言讲述一段又一段的故事。应用科学方面的展览由企业、政府和其他机构和组织承办。其次，世纪的进步世博会是第一个大量出售展位的世博会，这就需要特别的销售能力，虽然经济萧条给展位销售带来了困难，但是世博会在经济方面是否成功在很大程度上要取决于这样的销售能力。最后，世纪的进步世博会是第一个多方齐心协力，使每一个展览既充实完善，又不相互抄袭的世博会，这需要展商之间的广泛协商和相互妥协，这一点很重要，因为世博管理层要让展商尽可能多地从参展中受益，这在经济萧条时期尤为重要。

两次世博会在同一座城市举办，甚至同样都经历了经济大萧条时期。虽然，它们在其展览中都强调了科学、技术和进步的主题，但各自又有截然不同的展示方式。哥伦布纪念世博会采用了百货商场式的静态展示模式，展示直至1893年取得的科技进步，在这里，工业产品在货架上或展柜中陈列展示，各企业为使其产品获奖而展开激烈的竞争。看到美国产品优于外国产品胜出，一种民族自豪感油然而生。

如果将哥伦布纪念世博会比作一个百货商场，世纪的进步世博会就是一个实验室，在这里，最好的展览是让展品在观众面前定向运动，制造成型，或通过视觉手段或动画片演绎一段故事，这种展示有时达到了极致，似乎在展示“现代科学实践就是好莱坞电影加胡迪尼魔术表演”。本届世博会不颁发奖项，重点是展示过程而不是最终产品，展现“科学如何创造美好的事物”。

这两次世博会都成为经济萧条时期人们暂时的庇护所，是成人教育中心，是具有良好经营管理水平，应对时代挑战的成功的实业项目，它们像城中城一样地生息运作，在这里众多游客体验了快乐。它们为后来的世博会作出了榜样，如1935年圣迭戈博览会、1939—1940年纽约世博会和旧金山博览会从中受益匪浅。

## 后记

芝加哥原打算举办第三次世博会。1977年，芝加哥一些知名人士建议举办世博会庆祝哥伦布发现新大陆500周年，也正好纪念哥伦布纪念世博会100周年。1981年，芝加哥世博公司成立，这个由著名企业领袖、律师和建筑师组建的公司在没有公众和政府参与的情况下运作了几个月，策划主题，规划场地，计划在1992年举办世博会，并向国际展览局提出了申请。

到了1982年，世博公司的这种闭门造车式的决策过程招致了众多反对意见，多数批评集中在世博会的融资风险、对环境的影响以及对附近住区可能造成的干扰等方面。1982年下半年，州政府和市政府联合组成正式的1992年芝加哥世博局，取代世博公司。

然而，来自华盛顿当局和外界的批评意见主要集中在世博会所需的巨额公共花费上，例如，需要改变世博园附近的主要车行道，建设排污系统，提供安全保护和防火措施等。一些人对世博当局的参与程度和世博会的经济前景表示怀疑，对热心于举办世博会的人是否在利用世博会刺激与他们经济利益相关的附近地区的地价上扬提出质疑。

这类争论从1984年一直持续到1985年。当1984年新奥尔良世博会经济损失惨重的消息公布后，举办世博会的希望变得渺茫。最后，决定性的一击是在1985年6月，由伊利诺伊州众议院委托进行的一项可行性分析研究表明，酝酿中的世博会是一个可怕的风险投资，州政府不能承担。没有州政府的资金支持，世博会就不可能举办。1987年12月，国际展览局撤销了芝加哥世博会的许可。

# Chapter 4

# The 1933 Chicago World's Fair

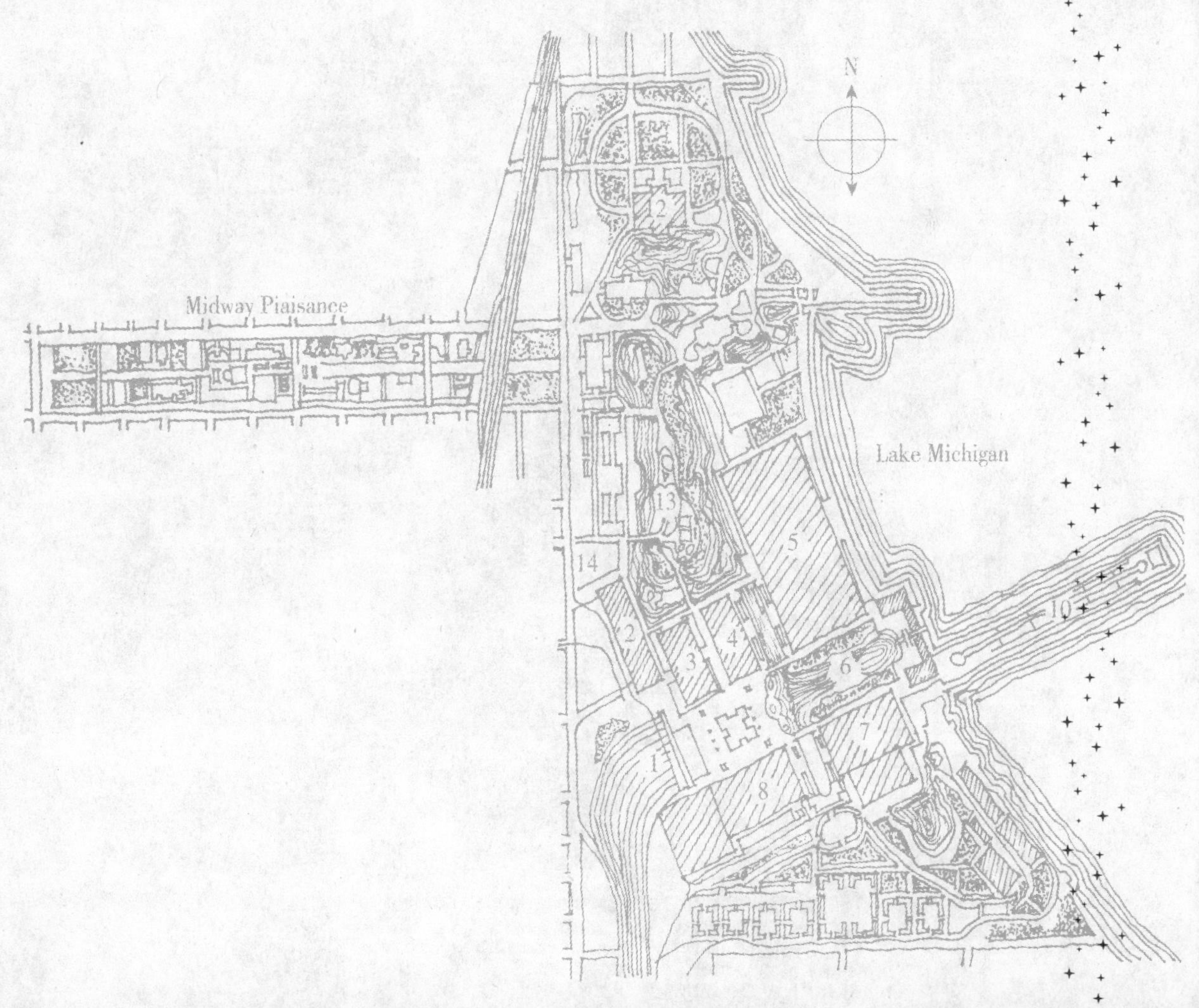

## Planning A Second World Fair

By the 1920s, the great era of fairs in America had passed. In that decade of blossoming modernism, the fair began to seem old-fashioned. The legacy of the World's Columbian Exposition that lived on into the twentieth century is seen in more indirect ways——the city planning movement, the Burnham's Chicago Plan of 1909, and the continuing development of Chicago as a commercial and cultural city.

Inspired by the fair, people saw a need to do something about the urban chaos brought on by the rapid and uncontrolled rebuilding of the city, and talked about the rebuilding the city like the fair. The unity of the fair's physical organization gave people confidence that the lessons of the fair could be used to reform urban life——cities could be made subject to planning just as the fair had been.

The Chicago Plan of 1909 recognized the commercial importance of Chicago by emphasizing transportation in, out, and around the city, and it also recognized the need of working-class people for rest and relaxation and the importance of a city being able to maintain a certain dignity; hence, provision were made for parkland and public buildings, artfully arranged. The plan guided Chicago's development for fifty years after its adoption. However, the plan encountered major financial and legal obstacles that prevented its immediate and even long-term implementation in many respects.

In 1923 and 1925, some Chicagoans suggested celebrating the centennial of Chicago's founding in 1833 with an international exposition. It was believed that such an event would bring about the final realization of Daniel H. Burnham's City Beautiful plan. The proposal strongly supported by the general public was approved by city council, and an organizing committee was appointed in 1927. The decision was made that civic improvements should accompany the 1933 celebration. The Plan of Chicago's consideration of public buildings, cultural venues, and recreational space was quite fully implemented prior to the Century of Progress, which played a role in the staging of the exposition. The year between the Plan of Chicago and the Century of Progress witnessed a major commercial building boom in Chicago, which came to an end with the arrival of the stock market crash of October 1929 and the ensuing depression.

Starting from 1928, the organizing committee moved quickly. The Board of Trustees of the committee was formed, which was the central nervous system of the fair organization for the next six years. A wide array of fair-related activities was launched.

The Science Advisory Committee of the National Research Council——an umbrella organization of scientists formed in 1916 to advise the government during World War I——was approached to come up with ideas for exhibits and develop the general theme of the fair, with the focus on scientific progress over the past hundred years.

Generating public interest through the news of the fair was important because the organizing committee had decided not to utilize any of their limited funds on paid advertising, a technique that had worked well for the World's Columbian Exposition and San Francisco's Panama-Pacific Exposition in 1915. A committee on public information was created in April 1928 that kept newspapers and magazines well supplied with exposition information through press releases and news features. On 1 April 1931, the committee on public information began publication of a weekly newsletter named **Progress**, which continued to appear until the fair opened, when it became known as **World's Fair Weekly**, oriented more toward informing visitors about the fair.

In May 1928, the board fixed June 1, 1933, as the opening day for the fair, noting that in 1893 the World Columbian Exposition had opened on May 1 and suffered poor attendance because of cold, rainy weather and the fact that schools were still in session.

In June 1929, the fair board, responding to a suggestion from a group of citizens, changed the name of the exposition from Chicago's Second World's Fair to the Century of Progress Exposition. This name reflected both the centennial celebration of the host city and the theme of progress through science.

## Financing The Fair

The process of financing the fair began through the initiation of a drive to sell $5 shares to the general public, for which the purchaser received a certificate of The World's Fair Legion membership that could be exchanged for ten admission tickets when the fair opened. It was a door-to-door drive to sell the $5 Legion shares in a campaign similar to wartime Liberty Bond drives. Although the campaign began slowly, a total of 118, 773 shares were sold over the next few years, generating, with interest, $637, 754 for the board. More importantly, the campaign served to build public interest in the centennial celebration by giving the ordinary citizen a stake in what was happening. Then a Founder Members' drive, soliciting $1, 000 from wealthy Chicagoans followed.

Nevertheless, more money was needed than could be raised in this manner. Consequently, a new form of financing was devised. This was a $10 million bond issue authorized in October 1929. The bonds, known as gold notes, were to be secured by 40 per cent of the gate receipts of the fair. These infusions of capital were important in financing the projects of the fair, such as the construction of an Administration Building, thought necessary so that fair officials could be on the site and the $40, 000 annual rent on their downtown office suite could be saved.

In addition the board wanted to have some popular exhibits open, before the fair, to generate public interest and additional income. To this end, a replica of Fort Dearborn was built, representing the Chicago of 1833, and a transportation exhibit organized. The board decided that spending the $10 million should be done in way that would raise still more money in order to complete the fair as planned.

In April 1929, the board created the position of general manager for the fair, and hired Major Lenox Lohr, an army engineer and former editor of Military Engineering to fill the post. He was responsible for running the day-to-day operations of the fair in a highly organized and business-like manner. After the stock market crash and onset of the depression, it was the manager's steadfast sense of money management and the ability to be all things to all people that found ways to cut costs and generate more income.

Comparison with the World's Columbian Exposition was inevitable. The fair managers spent a great deal of time and effort studying some other fairs, held in North America and Europe from 1904 to the early 1930s, with regard to daily attendance, weather reports, financial information, attractions, entertainment, color, lighting and night-time view etc.

Although the depression in early 1930s slowed the pace of subscriptions to the bond issues, a substantial amount of money had been received. This money had enabled the fair managers to build the Hall of Science, the Travel and Transport Building, and the Electrical Group, and make space available for industry to rent for their exhibits. The notion of having corporations, states, and other organization pay for the use of exhibit space was first suggested to the Century of Progress organizers in 1928. Planners were operating under the assumption that industrial exhibits would be put together co-operatively by trade associations, who were accustomed to paying for space at annual trade shows. The World's Columbian Exposition had offered free space, as had other past fairs, but this was no longer customary. The Century of Progress board adopted the suggestion, and the rental of exhibit space in one building was used to pay for the construction of the next building. The success of the Century of Progress in coaxing advance payment for space rental became an essential financial ingredient in completing the fair as planned by its opening day.

The depression did bring with it certain advantages. There was a ready and willing supply of labor that would work very cheaply. The board could buy supplies and equipment for less money and could negotiate cheaper contracts for services, as contractors were looking for work to do, regardless of the profit margin. The board was frequently paying its vendors or service providers part of what they were due in gold notes or admission tickets. The depression also reduced the grandiose expectations the public might have had about a large world's fair, so that when the fair did open, it overwhelmed visitors by exceeding their pre-conceived notions.

Meanwhile, a series of schemes were devised, which enabled the board to make a substantial amount of money from fees paid by concessionaires in the midst of the hard times. In some cases, collection of royalties due the Century of Progress was deferred until the concessionaire had recouped most of his investment. In others, businesses sponsored their products to be sold on the fairgrounds, in return for the privilege of advertising and the assurance that no other brand of the same products to be sold at the fair. For example, postcards were commonly printed up as a means of publicizing the fair. They also served as advertisements for the companies whose buildings they depicted with the company's name displayed prominently. By distributing images like this, companies were able to identify themselves with the idea of progress symbolized by this architecture of modernity. Indeed, corporate sponsorship was a big business in the Chicago World's Fair of 1933, which frequently utilized corporate financing for the purpose of endorsing certain products which exemplified the advancement of America. In 1933, the fair received $3.02 million from concession; in 1934, it received $3.8 million.

The various concessions and entertainment programs were an important element in the financial impact of the fair. Indeed, the Century of Progress had been beneficial for Chicago in 1933. Up to 1 November——the scheduled closing day, the total number of paid admissions was about 23,000,000. Visitors had spent about $35 million in admissions, concessions (including food and drink), and special exhibits on the grounds. During the peak of the 1933 season, 22,000 people were employed at the fair, and the fair had created, directly or indirectly, 100,000 jobs. $400 million of business brought to the city and an increase of 17 per cent in bank deposits (against a national average increase of 7 per cent). Department store sales increased 19 per cent, turning around a decrease of nearly 25 per cent for the same period in 1932.

According to a Century of Progress press release, Chicago hosted 1478 conventions in 1933, with a total of roughly 1.6 million visitors, more than double the number of conventions and visitors the year before. About 90 per cent of the conventions were held during the period the fair was open. From that time forward, Chicago became known as a 'fair' town.

## Building a Century of Progress

From the beginning, it was clear to all concerned with the Century of Progress that the fair's architecture would be highly distinctive and reflective of the theme of scientific progress. Aware of the architectural success of the World's Columbian Exposition designed by a committee of leading national architects, the Century of Progress board chose to follow the same course and appoint an architectural commission composed of architects from both Chicago and other parts of the country.

In May 1928, at their first meeting, the commissioners decided to create a composite design for the exposition, adopting architectural principles, which reflected the development of architecture in the world since 1893 in their designs, including new modes of construction, new inventions, and advances in the use of artificial lighting, emphasizing economical and fireproof construction. In addition, given the lakefront site on the edge of Lake Michigan (Figure 7), the commissioners agreed to maximize the use of water as a design feature. At this time, with country still in the full bloom of prosperity, the architects conceived of a fair of great extravagance. The commission agreed that the site should be divided among the several members of the commission, with each architect being responsible for the design of buildings within his sector. It became clear that there would be no distinctive 'style' of architecture, as there had been for the major buildings of the World's Columbian

Exposition.

The commissioners also sensed that previous fairs had covered too much area, contributing to visitor fatigue, and therefore thought it important to consider designing multi-story buildings in order to concentrate exhibits. Discussion continued about transportation on the fairgrounds, the movement of visitors through multi-storied buildings, the landscaping, and color studies of the buildings.

It was not until October 1930 that the oncoming global economic depression became a serious threat to the fair. Consequently, some changes were made to the original plans, e. g. the plan for a signature structure for the fair was cancelled.

### 1. Development of Modern Style

The depression also served a very positive purpose. It forced the architects to focus on one of their original principles, the construction of economical buildings. Rather than repeat the classical architectural models as had been done in 1893, the fair buildings would have a new beauty of their own, creating opportunities for the use of new materials and techniques, including suspended roofs, as in the Travel and Transport Building, and prefabrication, as in the Administration Building.

The construction got underway on most of the major buildings in 1931 and 1932. The work to economize on building costs involved the application of two principles: the efficient use of labor, and the utilization of lightweight materials to lesson the amount of structural steel and foundation work. On-site labor could be substantially reduced by the use of prefabricated trusses, wall sections and the like. Other factors contributed to the success of this cost-cutting effort. The fair buildings were meant to be temporary, as are most exposition buildings; the freedom of an asymmetrical site plan also allowed for creative cost-cutting and experimentation. As a result, the major buildings were constructed at about one-sixth the cost of conventional commercial construction. These building methods employed at the Century of Progress would have a great impact on the construction technology of the future. Even the future skyscrapers, built of lightweight, unornamented, prefabricated sections, could benefit from it.

Principally because of cost considerations, the use of new types of building materials, and the temporary nature of the buildings, this was a plainer, less elegant modern architecture, lacking much of the intricate geometry and stylistic bas-relief sculpture seen elsewhere. The purpose of the architecture was to house the exposition in the most effective and expeditious way, taking into account the conditions.

The architecture also complemented the movement of industrial designers into streamlining and the use of new materials, such as Bakelite, glass bricks, and Formica, which did not lend themselves to ornamentation. So it was left to Joseph Urban, a well-known designer of Broadway stage sets, to develop the intense and varied color scheme and the wide array of incandescent and gaseous tube lighting to substitute for more conventional kinds of ornamentation and provide the Century of Progress with a distinctiveness that fair visitors loved and architectural critics frequently dismissed as trivial and tawdry.

### 2. Color Schemes as the Principal Decorative Elements

As the depression cut into the funding available for constructing extravagant buildings, the architects were forced to look for alternative ways to decorate their buildings, and color schemes became increasingly more important as the principal decorative elements. In January 1932, Joseph Urban was called on to draw up an overall color scheme for the fair, and to co-ordinate light and landscaping with color.

When the Century of Progress opened on 27 May 1933, visitors saw a fair architecture that sharply contrasted with that of the World's Columbian Exposition. There was no attempt to bring uniformity to building size, cornice height, or color, but there was a general similarity in the architectural style. The fair was dressed in 'modern' architecture, based on the precepts basic to Art Deco or Art Moderne, seen primarily in Europe during the 1920s at the Paris Decorative Arts Exposition of 1925, in the German Bauhaus, in the work of Dutch architects of the De Stijl movement, and more recently in the architecture seen at the 1930 Gothenburg Exposition in Sweden and the 1931 Colonial Exposition in Paris.

Perhaps the strongest impression most visitors carried away from the Century of Progress was the rainbow of colors seen on the fair buildings and all the various decorative items splashed around the fairgrounds. Some of these smaller structures were important and popular additions to the fair. Chief among these was the huge thermometer, a 240-foot high tower with temperature gradations and a tube filled with what appeared to be red liquid that accurately told the temperature. The actual thermometer mechanism, however, was located in the base of the tower.

The use of color on buildings had no tradition in the history of world's fairs. The World's Columbian Exposition had been widely known and praised as the White City, and the dazzling whiteness of the classically styled buildings around the Court of Honor had been one of the strongest images of that fair. Pastel colors had been used at the Pan-American Exposition in 1901 and the Panama-Pacific International Exposition in 1915, but in neither case was color a dominant decorative feature. Some of the European fairs of the late 1920s and early 1930s had utilized color to a greater degree than ever before. The colorfulness of the 1931 Paris Colonial Exposition was so impressive that the board of Century of Progress fair decided to adjust the budget to allow for more color at the fair.

There were really two problems involved: the colors to be used and their relationship to one another, and the types of paint to be used, taking into consideration the vicissitudes of the weather and the variety of surfaces to be painted.

Urban's color scheme consisted of twenty-three intensely bright colors. These included white, gray, black, aluminum, and gold, as well as six shades of orange and yellow, three shades of red, and nine shades of the blue and green. Urban called for the use of three or four colors on most buildings. He wanted the colors used in ways that would emphasize the architectural characteristics of each building, while at the same time coordinating larger groups of buildings. In addition, the bright colors were also important in creating a carnival spirit for the fair.

For the most part, cool colors (blues, greens, violets) were used on the north sides of buildings, while neutral colors (white, gray, gold, aluminum, black) were used on the east and west sides, and warm colors (reds, oranges, yellows) were used on the south sides. This was done in part because of the way the colors would look under sunlight and partly out of concern for permanence; cool colors stand up least well under bright sunlight.

Weather conditions were an important concern. The paint to be used would stand up under weather that ranged from the cold rainy days of a late spring or early fall in Chicago to the bright sunny days of July and August, and adhere for at least eight months to a wide variety of surface.

Together with color, artificial lighting was a major decorative component of the Century of Progress. Night effects were also a consideration. Lighting had been an important feature of the World's Columbian Exposition, with the major buildings outlined with strings of incandescent lights. All the fairs after 1893 had achieved the desired effect by means of shining lights. The Century of Progress managers made the decision to place considerable emphasis on lighting for dramatic and decorative effects. Incandescent lighting had become brighter and more highly concentrated, color screens or filters of various materials were available to flood wall surfaces with colored light, and gaseous tube lighting, utilizing inert gases such as neon, could produce brilliant colors of lights in glass tubes that could be formed into any desired shape.

Interior lighting was also important, because the fair buildings contained practically no windows, a decision occasioned by economic considerations and the desire to have consistent lighting for the exhibits at all times of the day and in all kinds of weather.

The lighting for the Century of Progress was successful in achieving its main objectives. It helped bring together groups of buildings into a more unified whole. Lighting could be used to create the impression of greater height, or present a more dignified and restful effect. Lighting made the fair look different at night than it did in the day. Many varieties of light made the fair lovely at night. Searchlights were used to set the fairgrounds apart from the lights of nearby downtown Chicago.

Of the major fair buildings, the most distinctive were the Hall of Science, the principal 'theme' pavilion of the fair, and the Travel and Transportation Building, the most innovative structure at the fair, although many critics were distressed by its unconventional appearance. However, it was the Chrysler Building (Figure 8) that received the most praise. It was impressive with the spread out design, and the manner in which the building related to the nearby Travel and Transportation Building.

In a sense, the architecture of the Century of Progress may be seen as an architecture of transition. The raw modernism of the buildings and the bright colors used to paint them seemed to combine with the carnival spirit present in all expositions to recreate a mood that had disappeared with the stock market crash. At the same time, however, the architecture of the fair did serve to popularize modernism in America. It contributed its share to the blossoming of domestic and commercial architecture based on Art Deco and what was becoming known as the International Style, and to the trend in industrial design of streamlining, seen in everything from locomotives to toasters. And despite the claims of some critics, the use of new building materials and the emphasis on prefabrication left their marks on American building techniques. That the New York World's Fair of 1939—1940 adopted a very similar architectural style is ample testament to the architectural legacy of the Century of Progress.

## Science: the Key to Progress

When the idea of celebrating the centennial of the founding of Chicago with a world's fair was first broached in the mid-1920s, most of those involved spoke of such a fair in terms of showing off the progress of Chicago since the World's Columbian Exposition in 1893 and in what benefits a 1933 fair could bring to the city. However, fair leaders knew that a successful fair would have to have a broader theme than one limited to the past, present, and future of the host city. Hence, the National Research Council was asked to help determine a 'philosophy' for the fair, and organize the relevant scientific activities.

### 1. Focusing on Scientific Progress and Creating New Exhibitions

In August 1928, the board formally requested the advice and assistance of the NRC, which in turn appointed a committee, known as the Science Advisory Committee, to respond to the fair board's request. According to the SAC, the Hall of Science should be the central feature of the fair, an architecturally striking building, where visitors would receive a 'quiet unconscious schooling', learning how basic science connected with their daily lives. The exhibits should focus on the service of science to mankind and attempt to show the process by which modern industrial products were made, rather than simply displaying the finished products, as had been the practice at past exposition. Elements of science were to be combined whenever possible: biology and zoology might be appropriately presented together, for example.

Similarly, in August 1930, the board decided to invite the Social Science Research Council to help create an advisory committee on social science for the fair. A display showing groups of people from Eskimos to southwestern Indians was suggested, including reproductions of Maya buildings to represent the height of native American civilization prior to the arrival of Europeans.

The exhibits seen at the Century of Progress were meant to be educational, to carry out the theme of showing the progress of science and technology during the past century. Fair leaders worked hard to assure that exhibits adhered to the major theme. In 1932, a design section was set up to develop concepts of how the exhibits should be presented and to see that the exhibits conformed to the design standards established by the fair management. All exhibitors using space in the principal theme pavilions, such as the Electrical Group or the General Exhibits Building, were required to submit their final plans and color studies to the design section in order to avoid duplicated exhibits and to co-ordinate with related exhibitors. In some cases, however, exhibit ideas were developed by individuals on the exposition staff. They were then taken to the most likely sponsors, who were invited to present them.

## 2. Creating New Operation Mode to Realize the Theme

The Century of Progress was perhaps the first international exposition to take on the responsibility itself to produce a large number of exhibits. To remain faithful to the theme, the board created a Basic Science Division to handle the fair-sponsored exhibits in pure science, and an Applied Science and Industry Division that would work co-operatively with the Basic Science Division but be responsible for obtaining the participation of industry to sponsor and install the applied science exhibits. The initial response from American industry was good. The fair profited from the fact that the involvement of many individuals and organizations in the development of exhibit strategies led to many exhibits being donated or loaned by universities and industry.

As indicated earlier, the emphasis in exhibiting was on process rather than product, and this led to some spectacular exhibits by a number of large corporations. The $1.6 million General Motors Building contained an entire Chevrolet assembly line. Not to be outdone, the Chrysler exhibit contained a one-quarter mile oval testing track, on which visitors could ride in cars driven by famous movie stunt men or racecar drivers.

In practical terms, the model housing exhibit, developed and coordinated by the Century of Progress management and executed by private builders, was a nearly ideal expression of the theme of the fair. In the eleven model homes constructed by different builders, and in the nearby Home and Industrial Arts pavilion, visitors could see where science and technology had influenced domestic life in America.

Homes exhibit was considered an important exhibit, since homes affect everybody, and that therefore it should be treated differently from any other industrial exhibit. European architects should be involved in the model homes exhibit, since this was an important topic of concern there, and it would help secure European participation in the exposition.

Of the eleven model homes, eight were delightful small houses designed to be economical residences that in different ways showed the possibilities of prefabricated units and new building materials yet retained variety of style and individuality in taste. Two other homes, one with emphasis on modernity and the other classically-designed, were clearly intended to be more expensive dwellings. Finally, the 'House of Tomorrow' was a two-story glass and steel house, with many windows that did not open, owing to the central air conditioning. A central pillar supported the house and served as a chase for wiring, plumbing and gas lines. Everything in the house was waterproof and fireproof. It was billed as a ' daring conception, inside and out'.

Although scientific progress over the past century was the theme of the fair, organizers knew that every respectable world's fair in the past had included a fine arts exhibit. But with the coming of the depression and the knowledge that such a pavilion would be quite expensive, given the fireproofing and security needs, the idea of a fine arts building was quietly dropped, and in June 1932, a formal agreement between the Art Institute and the fair board was signed. This authorized the Art Institute to provide and manage an art exhibit in the name of the exposition. The institute would absorb all expense incurred in mounting the show, but the fair agreed to sponsor no other significant art exhibit, and to give the institute 20 per cent of any surplus funds after the end of the fair. As the Art Institute was about a mile away from the fairgrounds, shuttle transportation was provided.

The 1933 art exhibit at the Art Institute attracted just over 700, 000 visitors at twenty-five cents each during its five-month run. The exhibit based on the theme ' A Century of Progress in American Collecting' consisted of an array of artworks, borrowed from twenty-five museums and over 200 American private collections.

The emphasis on process makes exhibits that would normally be boring entertaining.

## Fun at the Fair

By 1933, the concept of a Midway, or entertainment zone, had become a staple feature of world's fairs. First popularized at the World's Columbian Exposition, the Midway came to be widely recognized as a place where visitors weary of serious industrial and agricultural exhibits could find refuge among a mindless mélange of rides, games of chance or skill, freak shows, and night club acts that often tested the moral limits of the time and place.

For the fair organizers, midway traditions posed something of a dilemma. They were trying to bring off a high-minded, educational exposition, based on a theme of science and progress; sleazy midway acts would certainly detract from that goal. On the other hand, they were well aware that their fair had to have broad public appeal in order to be successful; sleazy midway acts would probably contribute to that goal. In the end, they took the most reasonable course by sponsoring some entertainment programs themselves, which were generally faithful to the educational objectives of the fair, while at the same time, they rented space to commercial operations, which, for the most part, sponsored entertainment that was meant to be nothing more than fun. The concessions offered night time activities after people had been instructed by scientific exhibits during the day, and were especially important for the evening operations of the fair.

Among the fair-sponsored concessions, Fort Dearborn and the Chinese Lama Temple were open to the public, during the summer of 1932, when the fair board fixed a general admission to the grounds at ten cents. Some 600,000 people toured the site, watched the exposition being constructed, and visited the few buildings and concessions that had been finished. Fort Dearborn was a replica of the structure that was built when Chicago was founded, while the Chinese Lama Temple was a replica of a Chinese religious building that had been constructed in 28,000 pieces in China, broken down for shipment to Chicago, and then meticulously reassembled for the fair. Both were popular attractions in 1932. Other fair-sponsored attractions were an outdoor pageant on the history of transportation, a show named the World a Million Years Ago and etc.

At the far south end of the fairgrounds, there was an air show, called 'Third of a Century of Progress', in which a number of planes were exhibited to show the evolution of aviation since the Wright brothers' flight in 1903. The US Army Air Corps also displayed its latest planes. For the more adventurous visitors, they were taken on rides over the site. 70 percent of them flew for the first time in their lives. However, the worst tragedy of the exposition occurred on 11 June 1933, when a plane crashed, killing all nine aboard.

Most of the private concessions operated in two amusement areas. One called the Midway, while the other named the Rainbow Area. The Streets of Paris, which was highly successful during the 1933 season, consisted of a grouping of buildings, streets, and squares representative of Paris, with shops and cafes in the buildings, was created by a group of Chicago investors.

For children, the main entertainment venue was a five-acre site called Enchanted Island. It was a very popular attraction, with over three million visitors in 1933 and much favorable commentary in newspapers and magazines. Despite its orientation toward children and their activities, almost 70 percent of the visitors were adults.

Enchanted Island also contained an Art Gallery for children's art and handicraft exhibits and a 'Ship of Health', a center where licensed doctors provided health advice to children and their parents. In addition to the playgrounds, a Children's Theater that used amateur acts to draw crowds yet keep cost down was highly successful.

From the beginning, Century of Progress organizers were aware that involvement with sports would enhance the popularity of the fair. A great deal of effort was put forth to launch major football games and baseball games, and a large number of smaller events were scheduled, such as Sunday afternoon speedboat races on the lagoon, which were very popular. The organizers wanted to see sport as a part of the fair.

To try and derive a little more benefit out of 1933 season, concessionaires requested that the fair remain open past the scheduled closing date of 1 November, and the fair board granted this request, setting a new closing date of 12 November. It turned out to be a bad idea, as attendance dropped because of cold and rainy weather and the announcement that the fair would reopen in 1934. The fair board and concessions division tried their best to stimulate attendance with a number of special features. On 8 November, to celebrate the repeal of prohibition, free beer was distributed on a day ironically publicized as 'Personal Responsibility Day', when 50,000 people showed up, double the previous day's crowd. They drank all the beer and ate almost 200,000 free sandwiches. Sixty people were ejected from the fairgrounds for drunkenness. On 10 November, all persons on the relief rolls were admitted to the grounds free upon presentation of an identity card. Despite special events such as these, the fair extension did not draw enough additional visitors for most concessions to meet overhead expenses.

## A Second Season: 1934

Toward the end of the 1933 season, and particularly after President Franklin Roosevelt's visit on 2 October, the crowds were still heavy and demand for the fair was high. There was increasing interest and discussion about reopening the Century of Progress for a second season in 1934.

In late October, exhibitors were asked if they would be interested in returning for a second year, as plans for a renewal had been developed, and the fair board had voted to reopen the fair the following year, pending support of the Illinois legislature and sufficient commitment from the local business community. The Chicago Tribune noted the most important reason for a second season: that the total indebtedness had been reduced to about $5 million, a $21 million plant was already in place, and a second year of the fair would wipe out the remaining debt.

There was little public dissent with the fair board's decision, although some people felt that if the fair were opened for a second year solely for financial reasons, the renewal would be like 'a warmed over dinner'. However, the board felt that the 1933 season had been very beneficial to Chicago and that the fair was still obligated to its bondholders. Civic support was very strong, the fair buildings were in good condition, and the success of the fair in 1933 had been good for the national spirit.

To help generate interest for a 1934 season, important Century of Progress exhibits were sent to various places around the county in the winter of 1933—1934. About fifty-three exhibits were taken from the fair and put on display in some cities like Pittsburgh, Philadelphia, Clearwater and so on.

### 1. Creating Something New

There was neither the desire nor the money to make significant changes in the Century of Progress for the new season, and so visitors saw many of the same exhibits and shows that they had seen in 1933. Still, some of the changes that were made were quite evident. First of all, the new color scheme appealed to the visitors. The summer sun had badly faded the color of some buildings, and about 75 per cent of the exterior surfaces needed to be repainted. A new color scheme was developed, utilizing just ten colors, with no more than three, including white, on any building. The new color scheme allowed for a clearer 'zoning' principle, with a certain dominant color for each of the major buildings or section, helping visitors find their way around by using colors as a guide. The new colors were designed to make the fair seem more compact.

Additional lighting was installed, particularly in and around the lagoons. Nothing had been done to provide nighttime lighting in the lagoons for 1933, but for 1934, the north end of the lagoon area featured a bank of searchlights that replicated the aurora borealis. A new fountain, billed as the largest in the world, was constructed, with a 75-foot high column illuminated by five different colors lights. Meanwhile, on dry land, 300 trees and 51,000 new flowering pants, chosen to harmonize with the new color scheme, were added, and a variety of new concessions, including restaurants and an open-air theater, were built along the edge of the lagoons.

**2. Involvement of Ford——A New Spotlight**

By far the most significant addition to the 1934 fair was the Ford Motor Company pavilion. Henry Ford had planned to have an exhibit at the fair in 1933, featuring an assembly line, but when General Motors announced in July 1931 that its pavilion would have an assembly line, angry Ford said he would stay away from Chicago and hold his own exhibition. This was Ford Exposition of Progress, a strictly automotive exhibition staged in Detroit and New York City in late 1933. Almost 3.5 million visitors flocked to see the Ford show over three and a half weeks in the two cities. Aware that 10 million or more visitors had seen the General Motors and Chrysler pavilions at the Century of Progress in 1933, Henry Ford decided to jump in for 1934. The Century of Progress management was thrilled to have him, and he was given an eleven-acre site near the other transportation buildings, where he erected a \$2 million pavilion. In the center rotunda was a 20-foot high globe showing Ford's international operations and an exhibit of sixty-seven historical automobiles. An Industrial Hall featured the latest innovations in automatic machine tools, all busily whirring and clanging, contrasting sharply with a nearby exhibit replicating Ford's original workshop where he handcrafted his first automobile. In addition, there was a band shell in front of the pavilion where the Detroit Symphony Orchestra, sponsored by Ford, played a regular concert program for thirteen weeks, and a 2000-foot walkway through a five-acre garden area between the pavilion and the lake, with nineteen sections representing different historic roadways.

Henry Ford himself took a great interest in the exhibit, personally approving such things as the style of chairs visitors could relax in and banning any sales pressure, despite the fact that General Motors had sold over 3000 automobiles at its pavilion in 1933. After the fair opened, Ford made thirteen visits to his pavilion and often took the time to explain the display personally to young visitors, especially when there were newsmen and photographers nearby, asserting that a fair would help educate people and reduce ignorance. The Ford exhibit received abundant praise from newspapers and trade magazines. Figures show that in 1934, over 75 per cent of those who came to the fair saw the Ford exhibit, compared to some 45 per cent of visitors who went to the General Motors pavilion in 1933.

### 3. Emphasis on the Entertainment Aspect of Exhibits

Other changes in 1934 were more subtle. About 75 per cent of 1933's exhibitors signed up for 1934, and with new companies, such as Ford, coming in, the total number was actually greater than in 1933. With respect to the exhibits prepared for 1934, there was more emphasis placed on live entertainment and films.

This new attention to entertainment worked even in the staid Hall of Science. The Hall of Science was again one of the most popular buildings with its displays of basic scientific and mathematical principles. Improvements were made in the way exhibits were dramatized; many were simplified. New exhibits had to meet a guideline of three principles: 1) Is it simple? 2) Can it relate to some common experience of the visitor? 3) Does it move? The interdependence of scientific fields was emphasized in such displays as the giant periodic table of the elements, a 'Clock of the Ages', showing the geological history of the earth in forty-two seconds, and a large model of a molecule of simple table salt.

Commercial exhibitors were able to refine their presentation to keep the good from 1933 and alter the bad. Chrysler, for example, made much more use of its quarter-mile testing track, adding a grandstand and sponsoring stock car races. Standard Oil Company discarded its film about the petroleum industry in favor of a free wild animal act that told visitors nothing about oil but kept the company name in front of them. Hupmobile brought in a test-driving film that simulated real driving conditions. Visitors who completed the test drive were given a certificate. The Safety Glass Company dared visitors to break a window by throwing rocks at it. Armour, a meat-packing company, had a popular bacon sliding and wrapping demonstration, employing 'auburn-haired beauties' to run the machines. Visitors were more interested in seeing people do something or appear to do something.

In the Housing exhibit, George Fred Keck replaced his House of Tomorrow with the 'Crystal House'. This experimental glass and steel house was designed be to an ultra-modern, low-cost single family residence that could be erected quickly. Its plate glass walls and steel framing members were prefabricated and assembled on a concrete slab poured at the site. A central utility core contained mechanical equipment, and sliding draperies afforded privacy. Because of the glass walls, a sophisticated heating and cooling system was required, and while the house did have a rather dramatic appearance, its significance was more a symbol of modernism than as a practical prototype for residential housing.

In July, the fair sponsored 'A Century of Progress Better Housing Forum', involving discussion of local, state, and federal housing programs. On Home Modernization Day, 24 October, a century old house that had been moved from the city to the housing exhibit area was completely remodeled by volunteer workers in one day at an estimated materials cost of between \$750 and \$1,000.

The contract with Art Institute was renewed for the 1934 season, and the theme was 'American Art', viewed in the context of world art. The exhibit, said to be valued at \$75 million, showed more than 350 masterpieces borrowed from Europe. And a like number of American paintings from colonial times to the 1930s were at display.

The effects of the depression, however, limited official or semi-official participation in 1934 to just six foreign governments and eleven state governments. An effort was made to attract more foreign participation by turning the Hall of States into a Court of Nations and offering space there to foreign governments, but it was unsuccessful. Some blame for the decrease in foreign participation was placed on the 1928 Paris convention, as the extension of the Century of Progress was deemed to be a violation of the agreement. Some countries changed their participation from official to semi-official.

On 31 May 1934, just a few days after the season opened, over 500, 000 visitors attended the fair on Children's Day, with children admitted for five cents and given a free bottle of milk at the entrance gate. This attendance was higher than any day during the 1933 season and encouraged the management to declare that on every Thursday children would be admitted for a nickel. Toward the end of the 1934 season, the management set aside two days for families on relief to see the fair without charge.

With a 1934 attendance of 16, 486, 377, fair management ended the season with a surplus of $688, 165 to cover the costs of demolition, organizational expenses, and any contingencies. The Century of Progress was the only world's fair to pay off bondholders in full. Many concessionaires expressed their willingness to stay a third year, and others made plans to participate in future world's fairs or other amusement venues.

Very soon after the fair closed, the dismantling of the fair started, which involved three major elements. First, there was a series of sealed bid auctions to dispose of the furniture, fixtures, and other portable assets on the grounds. Second, there was the process of demolishing the many buildings and other structures on the site and returning the land to its pre-fair condition. And third, there was the final accounting for the fair, which involved settling remaining debts and disbursing the surplus according to a pre-arranged formula.

The city of Chicago continued to derive economic benefit from the Century of Progress in 1934. The fair had brought about $50 million of construction and maintenance work. Out-of-town visitors had left $700 million in the pockets of the Chicago business community, part of which had gone to increase local and state tax receipt. Meanwhile, the fair had provided a notable cultural uplift to the city.

## The Distinctive Features of the Two Fairs

Though styled somewhat after that famous Columbian Exposition, the Century of Progress was to be quite different.

First of all, the Century of Progress was mainly funded by Chicago's wealthy citizens, in addition to quite a few corporate sponsors, whereas the Columbian Exposition relied heavily on grants from government agencies. The Century of Progress was indeed a successful business venture. Throughout the planning, operation, and aftermath of the exposition, the fair management, acutely aware of the financial status of their project, worked in the midst of a global economic crisis of immense proportions and paid off their investors in full, accepting no government subsidies.

More importantly, the goals of the fairs differed markedly. The Columbian Exposition had created a utopia which, in many ways, glorified tradition and an idealized past, and its overall sense of nostalgia was overwhelming. By contrast, the Century of Progress Exposition of 1933 was planned to project the mind and imagination into the future. It was to be a projection, not a recollection. By creating a wonderland reflecting America's greatest advancements in art, literature, architecture, science, and industry, the fair served not only as a source of pride, but also provided some much needed reassurance that, despite the current situation, the future of America was full of promise.

In terms of architecture, unlike the Chicago World's Fair of 1893, which sought in its classical architecture and arrangement to recall the glory and grandeur of the past, the Century of Progress Fair attempted to create a fantastic city of the future, patterned on the concepts of light, lift, and color. In fact, if there is one unifying characteristic in the vast array of forms that appeared, it was the tendency toward lightness and motion emphasized by design. Each of the buildings demonstrated this upward, open line, reaching toward the heaven. Where cathedrals used to be the tallest and grandest structures in a city, here they were replaced by temples of progress, dedicated to science, industry, arts and etc. The commission defined progress as aspiration and movement, and this definition was reflected in each of its designs. The buildings were of a streamlined, high-tech modern style, with a special emphasis on clarity of form. The object here was to create something entirely new, reiterating the idea that this was not simply an imitation of 1893.

The Century of Progress differed from other fairs in the area of exhibits. First, the Century of Progress itself had undertaken the presentation of a large number of exhibits——those in the basic sciences—— and was using a new method of exhibition, ranging from models to slides to short films. Exhibits were arranged in the way they told stories in layperson's terms. Applied science exhibits were provided by business, governments, or other organizations. Second, the Century of Progress was the first world's fair to sell large quantities of exhibit space. This required a special sales force, and the depression made the selling job difficult, but the financial success of the fair was largely dependent on these sales. Third, the Century of Progress was the first fair in which a concerted effort was made to have each exhibitor's display complete but not be duplicative of another exhibitor's display, something that would necessitate extensive consultation and compromise among exhibitors. This was important, because the exposition management wanted business to derive every possible benefit from participating in the fair, especially during a depression.

Both fairs shared a host city, and even shared the experience of operating during an economic depression. Although they stressed science, technology and progress in their exhibits, each approached the matter of exhibiting in a distinctive way. In order to show the state of progress up to 1893, the World's Columbian Exposition used the department store method, wherein static exhibits of industrial products were lined up on shelves or placed in display cases, just as they might have been in a retail store. Companies competed with one another for the prizes that were awarded to those products judged the finest, and there was a good deal of nationalistic pride in seeing that American goods had been judged superior to foreign products.

If the Columbian Exposition was a department store, then the Century of Progress was a school laboratory. The best exhibits were those that moved in some purposeful way, or made a product as visitors watched, or used visual or animated aids to tell a story; at their extreme, the exhibits seemed to show that 'modern scientific practice is a combination of Hollywood and Houdini'. Prizes were not awarded at the fair, and the emphasis was on process rather than product, showing 'how good things grow out of science'.

Either of the fairs was at once an escape from the trials of the depression, an adult education center, a successful business venture that met the challenge of its time with sound business management. They worked well as a small city within a city, where the vast majority of visitors were very pleased with what they experienced. They served as important models for subsequent fairs in San Diego in 1935 and New York and San Francisco in 1939—1940.

## Postscript to the Fair

There was almost a third Chicago world's fair. In 1977, some prominent Chicagoans suggested a world's fair to celebrate the quincentenary of Columbus's discovery of the New World and incidentally, the centennial of the World's Columbian Exposition. In 1981, the Chicago World's Fair-1992 Corporation was formed. This corporation, which consisted of influential corporate leaders, lawyers, and architects, worked for several months without public or political input and planned the theme, site, and dates for a 1992 fair and prepared an application for obtaining the sanction of the BIE.

By 1982, the closed nature of the fair corporation's decision-making process generated opposition to the fair. Much of the criticism centered round the perilous financing of the fair, the environmental impact, and the effect that the fair would have on nearby residential neighborhoods. Late in the year, state and city officials combined to create a formal Chicago World's Fair-1992 Authority to replace the Fair Corporation.

However, criticism, both in and out of the Washington administration, revolved around the amount of public spending necessary for such things as altering major roadways in the vicinity of the site, building sewers, and providing police and fire protection for the fair. Others questioned the reality of the Fair Authority's attendance and economic projections, and whether the pro-fair forces were using the fair to boost land values in nearby areas in which they had financial interests.

Further debate continued through 1984 and into 1985, and chances for the fair dimmed further when news of the financial debacle of the 1984 New Orleans fair was publicized. The final blow came in June 1985, when a feasibility study, commissioned by the Illinois House of Representatives, concluded that the proposed fair was such a bad financial risk that it should not be underwritten with state money. Without state funds, the fair could not be staged, and in December 1987, the BIE withdrew its sanction for the Chicago fair.

# 第五章

## *1939—1940 年纽约世博会*

芝加哥两次举办世博会——1893 年哥伦布纪念世博会和 1933—1934 年世纪的进步世博会——让世人刮目相看。许多规模次之的美国城市也成功地举办了博览会，像巴黎这样的国际大都市就更不用说了。然而，以美国经济文化中心而著称的纽约自 1853 年以来一直未举办博览会。美国第一届博览会——1853 年纽约水晶宫博览会，以 1851 年伦敦博览会为样板，但是创造了美国式的非政府筹办博览会的模式。政府希望这届博览会能有助于国家的团结统一，结果，由于当时美国四分五裂的政治气候，这次博览会是一个经济失败与激情的破灭。然而，纽约这个熟睡的巨人一旦苏醒，便创造出一个宏伟奇观，这场奇观出现在一场全国性的灾难行将结束，另一场灾难还未开始的交替之际。

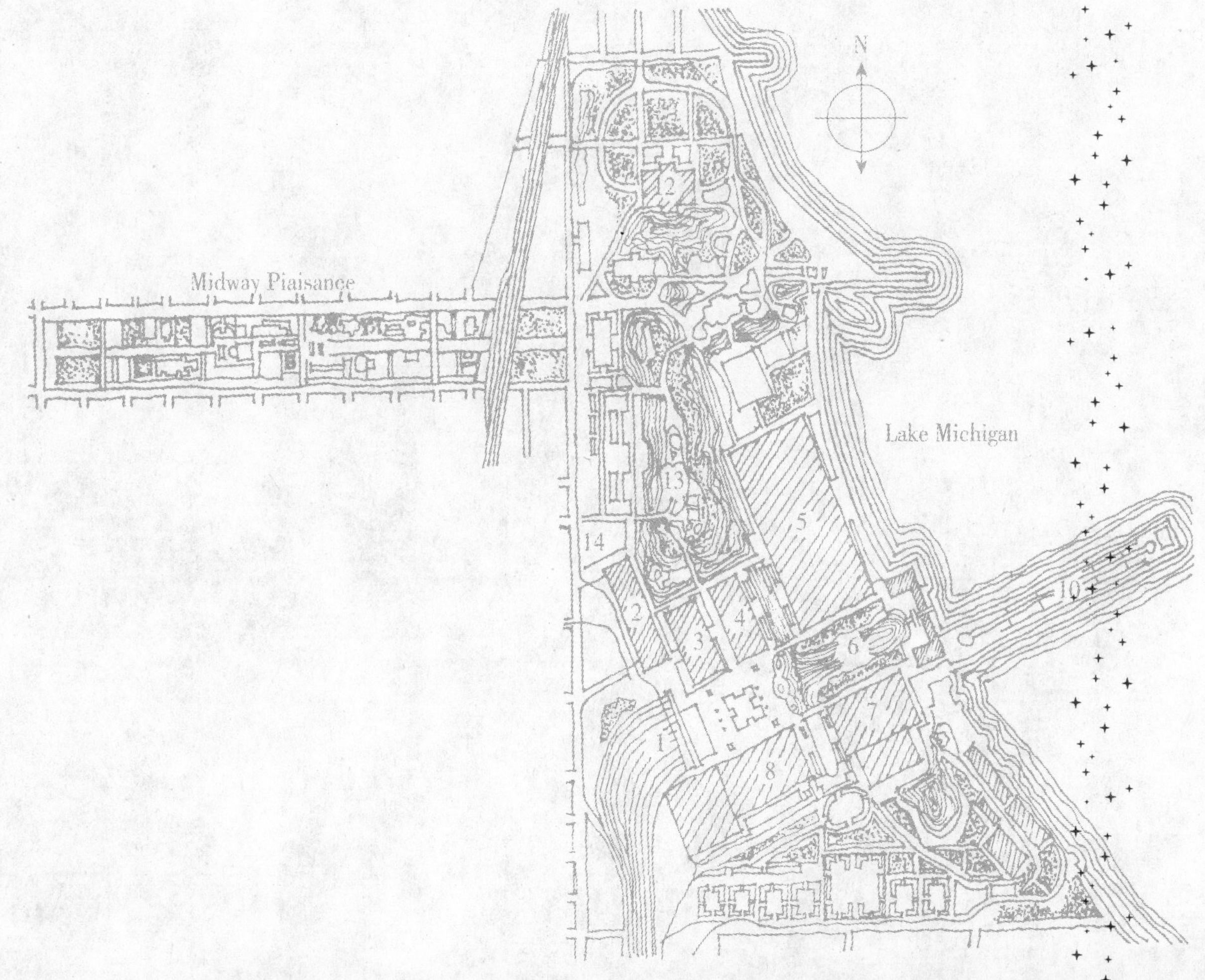

## 背景

虽然1939年世博会的创意诞生于美国企业界，其风格却来自新一代艺术家和建筑师。1935年正值经济萧条的高峰期，纽约一些商界人士认为举办国际博览会是这座城市和国家摆脱困境的有效途径。当年他们成立了纽约世博公司，推选Grouver Whalen为总裁。经过短期银行贷款，世博公司向企业、行业协会和公众销售了约2700万美元的债券（利率4%，1941年偿还），并从当地的富人那里获得了相当数量的私人赞助。

像19世纪和20世纪初的多数大型国际博览会一样，1939年世博会名义上是为了庆祝一个重大的历史事件，但是对投资世博会，组建世博公司的商界人士来说，其灵感既不是来自历史事件，或纪念日，也不是爱国主义的激情，他们的动机很简单，纯粹是为了商业目的：芝加哥1933—1934年世纪的进步世博会在经济萧条的艰难岁月取得了经济上的成功，如果美国第二大城市可以如此成功，还有什么力量可以阻止第一大城市纽约举办规模空前辉煌盛大的世博会呢？最终，世博会的主题确定：庆祝美国历史和纽约历史上的重要时刻——乔治·华盛顿在纽约（美国当时的首都）就职演说150周年纪念，世博会的第二个主题更加深入人心——“建设明天的世界”，但这是后来的构思。

1939年纽约世博会是在战争阴云密布的背景下举办的，对于仍然希望保持中立的美国来说，经济、安全和舒适才是他们关心的主要问题。1939年世博会无论是在庆祝民主政体的诞生，还是展示历史辉煌方面都未产生深远的影响，只有充满幻想的商业展示所颂扬的物质第一的信念令人难忘。这些展示之所以让1939年的观众为之振奋是因为当时人们对技术进步的好处深信不疑，这种信念在今天已几乎消失殆尽。但是，当年的中年观众出生在一个没有汽车、电灯、飞机和电话的年代，他们对速度、进步和新鲜事物惊叹不已。流线型、未来主义风格和锐意创新是1939年世博会的主要特征，1939年世博会自始至终都是设计师的博览会。

设计委员会包括工业设计界的“四大名师”：Norman Bel Geddes，Raymond Loewy，Henry Dreyfuss和Walter Dorwin Teague。大多数设计师都有舞台设计经验和艺术教育背景，他们以世博会为契机，宣传线条简洁、形式“纯净”的设计理念，这些理念在他们的产品设计中得以充分体现，小到牙刷，大到克莱斯勒流线型汽车。

世博会所展示的新技术对美国家庭产生了深刻影响，而当时著名建筑师菲利普·约翰逊和密斯·凡·德·罗等人设计的具有高度现代主义风格的建筑对美国的住宅设计影响却不大。通过世博会，现代主义以流线型设计的产品形式进入厨房、卫生间和车库，走进美国家庭。

## 世博会规划

单从规模、花费和持续的吸引力来看，1939—1940年世博会堪称最伟大的博览会，在诸多方面都产生了重要影响：古典式的对称性布局（虽然有的建筑评论家对此非常反感）；色彩作为分区符号，色彩标示的分区将世博会变成一个巨大的游乐城；巨大的三角塔和球形建筑简洁的几何造型和富有魅力的象征性。更重要的是，世博会对于一个经济技术即将起飞的时代是一部令人振奋的科幻作品。

关于世博会的场址，纽约园林局不允许世博公司使用现有公园绿地，而是要求世博公司在新址上建设世博园，世博会后交给园林局管理。世博会址选在Queens区曾经作为垃圾堆放场的Flushing Meadow沼泽地，这片3英里半长的沼泽地经过填埋平整，成为Flushing Meadow公园，在难以平整的地段布置设计了形态自然的人工湖。这个位于纽约大都市中心地理位置的垃圾堆放场碍眼又刺鼻，但却预示着一个巨大的机遇，展示了未来的发展将如何改造过去的残缺。这片垃圾场清理工程是美国东部最大的土地改造项目，投资预算高，优先重点发展。有了良好的铁路、地铁和公路交通，水路直通曼哈顿，在土地紧缺的都市区，这里显然是一个最佳的选择。公园规划始于1936年1月，破土动工仪式于当年6月29日举行。这项工程的另一个显著特征是，这是有史以来第一次按照预先计划，世博会后将世博园变成城市公园，交给地方政府管理的安排。

设计委员会对世博园的艺术风格和建筑风格作了规定，与世博会的主题与规范保持一致。建筑设计方案既体现了临时性建筑的特征，同时也保持了建筑、雕塑和景观规划方面的完美和谐。世博建筑大多采用无窗孔的单层结构，人工采光和通风，与纽约的摩天楼形成鲜明对比。为了借用远处曼哈顿的摩天楼景观，设计委员会为世博建筑规定了相对较低的天际线，只是偶尔伸出一个塔楼或标示塔，并且使三角塔成为世博园最高的建筑，这样观众可以“曼哈顿的空中天际线”为背景观赏世博建筑景观。

展馆采用直率的展览建筑风格，禁止模仿历史建筑或突出的传统建筑风格，只有政府展区和娱乐区除外。多数展馆立面完整，外墙无窗孔，采用空调制冷，因为窗孔会占据展馆的墙面空间，使得展馆夏季炎热。光秃的外墙采用雕塑、壁画和精心布置的藤本植物与树木形成的光影变化装饰，取得了“统一而不单一”的艺术效果。

由于世博建筑风格的变化受到世博设计规范的制约，各种艺术构思和技艺体现在大量的雕塑作品中，通过这些作品，20世纪30年代主流雕塑家的艺术风格得以充分展示。这些雕塑作品不仅对各类展馆和广场具有装饰点缀作用，而且体现了所在展区的特点，与世博主题和谐。例如，位于运输展区的一座雕塑，“车轮精神”，象征了人类在运输领域取得的进步。多数雕塑采用灰浆制作。

设计委员会在世博规划初期设计建造了几栋建筑，例如世博公司行政办公楼，成为众多建筑师效仿的样板。总的来说，世博园各类建筑多达 375 栋，包括 100 座重要的展馆和 50 个主要的游乐项目。

色彩的运用非常有趣。设计委员会为世博园巨大的中部展区制定了分地段运用色彩的方案。例如，主题中心区的三角塔和球形建筑是纯白色，周边是米色；世博园的主轴线采用不同层次的红色，由近及远逐渐加深，从玫瑰红渐进到葡萄酒红。

夜间照明也经过了精心设计。泛光照明只用于主题中心的球形建筑和其他几个景点，探照灯构成的华盖设置在联邦大楼附近的和平广场上空。其他地方的照明色彩丰富，富有创意，但有所控制，两处水面上的烟花和别出心裁的灯光展示除外。

设计委员会在世博总体规划和展览规范中创造了一个井然有序，结构完整的体系，这种设计理念自然也渗透到展览中，从而使展览成为“改造人的机器”。设计委员会的意图是创造一个“精心设计的迷宫”，这样可以“激发观众的兴趣，让他们有感而发”，在这方面，设计委员会非常成功。

当问及对 1939—1940 年世博会的感想时，人们常说世博会有种“魔力”，特别是在晚间，绚丽的灯光、绝妙的色彩构图和蔚为壮观的烟花表演被演绎到了极致的效果。

当 1939 年春天举办世博会的条件成熟时，开幕日定在 4 月 30 日——美国第一任总统华盛顿就职演说 150 周年纪念。一座国父的巨型塑像矗立在世博园，华盛顿的名字和形象随处可见。

在一个经济压力巨大，战争乌云密布的年代，罗斯福总统发出了盛情邀请，有趣的是，前苏联第一个作出回应，拨款 400 万美元建设国家馆，苏联馆最终成为国际展区最受欢迎的展馆。面对挑战，西欧国家也不甘落后，共有 60 个国家和国际组织参与了 1939 年世博会，德国除外。

## 规划明天的世界

时任纽约市园林局长的 Robert Moses 从 1935 年开始参与世博规划。当世博公司与他接触时，Moses 迅速将他们的世博方案纳入自己的公园计划。让 Moses 感兴趣的不是世博会本身，而是世博会带动城市建设的潜力，他把世博会看作是一个方便快捷、预算庞大、优先发展的项目，便于推进和实现他的主要目标：建设 Flushing Meadow 公园和道路设施。他构想了一个雄心勃勃的方案，要将 Flushing Meadow 地区的垃圾山变成一座城市公园。世博园北区建设的喷泉和道路将成为公园古典风格布局的一部分，用他自己的话来说就是“美国的凡尔赛宫”。公园南区的设计风格随意自然，并且布置了两个人工湖。垃圾场的大部分改造工程在不到两年的时间内完成，更多的工作要在世博会后进行。在 Moses 的鼓动下，园林局的许多景观设计师也阶段性地参与了设计委员会的工作。为了改善纽约的交通设施，Moses 还设计了新的道路交通总体规划图，该规划方案以位于纽约市中心区的 Flushing

Meadow 为核心，使之自然而然地成为这个道路网络的中枢。

1939 年世博会以“建设明天的世界”为主题，着眼于未来，强调人之间以及国家之间的相互依存关系，改善人们的福利，改进美国人的生活方式，为所有人创造一个更加幸福美满的地球。世博会的主题在其平面布局、建筑风格、色彩运用以及各类展览中得以充分体现，所有这些因素都预示着明天的世界将会发生怎样的变化。

**1. 主题中心的创意**

世博主题需要一个主题中心予以体现。哈里森（Harrison）和富尤（Fouilhoux）于 1936 年 11 月获得了设计委托，他们设计的主题中心具有展览功能，戏剧性地展示了世博主题。哈里森说：“世博会的实质就是表现未来生活，这正是我们试图以最现代的方式演绎的理念。”

主题中心由两座著名的世博建筑构成：700 英尺高的三角塔和直径 200 英尺的球形建筑（图 9），称之为“视觉糖果”，其知名度仅次于水晶宫（1851）和埃菲尔铁塔（1889）。选择球形是因为它是耗费材料最少，创造空间最大的理想形体，塔楼是球形的天然参照物。这两座简洁自然的建筑造型令人为之振奋，影响深远，该方案在 1937 年第一次公布时就被誉为“未来的符号”。正如世博公司总裁 Grouver Whalen 所说，“我们以世博建筑的形式向世界承诺创新，这就是——既完全不同，又基本与人们过去的经历相关。”

图 9　主题中心由两座著名的世博建筑构成：700 英尺高的三角塔和直径 200 英尺的球形建筑，具有展览功能，戏剧性地展示了世博主题

除了象征意义外，主题中心至少具有两个实用功能：世博园（面积 1216 英亩）的导向标志和最佳观景点（图 10）。各展区以主题中心为核心，呈放射状展开，从空中鸟瞰，世博园就像张开的五彩花扇，由三个片区构成：主展区、政府展区和娱乐区（图 11）。

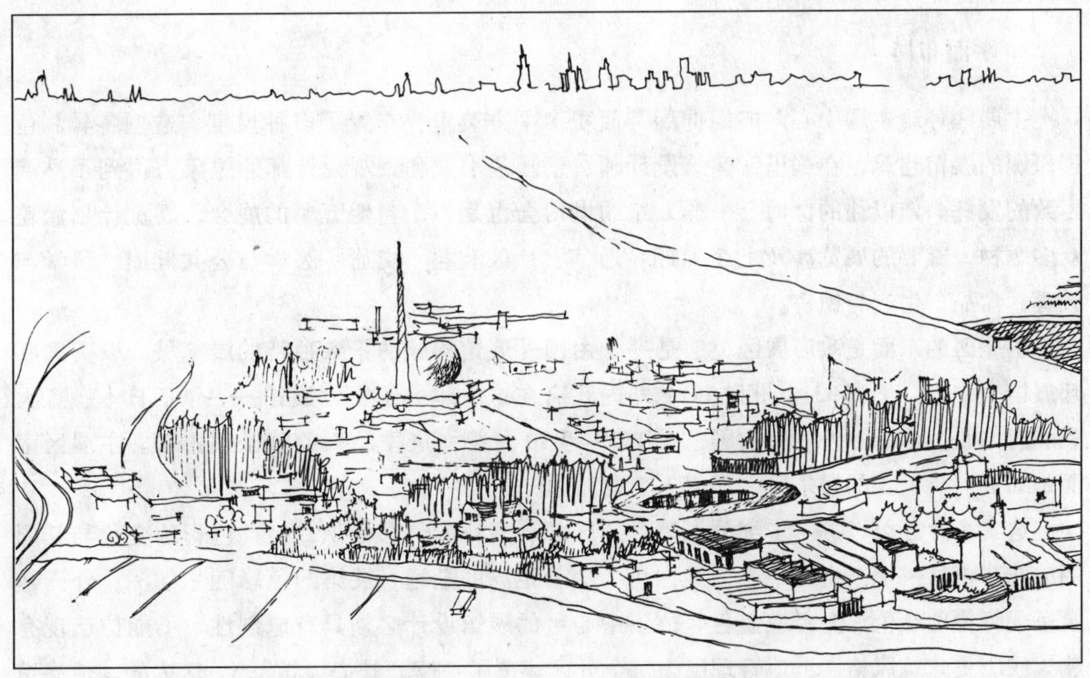

图 10　主题中心是世博园的导向标志和最佳观景点

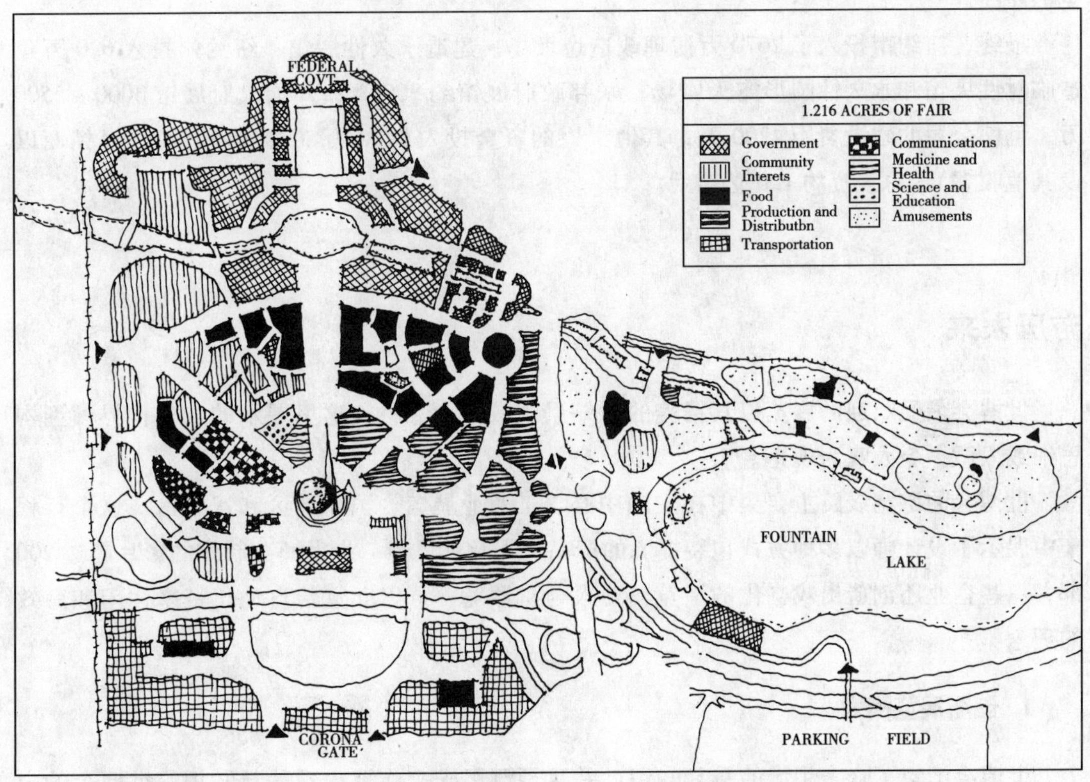


图 11　世博园由三个片区构成：主展区、政府展区和娱乐区，各展区以主题中心为核心，呈放射状展开

### 2. 平面布局

主展区环绕主题中心向四周伸展，面积1平方英里，布置了多种尺度、造型各异、色彩斑斓的展馆建筑，在这里，建筑设计师、壁画艺术家和景观设计师的想象力得到了淋漓尽致的发挥。像以往的世博会一样，纽约世博会也是一个包罗万象的展会，展览计划涵盖众多题材，重要的展览涉及七个专题：通信、社区利益、交通、医学与公共健康、科学与教育、食品、生产与销售。

主展区的东面是政府展区，这是一个由国外展馆构成的景致独特的展览城，以美国联邦展馆为中心。美国33个州和58个外国政府在这里建造了官方展馆——包括日本、意大利和前苏联，德国除外。有的国家在1939年10月第一展季结束前就已被占领。主展区南面是绵延一英里长的娱乐区，环绕人工湖而建。

这三个片区可以进一步细分，每个片区都有醒目的色彩标识，而且色彩的变化与其周围的花草植物搭配。主题中心为纯白色，随着距离的渐远，展馆的色彩随之加深，外围建筑呈现鲜艳的红色、金色或蓝色。位于中心区的展馆设计必须具有原创性，不能仿造现有建筑或历史建筑风格。世博管理层为每个分区建造了一座“核心展馆”，分区内的其他展馆由参展商自行建造。每一座核心展馆都成为世博会推出的科学与艺术、工业与成就系列展览的序曲。

最终，纽约市投入了2670万清理改造垃圾场，建造永久性展馆；纽约州投入620万建造临时性展馆和永久性圆形露天剧场；联邦政府展馆约300万；外国政府展馆3000～3500万；世博公司的建设费用4200万；其他渠道的资金投入5200万（参展商、特许经销商以及其他收费）。总投资约1.6亿美元。

## 游历未来

世博会最受欢迎的展览以其精美的微缩景观效果而著称，这里展示的未来世界模型构思细致入微，令人叹为观止。

世博会的游览线路主要集中在主题中心、工商业展馆、国际展区和娱乐区。这个行程集中展示了设计师以多种方式包装提炼的产品、人及其思想。为世博会制作的影片超过200部，一些企业还创造出戏剧化的展览，让人与机器竞赛，以此宣传自动化带来休闲和高效的理念。

### 1. 创新展览模式

世博会汇集了众多领域的最新知识，并且预测了未来将要出现的新知识。世博会的中心思想集中体现在两座白色建筑上：球形建筑——人类建造的最大球体；塔楼——修长的三棱尖塔。主题中心庞大而独特的造型数英里外清晰可辨，球体象征着我们的世界，尖塔象征着我们的渴望。球形建筑内的主题展览奠定了世博会的基调：未来城市全景模型（Democracity），这是一个理想世界的景观。

塔楼与球形建筑之间有一座巨型坡道连接，观众通过坡道返回地面。进入主题中心需要搭乘当时世界上最大的电动扶梯登上塔楼，观众从这里进入球形展厅观赏名为“Democracity”的“未来城市及郊区规划”，这是一个布置在展厅地面上的微缩模型，与世博园的规划很相似。观看展览的同时，播放一段6分钟的关于未来的解说，接着是电影放映，展示“快乐的农民和工人”，他们代表了富裕起来的美国人，观众在不远的将来便会融入其中。塔楼和球形建筑体现了当代工业设计师所强调的纯净形式。

主题中心周围布置了工商业展馆，规模和数量最大，占据了展区的大部分面积，这种布局表明美国城市的未来依赖于企业的经营与技术支持。在世博会的众多展览中，引起最大反响的是通用汽车公司的名为Futurama的未来生活全景展览，Norman Bel Geddes设计。

未来生活全景展览是一个尺度为36,000平方英尺的微缩景观模型，展示了未来——也就是1960年——美国的生活场景，包括未来的住宅、市政建设、桥梁、水坝和景观环境，特别是先进的公路交通系统，汽车的行驶速度可以达到每小时100英里。观众坐在配有扬声器的传动椅上观赏展览，好似坐飞机在某个城市上空降落，从舷窗向外望去，一幅代表了3000平方英里的美国繁荣进步的景象尽收眼底，这是未来的人间仙境。同时，观众还看到了美国企业与这片奇景的联系。通用汽车展馆所传达的信息，不仅永远地改变了广告和营销的形式和规模，而且也改变了美国人的生活、出行和建造方式。

威斯汀豪斯公司创造了一种崭新的展示技术，故弄玄虚地将其主要展品掩埋地下——一个子弹造型的时间盒，包括了压缩在微缩胶片上的几百万页文献资料，以及20世纪初的文化标志：爱因斯坦和托马斯·曼的文章、连环漫画、《生活杂志》、一盒骆驼牌香烟、一个塑胶洋娃娃、一个美元以及大量其他制品。时间盒要保存到公元6939年才能开启。展商的目的很明确：为后人留下现代人所熟知的这个世界的完整纪录。这种以实物纪录和展示历史的方式引起轰动，令人难忘。

**2. 创造一种展商与观众互动的文化**

Walter Dorwin Teague和Albert Kahn设计的福特展馆外立面是一段盘旋而上，半英里长的车道，十分醒目，称之为“明天的道路”（图12），游客可以在此试驾福特、水星和林肯—西风等品牌的汽车，在这里，福特展馆创造了一种观众与厂商互动的文化。福特展馆的重点展览是“福特生产链”，这是一个直径100英尺，浮在水面，可以自由转动的圆盘，讲述了汽车工业如何扩大就业领域的历程，从原材料制造商，到零部件供货商，到流水生产线上的工人，到经销商，形成一个巨大的就业链。

在通信展区，美国电话电报公司展示了长途电话的最新技术，并且向抽签中奖的观众提供拨打免费长途电话的机会，这项活动的核心是让观众，让普通美国人体验长途电话的

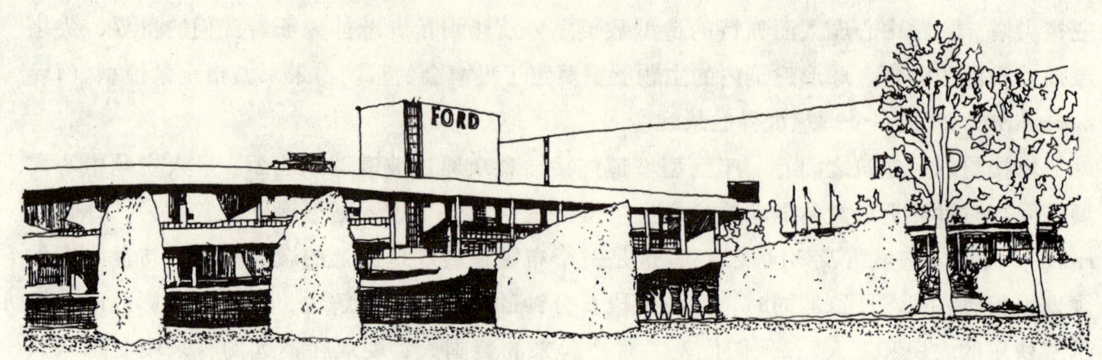


图 12　福特展馆外立面是一段盘旋而上，半英里长的车道，称之为“明天的道路”

妙趣，引发情感上的共鸣。

的确，世博会“汇集时空与历史、工业与艺术、加之狂欢作乐为一体——是一个色彩斑斓的世界，具有广阔的发展前景”。(纽约时报，1939 年 4 月 30 日)

## 营销未来

1939 年世博会从开幕的第一天起就是一个商业经营活动，但是带有国际合作与技术进步的色彩，并且动用了科学界的重要人物来传递这样的信息。爱因斯坦出席了世博会，他在演讲中说道，“如果科学能像艺术一样完全彻底地完成自己的使命，科学成就一定不是表面地，而是深层次地进入人们的意识。”

每一天，庆祝游行和烟花表演让世博会的活动达到高潮，这些活动是专为吸引国内外游客而设计的。特别是，世博公司总裁 Whalen 和纽约市长一直不遗余力地在媒体上宣传推介世博会，例如与到访来宾和参展商照相，在福特馆庆祝日当天与亨利·福特合影等。他们的目的不仅是要宣传世博会，而且是要推动纽约市的旅游，对潜在的游客说，“纽约与美国的其他城市没有什么不同，但是，我们能以更低的价格，提供更好的食宿。”

1939 年世博会是消费者的博览会，充满了专为世博会设计的产品，在会场和专卖店销售。主办方希望世博会的游客会给纽约市带来 10 亿美元的资金流量，而且也有助于消除纽约市孤傲冷漠，与美国其他地区格格不入的坏名声。

1939 年世博会举办了两个展季，于 1940 年 10 月 27 日正式闭幕。世博会吸引了 4500 万观众，创造了 4800 万美元的收入。然而，这个数字远远低于预期，虽然世博会也采取了一些措施——降低门票价格，特价电影，竞赛与颁奖等活动，所有这些吸引游客的措施都未奏效。长时间的恶劣天气，国际展区发生变故，尤其是不断传来的战争事态起了至关重要的作用，萦绕在人们头脑中的战争阴云妨碍了他们寻求其他形式的“娱乐活动”，所有这些因素都导致了世博会的失败。

虽然世博公司在工程建设、宣传运作方面投资了6700万美元（再加上其他渠道的投入1亿美元），这个Whalen称之为“20世纪最伟大的土木工程盛事”还是以经济失败而告终，世博公司也宣告破产。只有几座世博建筑被保留下来：纽约市展馆和纽约州建造的圆形剧场，它们都是Moses最感兴趣的建筑，成为永久性的娱乐设施。1964—1965年世博会也在这座公园举办，纽约市展馆和纽约州建造的圆形剧场发挥了同样的作用。

尽管1939年世博会是一场经济失败，但是参与世博会的政治家、企业名人、艺术家、设计师和社会活动的策划者共同在“Flushing Meadow创造了一个未来的运作模式”，在这方面，他们获得了成功，为未来的世博会树立了榜样。世博会的展览和世博会的参与者对设计、艺术、建筑、广告、营销、城市建设以及文化研究等领域产生了深刻影响。

# Chapter 5

## *New York World's Fair 1939—1940*

Chicago had dazzled the world with its Columbian Exposition of 1893 and Century of Progress in 1933—1934. Many smaller American cities, not to mention world capitals like Paris, had put on successful shows. Yet New York City, reputed cultural and financial center of the nation, had housed no fairs since 1853. The first American fair, New York's Crystal Palace of 1853, was modeled after the 1851 London Fair, but established the non-government approach to fair planning in the United States. The government hoped that the Fair would be useful in unifying the nation. Instead, the Fair was a financial and inspirational failure, due to the divisive national political climate in the 1850s. However, when the sleeping giant was roused, it produced a spectacle, brilliantly conceived on a colossal scale, which occurred at a time when one great national trouble was ending and another had not quite begun.

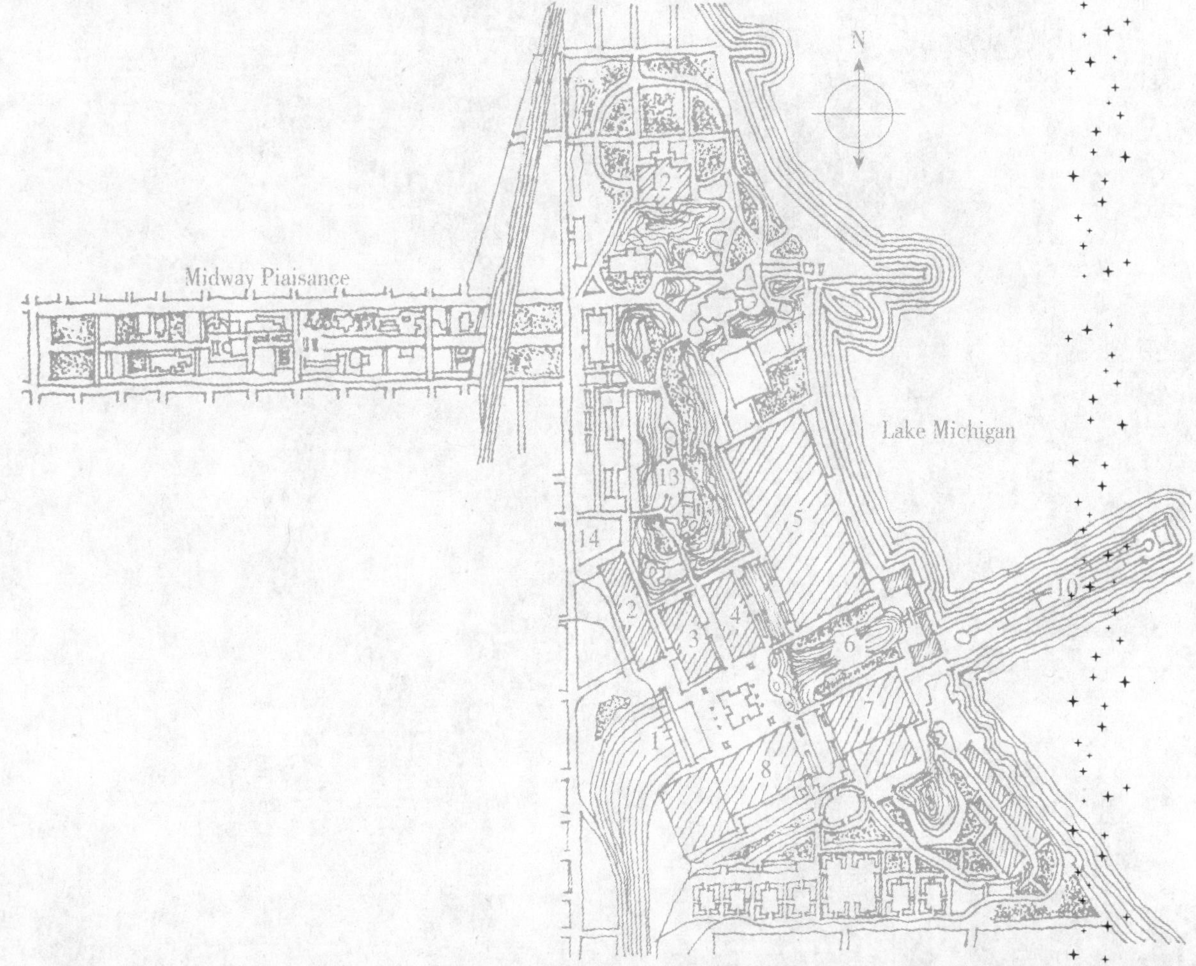

## Background

The idea for the Fair was born in the mind of corporate America, but its style was derived from a new breed of artist/architect of the day, the industrial designer. In 1935, at the height of the Depression, a group of New York businessmen decided that what the city and the nation needed to lift itself out of the difficulties of the times was an international exposition. That same year they formed the New York World Fair Corporation, electing Grover Whalen the president of the organization. After a temporary bank loan, the Fair Corporation sold about 27 million dollars' worth of bonds (at four percent, payable in 1941) to businesses, unions and the public, and received sizable private contributions from local millionaires.

Like many of the massive world's fairs of the nineteenth and early twentieth century, the fair was nominally to be organized around a momentous historic occasion. But to the businessmen who financed the fair and created the New York World's Fair Corporation to administer it, the inspiration was neither an occasion nor an anniversary, much less a patriotic impulse. The motive was business pure and simple: the Chicago Century of Progress Exposition of 1933—1934, financially successful against great odds in the worst years of the Depression. If the second city could perform so admirably, what could prevent the success of an even more glorious event in an even greater city? The rationale for the fair eventually became the celebration of an event unique in the history of America and the history of New York City——the 150th anniversary of George Washington's presidential inauguration in the city that was, in its day, the capital of the United States. Its secondary but best-remembered theme, "Building the World of Tomorrow," was an afterthought.

The 1939 New York World's Fair was held against a background of war and yet, to Americans still hoping against hope for neutrality, the very matters of economy, security and comfort were their major concerns. Neither the celebrations of democracy nor what history was shown at the fair made a lasting impact, but the exalted materialism of the visionary commercial displays did. What made these displays thrilling to the fairgoers of 1939 was a general credulousness, born of a belief in a beneficent technology that has all but vanished in today's world. The average middle-aged fairgoers of the time, born into a world without automobiles, electric lights, airplanes or telephones, were therefore dazzled by speed, by progress, by the new. The outlines of the fair were streamlined, futuristic, and intentionally original. It was a designer's fair from first to last.

Among the members of the Board of Design were the "big four" of industrial design: Norman Bel Geddes, Raymond Loewy, Henry Dreyfuss and Walter Dorwin Teague. Most of these men came from theatrical design or artistic backgrounds. They seized the fair as the opportunity to promote the belief in clean lines and "pure" forms which they demonstrated in their commercial products, from toothbrushes to the Chrysler Air-flow automobile.

The technologies displayed at the fair have had a profound impact on the American home. While the high Modernist architecture of the day, designed by figures such as Philip Johnson and Ludwig Mies van der Rohe, did little to influence the architectural design of the American home, Modernism, via the fair, entered the American home through kitchen, bathroom, and garage doors in the form of the industrial designers' streamlined products.

## Planning the Fair

For reasons of sheer scale and expenditure, as well as its enduring place in popular affections, the World's Fair of 1939—1940 could claim to be the greatest exhibition ever held. It achieved its powerful impact in many ways: the classically symmetrical ground plan, though detested by some architecture critics; the color-coded zones, which turned the Fair into a large playland; the vast size and attractive symbolism of the Trylon and Perisphere, with their geometrical simplicity. Above all, the Fair was a stunning piece of science fiction for an age poised at the brink of an economic and technological leap.

For the site of the exposition, the New York Parks Commission would not allow the Corporation to use an existing park for the fair, instead, required the Corporation to build a park on a new site, which the city of New York was to inherit when the fair closed. The Corporation's site was established on what had once been a trash heap in the Flushing Meadow area of Queens. A large tract of marshland three-and-a-half mile long was leveled and filled to create the new Flushing Meadow Park. The artificial lagoon and lake had been created, informal and natural in style, on those marshy areas that would have been hardest to fill. The location with high-piled mountains of garbage, offensive to the eye and nose, at the geographic dead center of the New York metropolitan area, was seen as an enormous opportunity to demonstrate how the promise of tomorrow was to reform the debris of the past. The clearance of this site for the Fair was the largest land reclamation project in the eastern United States, and a high-budget, high-priority enterprise. With good railroad, subway, highway, and water access from Manhattan, it was an obvious place to choose in a land-hungry urban complex. Park planning began in January 1936, and the ground-breaking ceremony was held on June 29, 1936. Another remarkable aspect of the enterprise was that, for the first time in history, arrangements had been made to turn over the exposition grounds to the local government after the Fair for a major new park.

The Board of Design regulated the artistic and architectural organization of the fair, making it consistent with the themes and principles adopted by the Corporation. The architectural scheme of the Fair was executed in the manner that frankly expressed the temporary nature of the buildings and at the same time maintained complete aesthetic harmony in the architectural, sculptural, and landscaping plan. By way of contrast with the skyscrapers of adjacent New York, Fair buildings consist largely of windowless, one-story structures, artificially illuminated and ventilated. With the spires of Manhattan visible in the distance, the Board established a relatively low maximum line of height for the buildings, broken here and there by towers and pylons, with the Trylon as the highest structure on the grounds, in order to allow visitors to view the fair's architecture against backdrop of "Manhattan's spires."

The pavilions were to be outspoken exhibition architecture. Replicas of historical buildings and extremely traditional structures were outlawed, except in the Government Zone and the Amusement Area. Since windows would eat up exhibition wall space and would make the buildings too hot in the middle of the summer, air conditioning was generally used and most of the pavilion exteriors had extensive unbroken surfaces. The barren aspect of blank surfaces was overcome through the application of sculpture, murals and shadows cast by appropriately arranged vines and trees. The result is "unity without uniformity."

Since the Fair buildings varied so in their conformity with the Board of Design's ground rules, infinite variety in artistic conception and technique was embodied in the scores of sculptured pieces by which the leading sculptors of the 1930s were represented at the Fair. The sculptured works, adorning the various buildings and plazas, fit into the Fair's general theme, giving expression to the particular section of the exposition in which they are located. In the Transportation Zone, for instance, 'The Spirit of the Wheel', symbol of man's progress in transportation. Most of these sculptures were made of plaster.

The Fair Corporation Board of Design conceived and constructed a number of buildings, such as its own administration and operation buildings, at an early stage to show the way. Many architects followed suit. All in all, there were about 375 structures of all types at the Fair, including 100 major exhibit buildings and 50 major amusement concessions.

The regulation of color was of great interest. The Board of Design laid down topographical prescriptions to exhibitors in a large central area of the Fair. For example, the Trylon and Perisphere, the Theme Center, were to be stark white, the immediately surrounding area off-white; the main axis of the Fair was conceived in reds, growing deeper——from rose to burgundy——with remoteness.

Night lighting was also carefully planned. Floodlighting was allowed only on the Perisphere and a very few other spots. A searchlight canopy played over the Court of Peace near the Federal Building. Otherwise only relatively restrained illumination was allowed, though it was bright, colorful and inventive, not counting fireworks and special light shows over the two main sheets of water.

The Board of Design created a highly ordered and structured environment in the overall plan of the fair and in the regulations for the exhibits. The same philosophy would filter into the exhibits, which became "machines for processing people". The Board's intention was to create a "craftily planned maze" so that "the spectator's interest is stimulated and his responses are involuntary," and to that extent the Board was highly successful.

When people were asked what they liked about the 1939—1940 Fair, they frequently said there was something "magical" about it, especially at night when dramatic lighting, ingenious color-patterns, and spectacular fireworks played to maximum effect.

When it appeared that it would be possible to open the fair in the spring of 1939, the opening day was settled, April 30——the 150th anniversary of the inauguration of George Washington as the first president of the United States. A huge statue of the Father of His Country was commissioned, and Washington's name and face appeared here and there at the exposition.

In a period of financial stress and gathering war clouds, President Roosevelt issued a hearty invitation. Curiously enough, the Soviet Union was the first foreign country to comply, and allotted four million dollars for its pavilion, which proved to be the most popular in the foreign area. Western Europe, thus challenged, could not lag behind, with Germany as an exception. Altogether, a record of 60 nations and international organizations took part in the Fair.

## Planning the World of Tomorrow

Robert Moses, the then-city Park Commissioner, became involved with the fair in 1935, when he was approached by the Fair Corporation, he quickly fused their plans with his own park scheme. He was more interested in the Fair's potential to generate permanent civic improvements than the event itself, and regarded it as a convenient, high-budget, high-priority enterprise to advance his main business: Flushing Meadow Park and roadway construction. He envisioned a great plan for an ambitious new city park out of a mountain of ashes in the Flushing Meadow area. To the north, the fountains and walkways constructed for the Fair would become part of a unique formal park layout, "the Versailles of America" in his own words. The south section of the park, with two artificial lakes, was to be relatively informal and natural in style. Much of this transformation from garbage dump to "Versailles" took place in less than two years. More work would follow the closing of the Fair. With his encouragement, many of the landscape architects and designers from the Park Department had temporarily joined the Fair design staff. To improve New York's transportation infrastructure, Moses also developed a new roadway master plan, with Flushing Meadow, at New York's center, as a natural hub for this network of roads.

With the theme "Building the World of Tomorrow", the fair looked resolutely ahead and aimed at recognizing the interdependence of men and nations, improving human welfare, bettering the American way of living and making this planet a happier one for all concerned. It expressed the theme in its ground plan, its architecture, its use of color, its exhibits, all of them broadly hinting at what the world may be in years to come.

### 1. Creation of A Theme Center

The idea of the theme suggested a Theme Center. When Harrison and Fouilhoux were awarded the commission to design a theme center for the Fair in November 1936, they proposed a design that would function as a practical exhibition hall in which the overall theme of the Fair could be dramatized. "The essence of the Fair is the expression of the life of the future, and this is the idea we will try to develop in the most modern way." Harrison said.

The Theme Center was a pair of the most famous world's fair structures, often referred to as "eye candy", only less famous than the Crystal Palace of 1851 and the Eiffel Tower of 1889: the Trylon, 700 feet high, and the Perisphere, 200 feet in diameter (Figure 9). The sphere was chosen because a ball is the ideal form for enclosing the largest possible amount of space with the smallest amount of material; a tower was seen to be the natural contrasting form to a sphere. Together these two simple and natural forms appeared instantly striking and permanently impressive and were hailed upon first publication of the plan in March 1937 as "an icon of the future". As Grover Whalen put it, "We promised the world something new in Fair architecture, and here it is——something radically different and yet fundamentally as old as man's experience."

Aside from its symbolic meaning, the Theme Center served at least two practical purposes: it served as a visible locus for finding one's way about the Fair's 1216 acres, and it provided a superb view of the Fair itself (Figure 10). From here, the zones of the exposition radiated. Viewed from the air, the Fair looked a bit like a many-colored fan spread over a space, containing three general areas, one for the main exhibits, one for government, and the other for amusement (Figure 11).

### 2. Layout

The Main Exhibit Area extends in all directions from the Theme Center, and covers a square mile filled with buildings amazing in size, shape and hue, where architects, mural painters and landscape designers have turned their imaginations loose. Like several earlier fairs, the New York World's Fair was an encyclopedic exposition, with a plan that reflected the various subjects selected for exhibit. Here are found the seven focal exhibits: Communications, Community Interests, Transportation, Medicine and Public Health, Science and Education, Food, and Production and Distribution.

Beyond the Main Exhibit Area to the east is the Government Area, a city of picturesque pavilions of foreign nations, centering on the Federal Building. Here thirty-three states and fifty-eight foreign countries——including Japan, Italy and the Soviet Union, but not including Germany——built official pavilions. Some of the countries were conquered before the fair closed for its first season in October 1939. Away to the south of the Main Exhibit Area for a mile or more stretches the Amusement Area, built around an artificial lake.

The three major divisions, which were in turn subdivided, had their own distinctive color, echoed in the flower plantings, which deepened in hue the further the buildings got from the pure-white Theme Center until the outermost buildings were vividly red, gold, or blue. All these central buildings had to be original in design, imitating neither an existing building nor a historic style. The fair management built a "focal exhibit" for each subdivision, the other buildings being the work of the private exhibitors. Each of the focal exhibits serves as a prologue to the drama of science, art, industry and accomplishment the fair unfolds.

Eventually the city spent about 26.7 million dollars for reclamation and its permanent Fair building. New York State, which offered its own temporary building and the permanent amphitheater, spent about $6.2 million. The federal government, some three million. Foreign nations paid between 30 and 35 million for their pavilions. The Fair Corporation's construction outlay was about 42 million, and 52 million came from other sources (exhibitors, concessionaires and so on). Total investment: about 160 million dollars.

## Touring the Future

The most popular exhibits were notable for their brilliant effects of miniaturization. The Fair was full of breathtakingly detailed models of the World of Tomorrow.

The virtual tour of the fair focuses on the general areas of the Theme Center, the commercial and industrial buildings, the complex of international exhibits and the Amusement Area. The tour was a display of products, people, and ideas which its designers encapsulated in a variety of ways. Over 200 films were produced for the fair. A number of corporations produced theatrical exhibits pitting woman or man against machine to promote their vision of leisure and efficiency through automation.

### 1. Creating New Exhibit Modes

The fair brings the latest learning in countless fields and forecasts learning yet to come. It sums up the central idea in two white objects, immense and unique, visible for miles: the Perisphere, largest globe ever made by man, and the Trylon, a slender three-sided spire, one symbolizing the world about us, the other, aspiration. Inside the Perisphere the Theme Exhibit sets the keynote for the Fair: "Democracity", a panoramic prophecy of the city of the future, a spectacle in which the dream of an ideal world takes form.

Trylon and Perisphere were connected by a giant ramp, which led visitors back to the ground once they had visited the structures. Fair-goers entered the interior of the Theme Center by riding in what was, at the time, the world's largest escalator up to the Trylon. From there visitors were directed into the Perisphere in order to view "a planned urban and exurban complex of the future", a diorama which filled the floor of the buildings, entitled Democracity. The plan for Democracity was very similar to the plan of the fair. While viewing the Democracity, visitors listened to a recorded six-minute message of the future, followed by a film show presenting "happy farmers and workers", the prosperous Americans whom visitors would soon become. Trylon and Perisphere reflected the emphasis on purity embodied by industrial designers of the day.

The commercial and industrial buildings were the largest and the greatest in number, and they covered most of the fair's grounds. The existence of these buildings around the Theme Center made clear that the future of American cities was dependent upon the support of business and technological enterprise. Among the most popular exhibits of the fair, none receives as much discussion or attention as the Futurama exhibit at the General Motor Pavilion, designed by Norman Bel Geddes.

Futurama was a massive, 36,000 square-foot scale model of America in 1960, complete with futuristic homes, urban complexes, bridges, dams, surrounding landscape, and, most important, an advanced highway system which permitted speeds of 100 miles per hour. Visitors viewed the exhibit from moving chairs with individual loudspeakers, with the effect of looking from the window of an airplane as it was descending toward a city, taking in what was supposed to be 3000 square miles of American progress and prosperity, the virtual wonderland of the future. What they also took in, though, was Corporate America's connection with that wonderland. The message delivered by General Motor not only changed the face and the scale of advertising and marketing forever; it changed the ways in which American live, move, and build.

The Westinghouse Corporation created a new twist in display technique by ostentatiously burying its chief exhibit——a bullet-shaped Time Capsule, containing millions of pages of text on microfilm as well as cultural emblems of the earlier twentieth-century: writings by Albert Einstein and Thomas Mann, comic strips, copies of Life magazine, a pack of Camel cigarettes, a kewpie doll, a dollar in change, and a host of other artifacts. The Time Capsule was not to be opened until the year 6939 A.D., and its organizers made very clear that their intention was to provide an organized record of the world they knew for future generations. It was such material things, so sensationally presented, that most people remembered.

## 2. Creating A Culture of Interaction Between Audience and Exhibitors

The Ford Exposition, designed by Walter Dorwin Teague and Albert Kahn, was outwardly dominated by a winding, half-mile road, also called the Road of Tomorrow (Figure 12), on which visitors road-tested Fords, Mercurys, and Lincoln-Zephyrs. The Ford Exposition also created a culture of interaction between the audience/customer and the company. Its central exhibit was The Ford Cycle of Production, a turntable 100 feet in diameter, floating in water. The Cycle rotated, telling the story of how the automobile industry spreads employment, from the producers of raw materials to parts suppliers to assembly workers to sales associates.

In the Communication Zone, the American Telephone & Telegraph exhibition demonstrated the latest advancement in long-distance calling by providing opportunity for fair-goers, chosen by lot, to make a free long-distance call. The focus of the activity was to create an emotional reaction by having the audience and average American enjoy the wonder of long-distance telephone calls.

Indeed, the Fair is "a library of time, space, history, industry, art and high jinks——the universe in full color with a wide perspective on the future to boot." (New York Times, April 30, 1939)

## The Marketing of the Future

From the first day, the fair was a money-making operation linked with a message of international cooperation and the benefits of technology. It appropriated major scientific figures to promote its message. Einstein's visit included a speech that began with "If science, like art, is to perform its mission totally and fully, its achievements must enter not only superficially but with their inner meaning into the consciousness of people".

Each day parades and fireworks highlighted the fair's activities, designed to draw visitors from across the nation and the world. Whalen and the Mayor of the New York City in particular continued to aggressively market the fair in the media, posing with guests as well as with sponsors of exhibits, such as Henry Ford on Ford Day. Their intention was not only to promote the fair, but also to promote tourism for New York City, stating to perspective visitors that "New York City is like every other town in this nation, except that we can give you better accommodations and better food for less money."

The 1939 Fair was a consumer's fair, filled with material goods designed especially for the Fair and sold there and in selected stores. It was hoped that visitors to the Fair would set about a billion dollars flowing through New York City, and that the City would loose some of its bad reputation for aloofness and remoteness from the rest of the country.

The Fair was open for two seasons and was officially closed on October 27, 1940. It attracted 45 million visitors and generated roughly $48 million in revenue. The number was far below expectations. Reduction in admission charges, bargain features, contests and prizes, and etc. ——all these measures to attract visitors failed. Long stretches of bad weather, the disruption of the international area, the fatal attraction of the war news which kept people's minds so occupied that they look less for other 'amusements' ——had taken their toll at the expense of the Fair.

Since the Fair Corporation had invested $67 million (in addition to nearly $100 million from other sources) in the construction, promotion, and operation of the fair, what Whalen called "the greatest civil engineering feat of the century" had failed economically, and the Corporation declared bankruptcy. Few of the original structures remain; the New York City Building and the New York State Amphitheatre, in which Moses had taken special interest, were scheduled to remain as permanent recreational facilities. In 1964—1965 another World's Fair was held in the park, with the old New York City Building and New York State Amphitheatre filling roles analogous to those of 1939—1940.

Despite its economic failure, the politicians, corporate figures, artists, designers, architects, and social planners involved with the fair attempted to create a "working model of the future in Flushing Meadow," and to some extent they succeeded. It has served as a model for future world's fairs, and its exhibits and the people involved with it profoundly influenced movements in design, art, architecture, advertising, marketing, urban development, and cultural studies.

# 第六章

## 1964 年纽约世博会

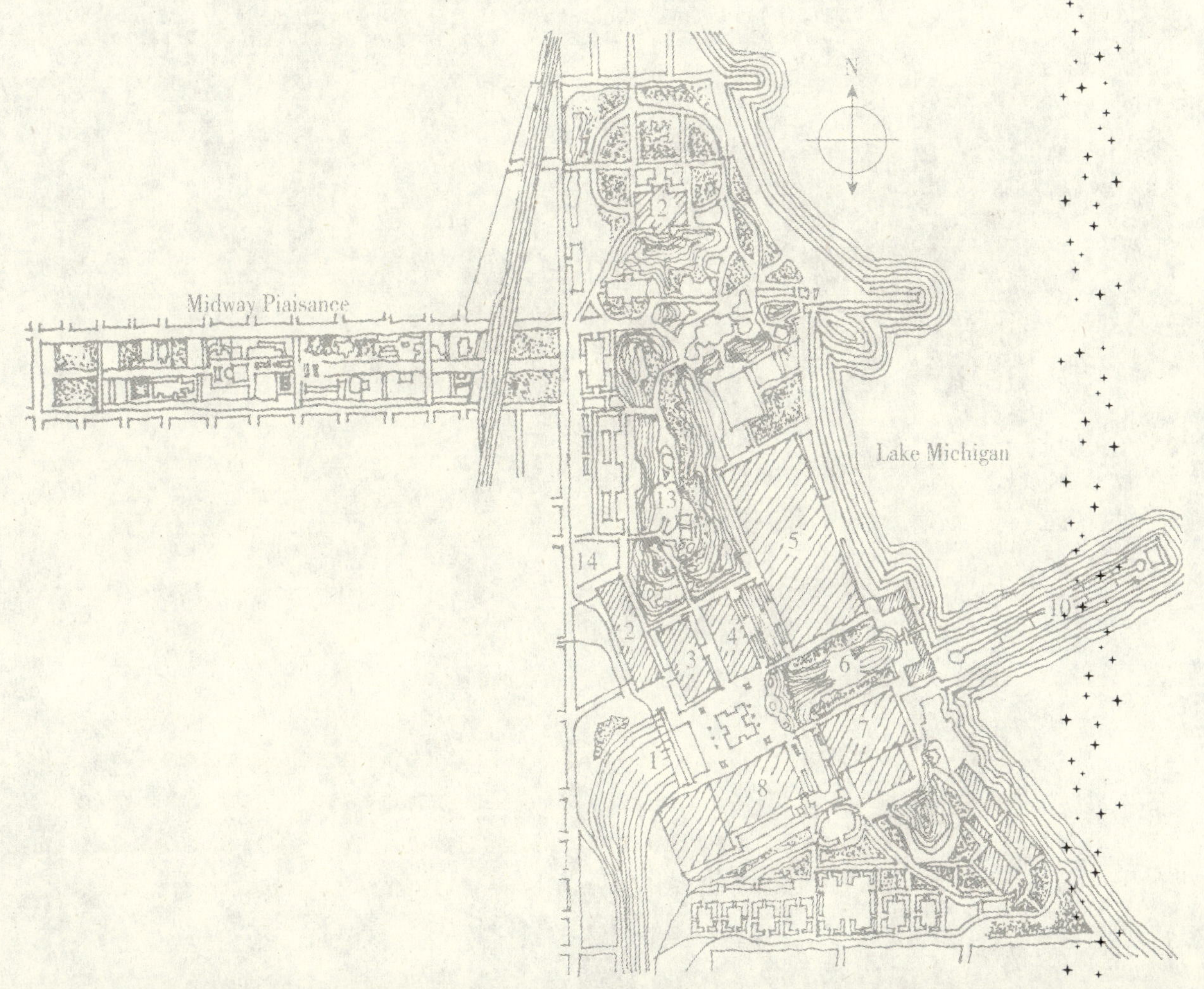

## 背景

1964 年纽约世博会是 20 世纪在纽约 Flushing Meadow 公园举办的第二次世博会。世博会于 1964 年 4 月 22 日开幕，进行了 2 个展季，每个展季 6 个月，于 1965 年 10 月 17 日结束。这是一届极尽奢华的世博会，占地面积近 1 平方英里（2.6$km^2$），创造了世博会规模和造价上的新纪录。这届世博会的举办未得到国际展览局的认证，是唯一未获批准的世博会。

第二次世界大战以后，无论是美国还是世界其他地区举办的博览会都更加趋于国际化，在强调人文精神的同时，潜移默化地扩大企业参与的领域，推动全球化进程。虽然 1964 年纽约世博会以商业展示为主导，却被冠以“通过理解走向和平”的主题。20 世纪 60 年代的国际竞争以美苏之间的冷战为主要特征，1964 年世博会的主题思想正是在这样的背景下产生的。此时的美国人正陶醉于人类登月空间计划，对计算机和信息时代的美好前景充满期待，并且投入开发利用核能，制造“成本微乎其微”的电力。

## 融资策略

1964—1965 年纽约世博会是由一群纽约商界人士策划的，他们时常追忆起孩提时代经历的 1939—1940 年纽约世博会，希望为后代创造同样的体验。同时，促进旅游，刺激城市经济发展也是在时隔 25 年之后再次举办世博会的重要原因，而且，1964 年恰好是纽约建市 300 周年纪念。

由于美国的世博会是非政府投资，主办方必须向私人融资，发行债券，筹措巨额运作资金，因此聘请了纽约“建设大师”Robert Moses 领导世博公司运作，因为他在大型公共建设项目的融资方面经验丰富。Moses 自 20 世纪 30 年代进入政府工作以来一直是一位令人敬畏的人物，他主持了纽约大部分的公路基础设施建设，在担任纽约市园林局长的几十年间，他规划设计了纽约市大部分的公园绿化带。有 Moses 掌舵，投资人相信他能够再现其当政时期创造的辉煌，纷纷鼎力资助，世博会高速运作。

为了确保获得足够的利润完成 Flushing Meadow 公园建设，主办方需要招揽 7000 万观众才能带来足够的利润，使世博会产生最大的经济效益。要想吸引如此大量的观众，世博会必须举办两个展季，达到 1964 年 4000 万观众，1965 年 3000 万观众的目标。此外，世博公司还决定向所有在世博会建设展馆的参展商收取场地租金。这些看似审慎的决策使世博会与国际展览局陷入冲突的境地。美国当时还不是国际展览局的成员国，但是主办方知道获得国际展览局的认证就意味着近 40 个成员国的参与。

## 招展策略

根据国际展览局的规定，每届世博会只能进行6个月，不能向参展商收取场地租金，一个国家在10年内只能举办一次世博会。1960年纽约申办世博会时，国际展览局已经批准西雅图和蒙特利尔在1962年和1967年分别举办世博会。Robert Moses不顾这些规定的限制，前往巴黎争取国际展览局的批准，当纽约的申请未被国际展览局批准时，一向自行其是的Robert Moses便向媒体公开了此事，表现出对国际展览局及其规定的蔑视，此举激怒了国际展览局，随即采取报复措施，要求其成员国抵制纽约世博会。因此，1964—1965年纽约世博会是有史以来唯一未经国际展览局许可的世博会。

国际展览局的决定对纽约世博会来说几乎是一场灾难，没有加拿大、澳大利亚、大多数欧洲国家、前苏联以及所有国际展览局成员国的参与，纽约世博会的形象大受损害，而且，纽约还不得不与西雅图和蒙特利尔争夺外国政府与国际组织的参与，结果多数国家选择有国际展览局认证的西雅图世博会和蒙特利尔世博会，而不是纽约世博会。因此，纽约世博会只能求助这些国家的商会和旅游机构举办各自的国家展，替代官方举办的国家馆。

纽约市在20世纪中期就已经是一个经济巨头，享有很高的国际声望。作为联合国总部的所在地，纽约是世界的首都；作为世界最大的金融机构和企业总部所在地，纽约是全球的经济中心。参与纽约世博会是对实力与声望的展示，这是一个向潜在的7000万观众营销一个主题、一种产品或一个民族的机遇，具有十分诱人的前景。许多中小国家并不在乎国际展览局的规定，能够在世界上最负盛名的城市主办的世博会上举办展览对他们来说是一种荣耀。因此，中小国家，也就是所谓的第三世界国家占了国际展团的绝大多数。

由于国际展区主要由中小国家和部分缺席国家的企业展馆构成，他们缺乏举办这类大型展览的经验，世博会的国际部必须密切协助他们工作，从招展到展馆拆除的全过程，国际部的每个成员都要负责几个外国展团的参展工作。

最终，只有西班牙和梵蒂冈举办了国家馆，其他参展国家包括日本、墨西哥、瑞典、奥地利、丹麦、泰国、菲律宾、希腊、巴基斯坦等国。

## 世博会规划

20世纪30年代中期，Moses意识到纽约城市人口正在向东迁移，由此他认为，将巨大的Queens垃圾场改造成璀璨耀眼的1939—1940年世博园是在靠近纽约大都市的人口中心区创造一个大型城市公园的契机。Flushing Meadow公园是Moses负责建设的最宏伟的公园项目，他构想的这片大型公园，占地1300英亩（$5km^2$），位于纽约市中心地理位置，是市民的主要娱乐休闲场所。在这片巨大的沼泽地下布置了数英里长的煤气、水电和排污管道，地面上修建了绵延数英里的车道和道路，种植了大量树木和花草坪。世博会是暂时的，而这些公用设施、道路和绿化是永久性的。这些基本建设和世博会创造的巨大收益将为世博会后世博园复原改造成一座城市公园打下坚实的基础。当 1939—1940 年世博会以经济失败而告终时，Moses 没有足够的资金完成他的公园计划，Flushing Meadow 公园变成了一片荒野，而不是真实意义上的城市公园。怀揣着他的纽约公园规划，Moses 将新一届预算超过 10 亿美元的世博会视为推进他的市政工程建设，完成上一届世博会未尽事业的另一个途径。

1957 年 10 月 4 日，前苏联发射了世界第一颗人造地球卫星，1964 年的美国也正处于太空时代，1964—1965 年纽约世博会全方位地展示了科学技术发展的前沿：太空时代、信息时代（计算机和通信技术）、消费时代（新材料和日用消费品开发）和原子能时代，它表明科学技术是建设美好明天的希望。

如果说 1939—1940 年世博会是一项宏图伟业，1964—1965 年世博会则想要更大、更好、更动人心魄，它不仅要向世界展示纽约是美国的商业中心，而且要展示美国是世界的经济中心。

### 1. 最大限度地利用公园现有设施

与 1964—1965 年世博会形成鲜明对比的是，1939—1940 年世博会具有准确的知识定位，明确而统一的计划，围绕一个主题“建设明天的世界”展开。为了深化主题，世博公司自行建造主题展馆，举办主题展览，并且要求展商围绕主题办展。设计委员会深入细致地制定了一整套参展规则，确保展馆视觉效果统一。

1964—1965 年世博会采取了完全相反的策略，Moses 尽可能减少对世博会的统一要求，这个决策反映了他在经济方面对实现世博会后目标的考虑，同时也是想让新一届世博会富有变化和新意。新一届世博会不只是倡导某一个主题，用 Moses 的话来说，而是要创造“具有广泛意义的主题，让每一个人都从中受益”。从表面上看，世博会围绕着“通过理解走向和平”这个主题展开，实际上，Moses 为世博会制定了多项目标：“世博会的基本目标是通过理解走向和平，即让世界各国人民认识到，国家之间的相互依存是确保持久和平的基础。举办世博会是为了展示人类在一个距离不断缩小的星球上，在无限广阔的宇宙空间中取得的成就，展示人类的发明与发现、艺术与技术以及人类的渴望与抱负。举办世博会是为了庆祝纽约建市 300 周年；为了庆祝林肯表演艺术中心开业；为了提供有益身心健康的娱乐活动；为了实现纽约这个大都市的交通干线网络建设；为了完成 Flushing Meadow 公园建设，在世博会后留下永久性的娱乐设施。”

Moses 的计划是最大限度地创造利润，尽可能地减少建设。他坚持要在 1939—1940 年世博会的原址上举办新一届世博会。在他看来，让参展商自己建造展馆，重新利用公园的道路、喷泉和地下设施，世博公司可以增加收入用于世博会后的公园建设，而且，任何新建改建项目都要有利于公园建设最终目标的实现。他的这些观点与建筑设计委员会的理念不符，建筑设计委员会寻求创造全新的世博建筑形式，提出了一个形似面包圈的单体展馆建筑方案，可以容纳多种展览。Moses 否定了这个方案主要是出于经济方面的考虑：世博公司不想投资建设这样的大型展馆，1939—1940 年世博会的经济损失就是因为世博公司出资建造的展馆太多。无奈之下，建筑委员会不得不解散。

1939 年世博会建造了许多“展厅”，企业可以用低廉的租金租到展位，结果许多展厅处于半空置状态，使世博会蒙受经济损失。本届世博会发誓不再重蹈覆辙，规模较小的企业想要参与世博会就必须与想要建造展馆的私营机构签约，但是这样的展馆只能在找到足够的客户，私营机构有利可图的情况下建造，这类展馆有“运输馆”和“海洋中心”等。

高额的参展费用，国际展览局留下的尴尬，再加上世博会不愿为参展商提供任何经济帮助的态度，许多渴望参与世博会的企业不能参展。一些曾经夸下海口的重要展览悄无声息地从世博地图上消失，难怪世博地图上开始出现“幻影”般的展馆，因为许多展馆被取消，只留下一张新闻剪报、世博地图上的一个地名或几张建筑示意图。

从建筑的总体布局和景观效果来看，1964—1965 年世博会在很大程度上是 1939—1940 年世博会的继续（图 13），但在有的建筑评论家看来，1964 年世博会不要求风格统一导致了世博建筑风格凌乱，布局杂乱无章。事实上，20 世纪的世博会，国家馆的数量迅速增加。但是从 1939—1940 年纽约世博会开始，企业展馆的数量超过了国家馆，1964 年纽约世博会的情况正是如此，大规模的企业展馆使国际展馆和美国各州立展馆相形见绌，因为这两次

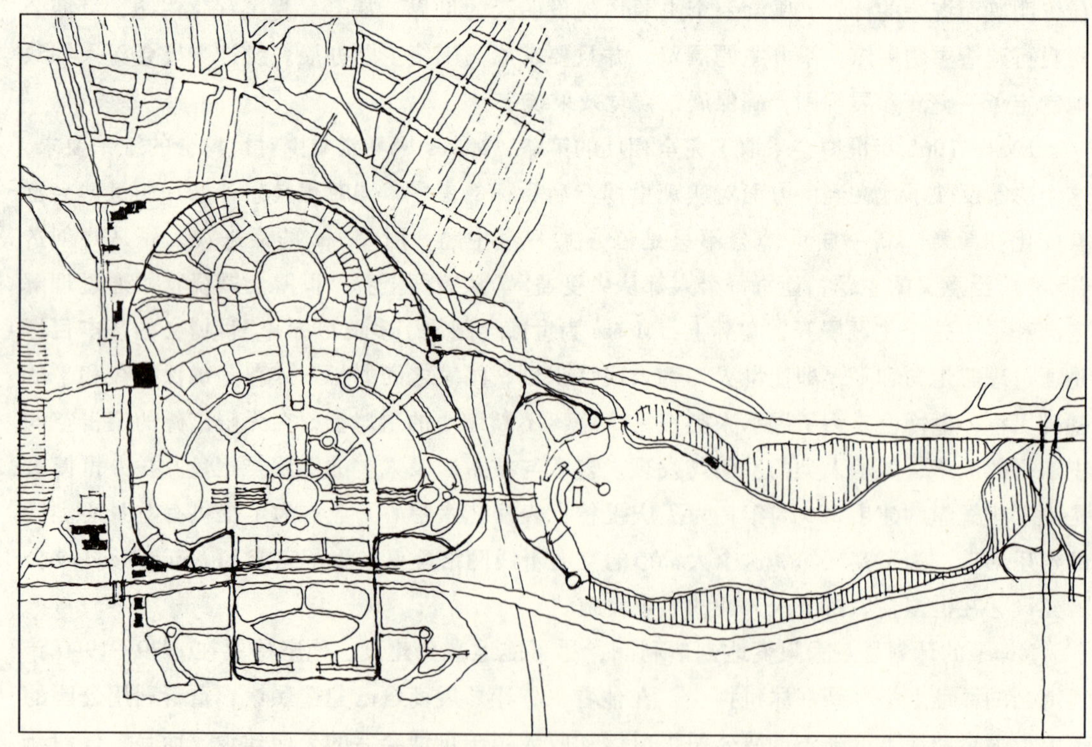

图 13　1964—1965 年世博会平面图

世博会的国际参展都不充分。

从1964—1965年间，160多座美轮美奂的展馆从 Flushing Meadow 公园拔地而起（图14），虽然1964年世博会不像1939年世博会那么让人留恋，有些展馆和展览还是值得关注的。世博会的标志性主题中心是一座140英尺高，90万磅重，不锈钢圈结构的地球仪（图15），称之为 Unisphere——一个新出现的英语词汇，环绕其周的三个巨型圈标志着第一颗人造卫星开启了太空时代。地球仪由一个位于圆形大水池中央的三角架座基支撑，环绕座基布置的喷泉喷出环形水幕，创造出动感势态，别出心裁的灯光设计强化了动感效果。从水

图14　1964—1965年世博会展馆

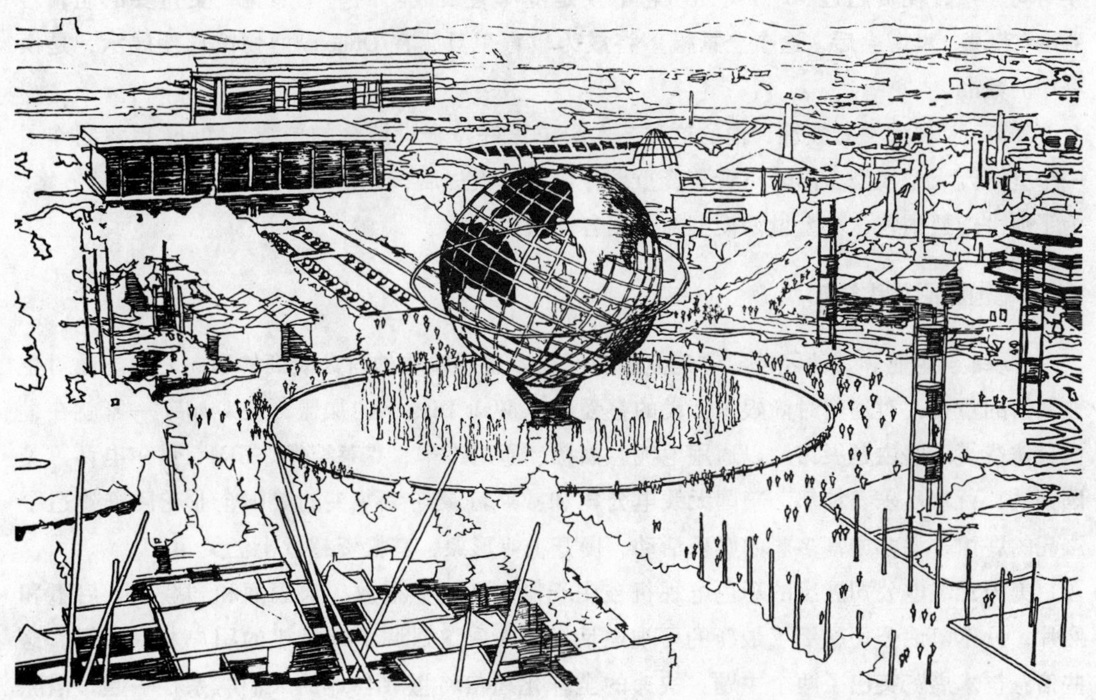

图15　1964—1965年世博会的标志性主题中心是一座140英尺高，90万磅重，不锈钢圈结构的地球仪

池边观赏 Unisphere 地球仪就好像在6000 英里的高空看地球。Moses 遇到的第一个，也是最艰巨的任务之一就是设计一个能与曾经辉煌的 1939 年世博会标志——三角尖塔和球形建筑（Trylon and Perisphere）——媲美的世博会标志。显然，Unisphere 地球仪正好符合 Moses 在他的主题中心备忘录中主张的那种“容易理解”的结构，“对一般人均有意义”。作为世界上最大的地球仪，Unisphere 满足了 Moses 对大尺度的偏爱，由于建造 Unisphere 地球仪需要运算速度极高的新型计算机解决复杂的技术问题，Unisphere 地球仪也迎合了 Moses 对工程技术的喜好。Unisphere 地球仪将成为雕塑品中的皇冠，永久性地装点 Flushing Meadow 公园。

科学馆是纽约市政当局根据 Moses 的建议建造的，Moses 对这个展馆很感兴趣，这座具有未来风格，令人耳目一新的建筑将作为 Flushing Meadow 公园的科学技术博物馆被永久保留。世博会期间，在科学馆举办了太空飞行、原子能技术和医学进步等展览，这些展览都是由政府部门主办的。最有吸引力的要数美国国家航空航天局主办的大型火箭和航天飞机露天展览。

纽约市展馆是 Moses 为 1939 年世博会建造的，他说服纽约市政当局在这座展馆中建造了一座规模宏大的纽约市全景模型，这座尺度为 9000 平方英尺的模型展示了分布于大都会五个区的 830,000 座建筑，十分精确地复制了纽约市。考虑到庆祝纽约建市 300 周年的需要，1964 年的纽约市展馆盛况空前。纽约市全景模型是当时世界最大的模型，花费了近 4 年时间建造，耗资超过 90 万美元。它不仅是世博会最成功的一个展览，更重要的是，对 Moses 来说，世博会后，这个全景模型将成为教育工具，在 Queens 博物馆长期展示，是模型中的精品。

Moses 对模型情有独钟，他的这种艺术品位正好符合世博会的传统，Moses 授意制作了一个世博园大型模型，向来访贵宾隆重推介世博建设进展，包括每一座新展馆的设计方案。为了促进门票销售，小型世博模型在美国各地巡回展出。

### 2. 企业展馆唱主角

Moses 与企业和其他经济实体建立的长期联系也反映在他对参展商的取向之中。他对企业展馆的重视，对通俗时尚娱乐活动的喜爱促使 Walt Disney 的加盟，仅 Disney 一家就在世博会建造了四座主题展馆。以通用电气、福特、通用汽车、克莱斯勒、IBM、贝尔电话、美国钢铁、百事可乐、杜邦、美国无线电公司和威斯汀豪斯为龙头的美国企业花巨资建造了漂亮的展馆，举办丰富多彩的娱乐活动，提升企业形象，其投资超过十亿美元。

美国无线电公司展出的彩色电视机被用于发布通知、播放庆典画面和刊登寻人启事和照片；贝尔电话公司展示了最新的可视电话；IBM 展馆强调了计算机的用户友好特征。这些信息技术展览突出了两个主题：快速的全球化通信将世界各地的人们联系在一起，消除了他们之间的沟通障碍；信息时代的产品，包括自动化，将为人类节省大量的时间和体力。福特、威斯汀豪斯、运输馆、通用电气，以及其他展馆都强调了原子能的未来发展前景和这种能源的最终用途。新崛起的太空时代及其发展前景也在展览中充分体现，这些展览是由联邦展馆、美国国家航空航天局、国防部和世博会共同举办的。

在 1939—1940 年世博会上，工业企业精心策划的大型展览占主导地位，1964—1965 年世博会，许多企业再次参展，并且比 25 年前的展览更精彩。因此，1964—1965 年世博会是对 20 世纪中期美国企业文化的最佳展示。

1939—1940 年世博会和 1964—1965 年世博会最具未来风格的设计不是某座展馆建筑，而是通用汽车的“未来生活情境”展览。这两次展览完全达到了世博会富于“幻想”和具有前瞻性的目标，“未来生活情境”展览 I 描绘了距当时还很遥远的 20 世纪 60 年代的生活，而“未来生活情境”展览 II 只是表明未来已经超出人类的期望和预期，正在成为现实。每次“未来生活情境”展览都是当年世博会最出色的展览。

克莱斯勒的波普艺术风格展馆是世博会最大、最富于想象力、最有趣的展馆之一，其设计岛上的主题展览是一辆 80 英尺长的巨型汽车，车轮高度超过 20 英尺，汽车底部高出地面 7 英尺，这里是展示区，这里的视觉展示突出了克莱斯勒的汽车款式设计风格（图 16）。

图 16　克莱斯勒的波普艺术风格展馆中，设计岛上的主题展览是一辆 80 英尺长的巨型汽车，车轮高度超过 20 英尺，汽车底部高出地面 7 英尺，这里是展示区，这里的视觉展示突出了克莱斯勒的汽车款式设计风格

为了庆祝世博会于 1965 年 10 月闭幕，威斯汀豪斯公司又安装了一个时间盒，埋在 Flushing Meadow 公园地下。第二个时间盒力求更新 25 年前制造的第一个时间盒中储存的信息，所选内容和实物是为了帮助 5000 年以后的人们了解我们目前的文明状况和飞速发展的

科学技术。

1964 年世博会被视为 1939 年世博会的延续，是对 20 世纪 30 年代—60 年代期间社会巨变——无论好坏——的宏伟展示。像以往大多数世博会一样，1964—1965 年世博会是一个购物的天堂，新技术产品和新材料得到充分展示。然而，对世博会的抱怨也不少：商业气氛太浓；美术展览太少，几乎没有表演艺术的展示空间；只有极少数几个欧洲国家的官方参展；世博建筑缺乏统一的风格；琐碎和粗俗的东西随处可见。这些指责大多属实，但都无关紧要，重要的是，1964—1965 年世博会是魔力与异想天开的美妙结合，非常值得一看。

## 世博遗产

1964—1965 年世博会创造了一些很有艺术品位的展馆，许多人建议将这些建筑永久性地保留在 Flushing Meadow 公园。实际上，早在世博园建设时期，世博公司、园林局和纽约市就对建设中的展馆是否保留进行了评估，经过世博官员 1964 年大半年和 1965 年全年对多种方案的调查跟踪和筛选，最终形成了公园总体规划方案。

根据 1965 年 7 月的“世博会后报告”：“世博会后的公园设计施工涉及需要保留一些建筑为公园所用。在这个问题上，世博公司的公园规划原则是，不保留与公园用途无关的建筑，除非它们位于公园边缘，并且从园外道路可以直接到达。另一个需要考虑的重要问题是，如果需要保留某个展馆，改造展馆的费用需由展商支付，数额应与展馆的拆除费用相当，不足部分通过其他渠道解决，世博公司不承担这笔费用。”

然而，这些展馆都是按照临时专门用途建筑的规范建造的，对几乎所有的展馆来说，将其改造成永久性建筑费用极高，对公园的用处也不大。

正当可口可乐展馆建设期间，世博公司想要说服可乐公司将其展馆的钟塔建成公园可利用的永久性建筑。1939—1940 年世博会失去了这样一个保留钟塔的机会，本届世博会不想再失去这个机会。遗憾的是，当世博公司完成钟塔项目的评估和改造方案时，还在担心可乐公司是否愿意承担这笔费用，钟塔的地基工程已完工，世博公司又失去了一次机会。

早在 1964 年，杜邦展馆就被列入可能保留的建筑，世博官员投入了大量资金，评估将其改造成木偶剧院的可能性，取代中央公园破旧老化的剧院。不幸的是市政当局不同意世博公司的成本估价和改造方案，世博公司只好作罢。

与 1939 年世博会的命运相同，1964 年世博会未能实现创造利润的目标，但还是给 Flushing Meadow 公园留下了几座著名建筑，为 Moses 实现他设想的建设都市中的绿洲打下了基础。两届世博会在这里举办把 Flushing Meadow 公园推上了国际舞台，联合国大会曾经连续 5 年在这里举行，这里也是世界职业棒球锦标赛和美国公开赛的举办地。今天的 Flushing Meadow 公园占地面积 1255 英亩，包括多种体育设施、景观绿地、湖面、喷泉、游乐场、露天体育场、博物馆和一个动物园，成为当地的一个文化娱乐中心。

## 结局

世博会的经济状况成为媒体争论的焦点。世博会在 1965 年展季之前花钱铺张，对急剧下降的观众数量没有引起重视，财务控制和监管不到位，结果第二展季开始时，世博会几乎破产。尽管如此，世博会还不得不为一些重要的展览提供运作资金，否则就会面临众多展馆关门倒闭的局面，因为许多参展商已无财力举办展览。世博会闭幕时，世博公司不得不勾销参展商的巨额欠款。只有在减少开支，提高门票价格之后，加上世博会结束前几天的大量人潮涌入，才减少了 1965 年展季的损失，从而也减少了整个世博会的损失。

超过 5100 万人参观了世博会，创造了世博会的新纪录，虽然这个数字远低于预计的 7000 万观众。但是，世博会没能创造足够的利润返还投资者，也未能完成 Flushing Meadow 公园的宏伟目标。多数责难归结于 Moses 没能与媒体搞好关系，以至于媒体对世博会非常挑剔，从缺乏美术展览到门票价格，可谓无所不贬。尽管遭受这样的经济失败，世博会还是为纽约市的经济注入了数十亿的资金，为许多市政基础设施改造提供了资金。

# Chapter 6

## The 1964—1965 New York World's Fair

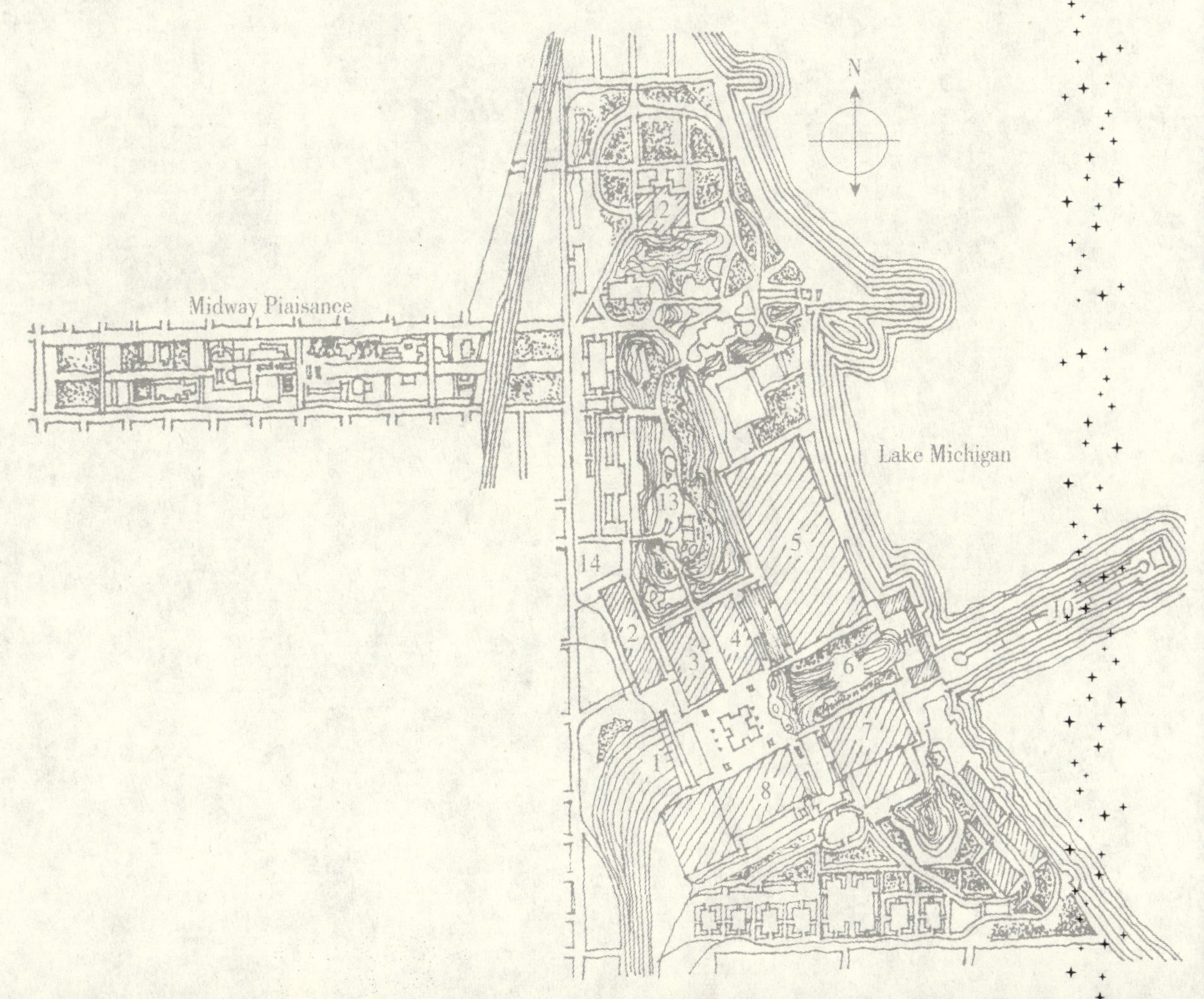

## Background

The 1964—1965 New York World's fair was the second world's fair to be held at Flushing Meadows Park in New York City in the twentieth century. It opened on April 22, 1964, and ran for two sixmonth seasons, concluding on October 17, 1965. It was one of the biggest international extravaganzas and set records for its size and cost, occupying nearly a square mile ($2.6km^2$) of land. The world's fair took place without sanctioning from the Bureau of International Expositions, the only one to do so.

After World War II, fairs both in the United States and abroad became more international in spirit. They emphasized the idea of a common humanity, while subtly advancing a domain of corporate exploits and globalization. Hence the New York World's Fair 1964—1965, an exposition overwhelmingly dominated by commercial exhibits, was given the theme of Peace Through Understanding. The competitive international system of the 1960s, which was powerfully shaped by the Cold War between the US and the USSR, was the context in which the 1964 Fair acquired its ideals. Americans were infatuated by the space program's goal of landing a man on the moon, intrigued by the promise of a computer and information era, and pursuing a nuclear power program to provide electricity "too cheap to meter".

## Financing the Fair

The 1964—1965 Fair was conceived by a group of New York businessmen who fondly remembered their childhood experiences at the 1939—1940 New York World's Fair and wanted to provide that same experience for their children and grandchildren. Thoughts of an economic boom to the city as the result of increased tourism were also a major reason for holding another Fair twenty-five years after the 1939—1940 extravaganza. The year selected, 1964, coincided with the 300th anniversary of the founding of New York city.

As world's fairs in the United States are not government financed, organizers must turn to private financing and the sale of bonds to pay the huge cost to stage them. The organizer hired New York's "Master Builder", Robert Moses to head the corporation to run the Fair because he was experienced in raising money for vast public projects. Moses had been a formidable figure in the city since coming to power in the 1930s. He was responsible for the construction of much of the city's highway infrastructure and, as Parks Commissioner for decades, the creation of much of the city's park system. Fueled by investors who were sure that Moses could repeat the success he had enjoyed at the helm of so many government agencies, the fair went into high gear.

To ensure profits to complete the Park, Fair organizers knew they would have to maximize receipts from the Fair. An attendance of 70 million people would be needed in order to turn a profit and, for an attendance that large to be feasible, the Fair would need to be held for two years, with 40 million visitors in 1964 and 30 million in 1965. The World Fair Corporation also decided to charge site rental fees to all exhibitors who wished to construct pavilions on the fairgrounds. These seemingly prudent decisions caused the Fair to come to blows with the Bureau of International Exposition (BIE). The United States was not a member of the BIE at the time, but Fair organizers understood that a sanction by the BIE would assure that its nearly forty member nations would participate in the Fair.

## Fair Promotion

BIE rules state that an international exposition may run for one six-month period only, no rent may be charged to exhibitors who wish to participate and only one exposition may be held in any given country within a 10-year period. Both Seattle and Montreal had already been sanctioned by the BIE to host World's Fairs in 1962 and 1967 respectively at the time New York put their World's Fair bid before the BIE in 1960. Robert Moses, undaunted by these rules, journeyed to Paris to seek official approval for the New York Fair. When BIE balked at New York's bid, Moses, used to having his way in New York, angered the BIE delegates by taking his case to the press, publicly stating his disdain for their organization and their rules. The BIE retaliated by taking the action of formally requesting their member nations not to participate in the New York Fair. The 1964—1965 New York World's Fair thus became the only significant world's fair in history to be held without BIE endorsement.

The BIE decision was nearly a disaster for the Fair. The absence of Canada, Australia, most of the major European nations and the Soviet Union, all members of the BIE, tarnished the image of the Fair. Additionally, New York was forced to compete with both Seattle and Montreal for international participants, with many nations choosing the officially sanctioned world's fairs of those cities over the New York Fair. The Fair turned to trade and tourism organizations within many countries to host national exhibits in lieu of official government sponsorship of pavilions.

New York City, in the middle of the $20^{th}$ century, was an economic power and enjoyed world prestige. Headquarters to the United Nations, it was the world's capital. Headquarters to the largest financial institutions and corporations, it was the economic center of the universe. To be a part of New York World's Fair was an expression of power and prestige. And the opportunity to sell a message, a product or a nation to 70 million projected visitors was a tantalizing prospect indeed. Unconcerned by BIE rules, smaller nations saw it as an honor to host an exhibit at the Fair in the world's most prestigious city. Therefore smaller nations and so-called third-world countries made up the majority of the international participation.

As the International Area of the Fair was defined by those smaller nations and privately sponsored pavilions of some absent nations, few of these pavilion sponsors had much experience with putting together an exhibit of such a large scale, the Fair's International Division had to work closely with them, from the time of the invitation to the Fair until the pavilion was demolished, with each member responsible for a group of exhibitors.

In the end, only Spain and Vatican City hosted a major national presence at the Fair. Other international participants included Japan, Mexico, Sweden, Austria, Denmark, Thailand, Philippines, Greece, Pakistan and so on.

## Planning the Fair

In the mid-1930s Moses realized that the population of the city was shifting ever further east. He saw the conversion of a vast Queens garbage dump into the glittering fairgrounds for the 1939—1940 World's Fair as an opportunity to create a vast urban park in an area which would be closer to the population center of the metropolis. Flushing Meadows Park was Moses' grandest park scheme. He envisioned this vast park, comprising some 1300 acres ($5km^2$) of land and located in the geographical center of the city, as a major recreational playground for New Yorkers. Beneath this huge expanse of marshy land was laid miles of gas, electric, water, and sewer lines. On the surface, miles of roadways, paths, trees and flower beds were created. The world's fair would be temporary. The utilities, roadways and plantings were permanent. They, and the huge proceeds from the fair, would provide the foundation for the site's restoration to a park after the Fair ended. When the 1939—1940 World's Fair ended in financial failure, he did not have the funds available to complete work on his project, and the park remained more of a wilderness area than a true urban park. Still brimming with plans for the city, Moses saw the new Fair, budgeted at over $1 billion, as another means to further his menu of civic improvements, and finish what the earlier Fair had begun.

On October 4, 1957, the Soviet Union launched the world's first artificial satellite into orbit around the earth. In 1964, the United States was in the midst of an era called the space age. The 1964—1965 New York World's Fair was all about the promise that science and technology were the keys to building a better tomorrow. It showcased, in many ways, new technological frontier: the space age, the information age of computers and communication, the consumer age of new materials and products for everyday life and the atomic age.

While the 1939—1940 fair was a massive undertaking on its own, the 1964—1965 fair was to be bigger, better, and more breathtaking. It was going to show the world that New York City was the center of American business, and that America was the center of the world's economy.

**1. Maximum Use of Existing Park Facilities**

The 1939—1940 Fair was marked by a precise intellectual vision, a clear and coherent program, and constructed around a single idea: "Building the World of Tomorrow". To successfully further the concept, the Fair Corporation constructed its own theme pavilions and exhibits, predicting future developments. Corporate pavilions too were expected to follow the theme. A design committee assured visual unity, carefully working out a set of rules that all fair participants were required to follow.

The 1964—1965 Fair took an opposite approach. Moses' decision to minimize central control of the Fair reflected the financial considerations related to his post-Fair goals, it was also motivated by his desire that the new Fair contain endless variety. Rather than proposing a single idea, the Fair aimed, in Moses' words, "to be universal, to have something for everyone." Ostensibly, the Fair was united around the theme "Peace through Understanding", Moses also set out diversified goals for the new Fair: "The basic purpose of the Fair is Peace through Understanding, that is education of the peoples of the world as to the interdependence of nations to insure a lasting peace. The Fair is dedicated to man's achievements on a shrinking globe in an expanding universe, his inventions, discoveries, arts, skills and aspirations, to the celebration of the $300^{th}$ anniversary of the founding of the City of New York, to the opening of Lincoln Center for the Performing Arts, to whole-some entertainment, to the realization of the Metropolitan arterial program, and the completion of Flushing Meadow Park with a legacy of permanent recreational facilities after the Fair."

Moses' plan was to maximize fair profits by minimizing construction. He insisted that the new Fair be held at the same location as the earlier 1939—1940 Fair. From his perspective, by having each participant build his own pavilion, and by reusing the park's roadways, fountains, and underground infrastructure, the Fair Corporation could increase profits for post-Fair uses. In addition, any change made was to be for the ultimate benefit of the park. This view did not sit well with the design committee, which sought to create an original new Fair and proposed a single doughnut-shaped building in which the various exhibits would be housed. Moses' rejection of this design was more likely financial: the Fair Corporation did not want to be responsible for such a large building. It was widely believed that the reason the 1939—1940 Fair had lost money was because the Fair Corporation had erected too many buildings with its own funds. In frustration, the committee had to resign.

The 1939 World's Fair had constructed "halls" where multiple industrial firms could rent exhibit space at a nominal fee from the Fair. Many of these fair-sponsored pavilions had gone half-empty and were money losers for the fair. This world's fair vowed not to make the same mistake. Smaller companies who wished to participate would have to sign on with private organizations looking to put up such structures as "The Transportation & Travel" pavilion and the "Marine Center". However, these structures could only be constructed if enough clients could be found to make the enterprise profitable for the sponsorship.

The high costs, the BIE fiasco and the unwillingness of the fair to provide financial support to any exhibitor made it virtually impossible for many eager participants to come to the fair. Some major exhibits, announced with great flourish, would quietly disappear from the site map with little or no comment. It's no wonder then that the map of the fair began to fill with "phantom" pavilions, as many pavilions simply disappeared leaving behind only a press clipping, a name on a map or a few architectural renderings.

In a general architectural sense, there was a great deal of continuity between the 1939—1940 and 1964—1965fairs (Figure 13). To some architectural critics, the Fair's decision not to impose a unifying approach resulted in a messy mélange of buildings. In fact, in the twentieth century fairs, national pavilions multiplied. Beginning with the New York World's Fair of 1939—1940, national pavilions were overwhelmed by corporate buildings. The same was true in 1964, with large corporate pavilions overshadowing smaller foreign and state pavilions, because neither fair had a full complement of foreign nations.

More than 160 fabulous structures rose from the grounds of Flushing Meadow Park between 1962 and 1964 (Figure 14). Though the 1964 Fair was not remembered with the same fondness as that of 1939, several of its individual buildings and exhibits were noteworthy. The visual theme center for the Fair was the Unisphere——a new word in the English language, which was a 140-foot-high, 900, 000-pound stainless steel armillary sphere covered with the representations of the continents and encircled by three giant rings denoting the first man-made satellites that had launched the space age (Figure 15). A tripod base supports the structure in a large, circular pool and fountains placed away from the base rise and fall in a circular pattern suggesting movement. Special lighting effects also suggest movement. Viewed from the edge of the pool, the Unisphere has the dimensions Earth would have if viewed from a height of six thousand miles. One of Moses' first and most difficult tasks was to come up with a visual logo to rival the highly successful Trylon and Perisphere. The Unisphere was clearly the type of "understandable" structure "with some significance or meaning for the average person" that Moses had favored in his theme center memorandum. As the world's largest global structure, the Unisphere appealed to Moses' love of huge scale. Since building the structure required the aid of newly invented high-speed computers to work out complicated technological problems, it also appealed to the engineer in him. The Unisphere was to be the centerpiece of a group of sculptures that would permanently adorn Flushing Meadow Park.

Moses was also interested in the Hall of Science that he convinced the city to construct for the Fair. This impressive futuristic building would be retained as a permanent Museum of Science and Technology in the post-Fair park. During the Fair, the Hall of Science contained exhibits on space flight, atomic energy, and advances in medicine that had been solicited from government agencies. Its highlight was a large outdoor rocket and spacecraft display provided by NASA.

For the New York City pavilion, which Moses had built in 1939, he persuaded the city to construct the ambitious "Panorama of the City of New York", a 9000-square-foot scale model showing all 830, 000 buildings in the five-borough metropolis, duplicating the city with remarkable exactitude. Given that it also celebrated the $300^{th}$ anniversary of New York City, the 1964 pavilion was particularly lavish. As the world's largest model at the time, the Panorama took nearly four years to construct and cost over $900,000. It was not only a successful fair attraction, but more importantly for Moses, it enjoys a long post-Fair life at the Queens Museum as an educational tool and a masterpiece of modelmaking.

Moses' love of models was an aesthetic taste that accorded well with the traditions of world's fairs. Moses commissioned a large model of the fairgrounds, ceremoniously used to show visiting dignitaries how the Fair was developing with each new pavilion design. Smaller models circulated around the country to promote ticket sales.

### 2. Corporate Pavilions Take the Spotlight

That Moses had long-standing relations with corporations and other powerful entities was reflected in his choice of Fair participants. His emphasis on corporate pavilions and his love of mainstream popular entertainment led to his personal recruitment of Walt Disney, who made major displays in four pavilions. It was U. S. industry, led by General Electric, Ford, General Motors, Crysler, I. B. M., Bell Telephone, U. S. Steel, Pepsi Cola, Dupont, RCA and Westinghouse that spent lavishly, erected handsome pavilions and stuffed them with entertainment that they hoped would boost their image with consumers. In all more than a billion dollars was invested.

The RCA pavilion presented color television, which was used for televising announcements, ceremonies, and photos of lost children. The Bell Telephone pavilion introduced the latest picturephone. The IBM's pavilion stressed the user-friendly aspect of computer. These information exhibits proclaimed two broad themes: that rapid, globalized communications would draw people together and breakdown barriers of misunderstanding, and that the products of the information age, including automation, would save much time and labor. Exhibits at Ford, Westinghouse, Transportation and Travel, the GE, and elsewhere made many of the same points concerning the future of atomic power and the end-uses of this energy. The nascent Space Age with its vista of promise was well covered by the exhibits sponsored by the Federal pavilion, NASA, the Defense Department, and the Fair itself.

At the 1939—1940 World's Fair, industrial exhibitors played a major role by hosting huge, elaborate exhibits. Many of them returned to the 1964—1965 Fair with even more elaborate versions of the shows they had presented twenty-five years earlier. Therefore, the Fair was best remembered as a showcase of mid-twentieth century American corporate culture.

The most futuristic design of both the 1939—1940 and 1964—1965 fairs was not an individual building, but General Motors's "Futurama" exhibit. In both instances it fulfilled most completely the expectations of the "visionary", predictive element of an international exhibition. The Futurama I depicted life in then far-off 1960, while Futurama II simply said its predictions were already "beyond the promise" and well on their way to becoming a reality. Each "Futurama" exhibit was the most popular display of its respective fair.

Crysler's Pop-Art pavilion was one of the largest at the Fair and one of the most imaginative and fun places to visit. Its Design Island was dominated by a giant car, 80 feet long. Its wheels were more than 20 feet high. Beneath the car, which sat seven feet off the ground, was an exhibit area in which visual displays stressed the company's automotive styling (Figure 16).

To mark the fair's closing in October 1965, Westinghouse Corporation again assembled a time capsule to be deposited below Flushing Meadow. Time Capsule II sought to update the story began by Time Capsule I a quarter-century earlier. The objects were chosen with the goal to aid people 5000 years from now in understanding our present civilization and the rapid pace of technological progress.

The Fair can be seen as a direct outgrowth of the earlier fair and a grand showcase of the dynamic changes, both good and bad, which took place between the 1930s and the 1960s. As at most world's fairs, the 1964—1965 event was a paradise for shoppers, where new technological products and materials were triumphantly revealed, though there are many complaints about the fair: it is too commercial; too little space has been set aside for the fine arts, and almost none for the performing arts; few European countries are officially represented; there is no architectural unity; triviality and vulgarity abound. Most of these charges are true; none of them matters. The salient fact is that the New York World's Fair 1964—1965 is a splendid concentrate of magic and malarkey, well worth seeing.

## Legacy

The 1964—1965 Fair produced some exceptionally artistic pavilions and there have been many suggestions that some of them be kept permanently in the Park. In fact, the Fair Corporation, the Parks Department and the New York City were carefully evaluating for retention of many structures while the Fair was still under construction. During much of 1964 and throughout all of 1965, Fair officials explored, pursued and discarded many ideas before they finalized their master plan.

According to the "Post-Fair Engineering Report", July 1965, "Inherent in the design and construction of the Post-Fair Park is the question of what buildings and structures should be retained for City Park use and related purposes. In this connection the Fair Corporation's planning for the Post-Fair Park has been based on the premise that buildings not useful for Park or closely related purposes do not belong in Flushing Meadow unless they are on the periphery reached independently of the Park interior road and path system. A further important consideration is that if an exhibitor's building is to be converted for permanent use, funds for the conversion should be provided by the exhibitor, up to the amount he would otherwise be required to spend for demolition, with any additional funds being provided by a source other than the Fair Corporation."

However, these pavilions were built under a special Building Code as temporary special purpose structures and in almost all cases, conversion for permanent use would be prohibitively expensive and would serve no useful Park purposes.

While the Coca-Cola Pavilion was still under construction, the Fair Corporation seriously lobbied Coke to make the carillon tower a permanent part of the Post-Fair Park. It seems that the 1939—1940 Fair had missed a similar opportunity to retain a carillon from that Fair and this Fair's management did not want to make the same mistake. Unfortunately, by the time the Fair Corporation had evaluated what design changes needed to be made to the carillon tower to make it permanent, and then agonized over the possibility that Coke would not pay for it, the tower foundation was already in place, and the Fair Corporation had once again missed the opportunity.

As early as 1964 DuPont building was given a lot of consideration for retention after the Fair. Fair officials were so serious about this that they spent a considerable sum of money evaluating its potential use as a marionette theatre after the Fair to replace the aging theatre in Central Park. Unfortunately, city officials disagree with the Fair Corporation's cost estimates and the steps necessary to bring the structure up to code. At this point the Fair Corporation had to give up.

Like the first one, the 1964 Fair failed to yield profits, but it left behind several prominent structures which have provided a foundation for the unique urban oasis Moses had envisioned. These fairs put this park on the world's stage, hosting the United Nations General Assembly for five years, baseball World Series, and the U. S. Open. Today, Flushing Meadow Park is 1255 acres of athletic fields, landscaped meadows, lakes, fountains, playgrounds, stadia, museums and a zoo. It has become a recreation and cultural hub for the region.

## Conclusion

The financial condition of the Fair was a matter of intense media debate. The World's Fair Corporation, prior to the 1965 season, operated lavishly and without heed to the consequences of a much reduced gate figure and without proper accounting controls and oversight in place. The result was that the Fair was nearly bankrupt as it entered its final season. The fair, nearly bankrupt on its own, was forced to bankroll major exhibits at the Fair or face the prospect of substantial numbers of padlocked and shuttered pavilions, as many exhibitors could not operate their exhibits. And at the close of the Fair it faced huge write-offs in uncollectable receivables from exhibitors. Only a combination of reduced spending, higher admission prices and a huge influx of visitors in the waning days of the Fair reduced the loss for the 1965 season and, in turn, for the entire run of the Fair.

More than fifty-one million people attended the Fair, a new record for international exposition, though much less than the hoped-for seventy million. However the Fair did not generate the money to pay back notes and to finish Flushing Meadow Park in ambitious style. Much blame was put on Moses' inability to get along with the press. As a result the press seemed unduly harsh on the Fair, criticizing everything from a lack of fine arts display to the prices charged for admission to the Fair. Despite that economic failure, the Fair pumped billions into New York's economy and funded numerous lasting improvements to the city's infrastructure.

# 第七章

# 2000 年汉诺威世博会

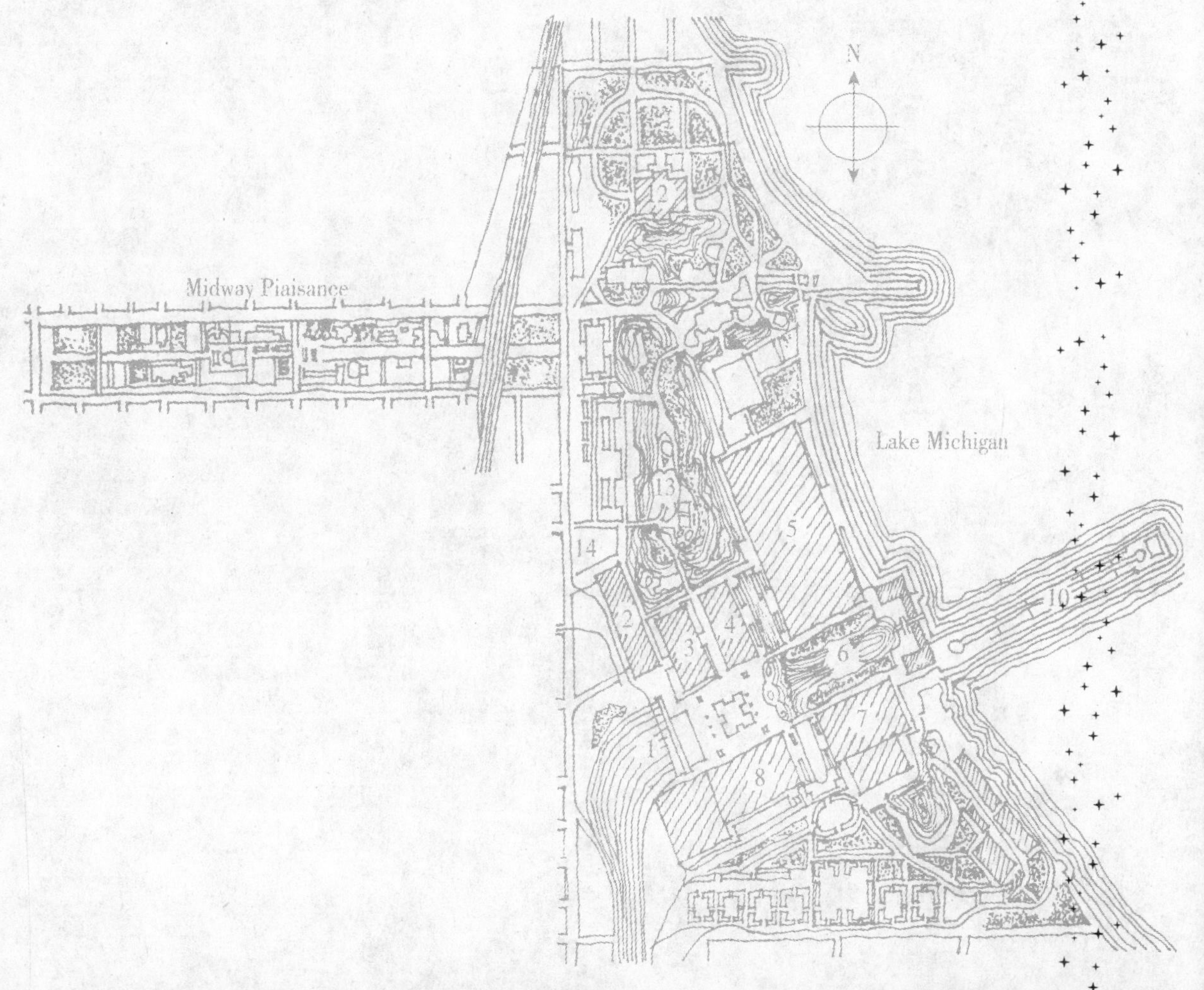

## 背景

柏林墙倒塌11年后，也就是第二次世界大战结束55年之后，德国有史以来第一次获得了主办国际博览会的机会。长期以来一直沉重地背负着20世纪"坏家伙"的恶名，德国期望借世博会的契机向世界展示一个崭新的民族形象：开放文明，面向未来。举办世博会就是要展现一个统一的德国。

汉诺威战后一跃成为重要的博览会中心反映了第二次世界大战后博览会在德国的快速发展，德国经济从战争的灾难中迅速复苏和崛起，成为世界最大的出口国之一。

战后的德国面临着毁灭性的灾难，工业废墟和蔓延的饥荒。西方战胜国认为德国经济恢复自足的唯一出路是出口自己的产品。因此，德意志博览会公司成立，第一届"汉诺威出口商品博览会"于1947年8月开幕，产生了重大影响。

最初，几乎所有人都对汉诺威能否超越莱比锡这个德意志帝国昔日的"展览之都"表示怀疑，但是几年后，汉诺威已发展成一座会展城市，吸引和聚集了众多的展览，包括世界最大的工业博览会（Hannover Messe）和世界最大的信息技术博览会之一——办公室设备博览会（CeBIT），这两个博览会在工业界引领潮流，是德意志博览会公司在汉诺威举办的众多展览中的旗舰展。汉诺威会展中心常年举办的其他展览也被视为各自领域的国际先锋。

## 人类·自然·技术

2000年世博会是新千年的第一次世界博览会，展示了人类在遵循可持续发展原则的同时，对人类社会、自然、科技和谐发展的关注，以及人类在描绘自身未来发展蓝图中发挥的极大潜力。

2000年世博会的总体策划由四个部分组成：参展国家（也包括企业）、主题展区、全球性项目、文化娱乐项目。

### 1. 全球性项目

汉诺威之所以赢得2000年世博会主办权是因为国际展览局认为其申博方案具有明显的先进性、创新意识和环保理念。获胜主题"人类·自然·技术——一个新世界的崛起"确定了本届世博会的目的：创造一个技术——与自然和谐相处——服务于人类的典范，在这个新的框架内，邀请各参展国就全球问题提供适合当地的解决方案。从这种意义上说，世博会不仅是在汉诺威而且也是在全球范围内同时进行，世界各地的人们都在为未来提供解决办法，并且付诸实践。全球性项目的理念是集中展示世界各地的典型方案。世博会大约征集到来自世界各地的700个全球性项目，其中280个项目来自德国。

与以往世博会重点展示技术进步不同，2000年世博会强调的是针对未来的解决方案，也就是针对当前的环境和发展问题提供解决方案，并且以充满魅力，真实而有趣的方式展示如何面对和把握21世纪的重大挑战。

关于未来，各国和各地区的解决方案各不相同。40个非洲国家在同一展馆共同展示了水资源保护和沙漠利用方案，纳尔逊·曼德拉为该展览剪彩。节地意识强的荷兰人建造了一座造型奇特的节地型多层展览建筑。

**2. 可持续发展**

为了确保与世博会相关的设计和施工符合城市、区域和全球的可持续发展，汉诺威制定了“汉诺威规范”，指导2000年世博会的国际设计竞赛，这个规范是设计师、规划师、政府官员以及所有相关人员制定城市优先发展战略时需要考虑的原则，为创新设计理念打下了坚实的基础。

可持续发展和资源保护的理念体现在世博规划过程的各个方面。汉诺威不会满足于照搬以往世博会的模式，过去的世博会有许多经验教训不容忽视，尤其是对世博会后的场址利用问题。因此，对原有的世界最大会展中心（汉诺威会展中心）和基础设施重新利用，并在此基础上对2000年世博会进行规划是在可持续发展和资源保护方面的大胆尝试。这种新趋势在世博建筑上也有充分反映，世博会不仅发展了新的节约能源的理念，促进了对自然资源的最大限度地利用，建造者使用的是可以反复利用的材料，如木材、纸制品等，而且进行了可供后人借鉴和效仿的试验，对世界各地的建筑师具有极其宝贵的激励作用，对参展国和投资者也具有良好的示范作用。多数展厅在世博会后将被赋予新用途，因为设计已对建筑的未来作出了预见性的安排，展示了建筑的非凡品质。汉诺威世博会表明，21世纪的建筑可以在坚持经济和生态原则的同时，达到设计品质的最高境界。

而且，世博会总体规划方案一直在不断完善，每6个月更新一次，通过这种方式加强对世博规划全过程的组织和构建，使之成为世博会的核心规划协调工具。

汉诺威的雄图胆略在于，为了可持续发展，避免世博会后留下像1992年塞维利亚世博会那样的“世博废墟”，德国要求参展国提供详细的世博会后展馆再利用方案。多数展馆设计都包括了后期再利用方案：尼泊尔的木结构庙宇将迁至汉堡，建成一个旅游信息中心；基督教堂展馆将迁至德国中部，建造一座修道院。最令人震撼的是，日本人用纸筒建造了一座面积38000平方英尺，造型轻巧的展馆，世博会后，整座建筑的材料可以回收再利用。

晚间节目的高潮是80英尺高的水幕，激光表演和影像展示，自行车骑手背负着孟加拉火焰包巡游，替代对环境有害的烟花。

这种绿色环保理念令人敬佩，与此同时，组办方还计划安排了大量的传统娱乐活动。

在世博会的153天里，每天都安排了100多个活动和节目表演，这些文化娱乐项目包括舞蹈节、戏剧节、电影节和体育运动节。除了世博会开幕式和闭幕式前后举办的文化活动外，各国还应邀在各自的国家庆祝日举办自己的文化活动。其他文化项目包括与主题展馆相关的会议。2000年世博会充分体现了传统与异域风情的融合，技术革新与乌托邦式的视觉幻想的相互渗透。

2000年世博会从6月1日开始，10月31日结束。近200个国家和国际组织参与了世博会，但不包括美国。美国后来改变了参与世博会的计划，因为没有筹集到足够的资金。因此，2000年世博会是第一个没有美国参与的世博会，但依然是参与国家最多的世博会。

## 世博会规划

1994年5月，2000年汉诺威世博有限公司（Expo 2000 Hannover GmbH）成立，负责世博会的建设和经营运作，资金大多由德国政府提供，1996年4月工程建设开始。

世博会场址位于汉诺威博览会原有的100万平方米场馆，这是一个减少场馆建设和拆除费用的措施，在此基础上又扩建了60万平方米的新展区。本届世博会意在展示一种新型的世博理念，即它不仅仅是一个临时的博览会，而且还能够把其基础设施作为一种资源和机遇，对汉诺威城市发展起到促进和推动作用。因此，所有规划都围绕着一个明确可行的目标进行，即这些场馆在世博会后仍然可以继续使用。

世博园划分为三个主要区域（图17）：

西区占地面积18万平方米，用来布置临时建筑，这里汇集了拉丁美洲和近东与远东地区国家的展馆，这片展区世博会后要清除，展馆或是搬迁，或是拆除。

东区面积28万平方米，包括30个欧洲国家的新建展馆，这个展区及其大多数展馆在世博会后将变成一个商务区，东西两片展区由称之为"Exponale"的人行天桥连接。

世博会广场位于东区的北端，面积11万平方米，在实现世博建筑理念中起着重要作用，成为联系汉诺威博览会公司原有场地与克隆斯堡周围新开发区之间的纽带。这座正方形广场让人联想起南欧典型的城市广场。世博会广场成为一个举办多种大型活动的重要场所，吸引游人驻足观赏。世博会后，广场将作为一个充满魅力的城市公共空间被保留，作为现代娱乐与服务设施使用。

中区是德意志博览会公司的原有展馆，世博会的主题展馆就设在中区的东部，称之为主题公园，由一排平行布置的五座相互沟通的展馆构成，包括26个展厅，面积10万平方米。虽然，这个名称让人产生嘉年华似的联想，主题公园实际上是围绕11个主题设计的展区，包括人类、知识、健康、基本需求、营养、能源等与未来环境相关的主题。主题展馆的目的是促进有关未来问题的讨论，教育同娱乐相结合。

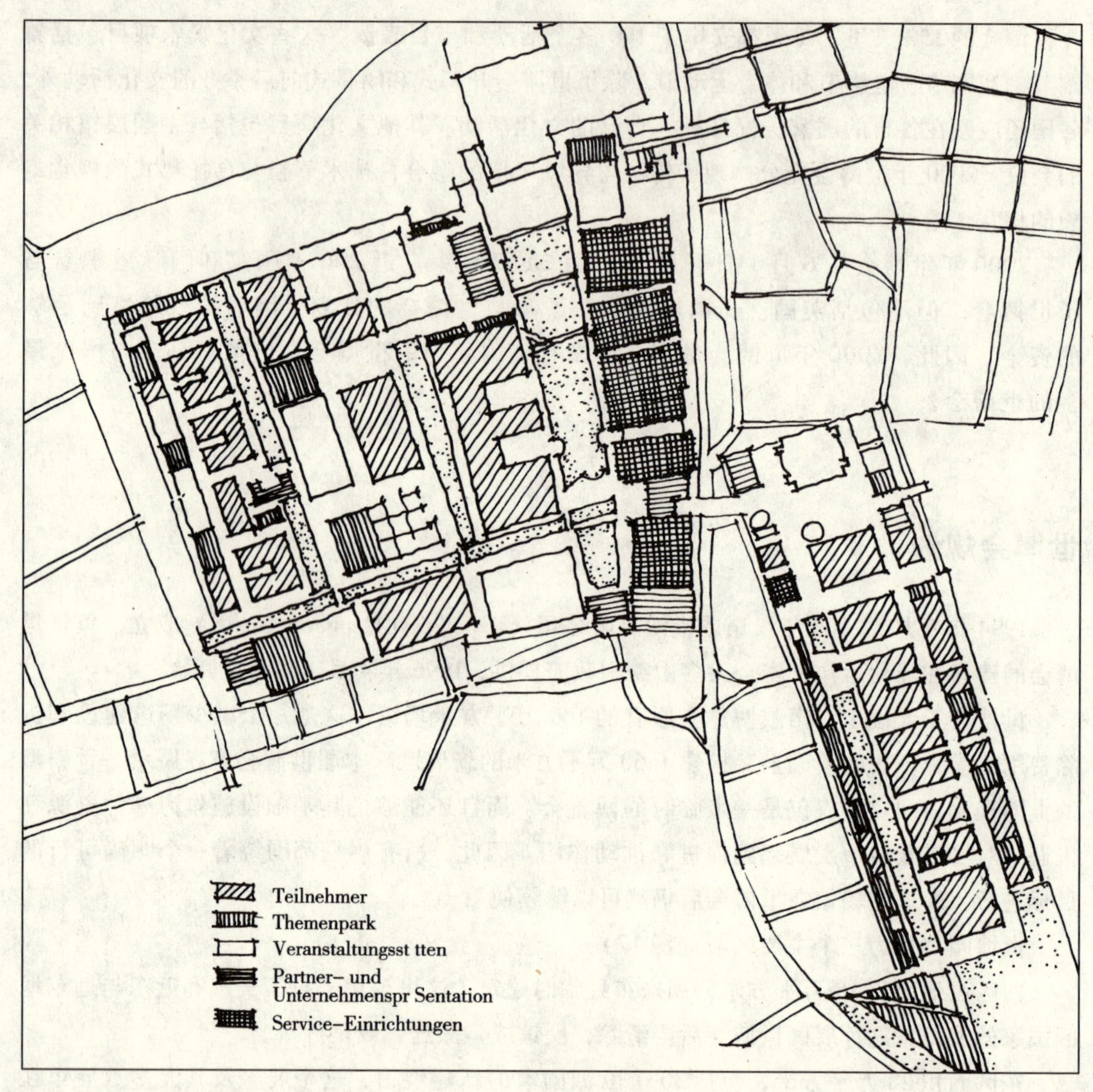


图 17　汉诺威世博园平面

许多国际展团及个人借此良机，租用理想的展位而不必耗资自建展馆。大约 130 个国家在这个展区举办了展览。

世博会总体形象塑造的重点之一是建筑与景观在空间上的融合贯通，成为一个有机的整体。设计的显著特征之一是按照相互垂直的体系布局的城区发展理念，以一条东西走向的林荫大道为脊骨，带状形绿地呈直角从林荫大道深入展区，构成了世博会场址的主要框架，创造出宽阔的公共空间。这些公共空间是接触、交流、对话、休息和放松的地方。而且，这些视野开阔、结构清晰的空间具有调节交通流量，指示方向和方便运作的功能。

将展厅和展馆集中布置在特定区域，其目的在于表现本届世博会集中紧凑的布局和城市化特点，方便游客观赏。深入这场风格迥异的建筑盛宴内部的是大片绿地，这些绿地被设计成了大大小小的公园和花园，如海浪公园、地球花园、会展湖公园等，每一座公园都各具特色。海浪公园以其波浪形的地形为主要特征，沿着西部展区起伏延伸；地球花园以一组绿色圆锥体为主要特色，由土堆积而成，顶部用抛光形铬钢帽装饰；会展湖公园是观赏每晚举办的“焰火晚会”的最佳观景点，湖岸边专为观赏烟花而建的大型舞台可容纳上万名观众，宽阔的伞形世博会屋顶遮盖了湖边大片地区，屋顶由 10 把巨大的木结构伞构成，顶棚由一种可回收的透明塑料薄膜覆盖，为观众遮阳挡雨，雨水顺流而下时形成一种喷泉的效果，世博会屋顶既是一个建筑作品，也是一件艺术品。

此外，绿地上还点缀着由来自世界各地的植物花卉构成的茂盛的花园，其创意在于给游客创造一个周游世界的体验。

许多国家的展馆都体现了环保主题，有些展馆采用纸制品、玻璃或简朴的旧木料建造，但造型各异。最让人耳目一新的是荷兰馆（图 18），赢得了国际上的赞誉。这座 36 米高的展馆（本届世博会最高的建筑）的主题是“荷兰创造空间”，由六个荷兰生态景观的片断叠置构筑而成，展示了这个国家最大限度地利用狭小空间的解决方案。游客从一层进入，通过宽敞的外置楼梯间（包裹建筑外表）游览各层展厅。顶层设置一个水面，风车环绕其周，为展馆提供能源。

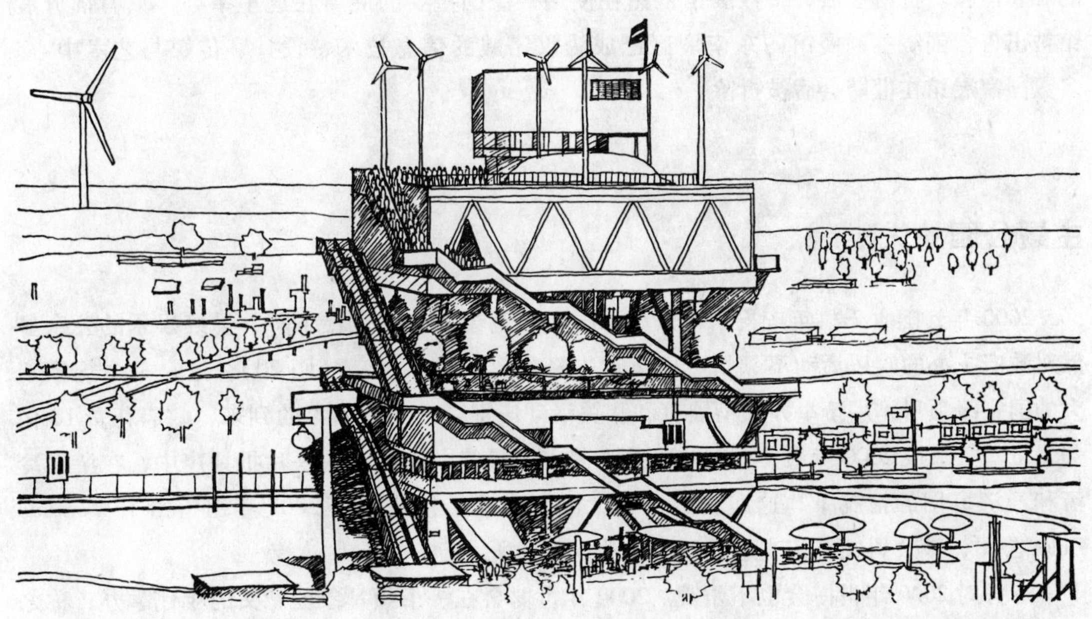

图 18　荷兰馆由六个荷兰生态景观的片断叠置构筑而成，主题是“荷兰创造空间”

日本馆（图 19）的结构由可循环利用的纸筒构成，创造了一座蜂巢似的建筑。由于德国方面拒绝纯粹的纸筒建筑——结构的接缝完全由纸筒拼接，所以又增加了一个辅助木结构才获得通过。整座建筑用 3 周时间组装，创造了一个长 72 米、宽 35 米、高 15.5 米的展览空间。

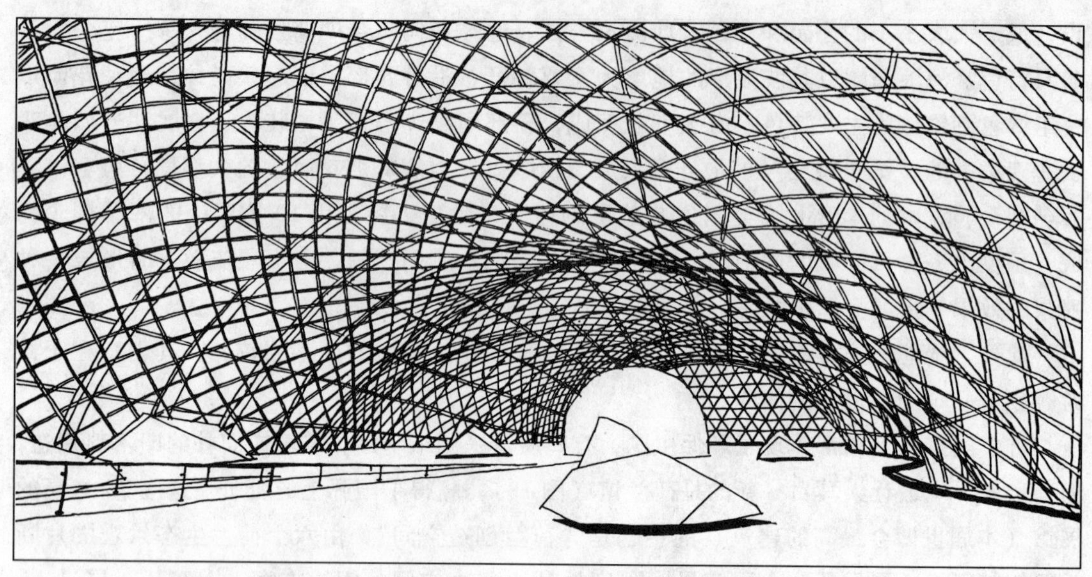

图 19　日本馆由可循环利用的纸筒构成，创造了一座蜂巢似的建筑

各参展国和国际建筑精英们的建筑细部设计和创作手法足以让世博之旅成为激动人心的难忘体验。世博会后，多数展馆依然在使用，德国重要的展事在这里举办，只有部分展馆被出售。围绕主题展馆的东南展区已成为汉诺威的信息技术、设计、传媒与艺术中心。多数国家展馆在世博会后被拆除。

## 主题公园的失败

2000 年，随着千禧年庆祝活动式微，国际博览会的热情也在下降，爱好娱乐的公众显然对政府主办的娱乐活动不领情。厄运首先降临英国的千禧宫（图 20），这是一个规模宏大的国家级项目，用于举办大型展览和相关活动庆祝第三个千禧年的到来，政府花费 10 亿美元将其打造成 2000 年最热门的一个旅游景点，最终，在媒体的一片批评声中，在游客冷清和经济窘困的情况下，这座世界上最大的穹隆顶结构建筑于 2001 年出售给了 Meridian Delta 公司，该公司又将其改造成一个运动休闲场所。

形势对 2000 年世博会也不乐观。2000 年世博会在一个颇具象征意义的年代举办，称之为千禧年世博会，主办方预计能吸引到 4000 万观众，但实际只有 1721 万观众入场参观。根据《时代周刊》欧洲版（Time Europe）的报道，组办方多次预测 4000 万观众将产生 8.7 亿美元的门票收入，1.45 亿美元的特许经营收入和 4.6 亿美元的赞助费。然而，观众数量少，又缺乏大企业的赞助，世博会的亏损超过 2 亿美元。

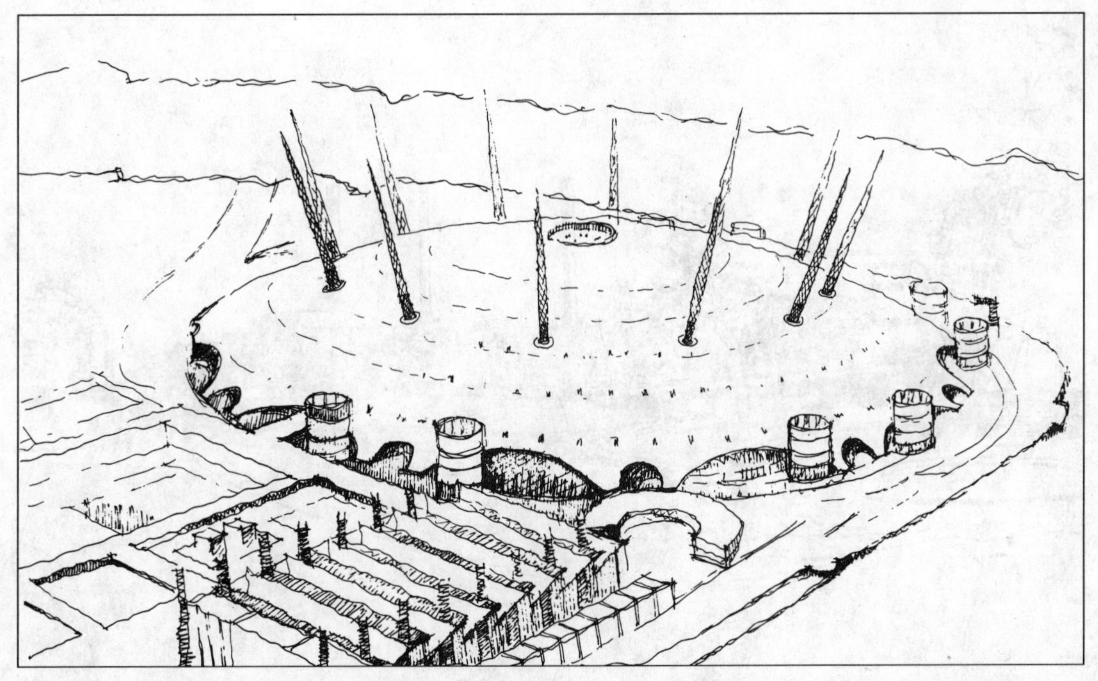

图 20 千禧宫是一座大型会展中心，为庆祝第三个千禧年而建

### 1. 主题公园模式

但是，位于汉诺威以东 80 公里外的沃尔夫斯堡，一座占地面积 62 英亩的主题公园在 2000 年 6 月与汉诺威世博会同时开幕，取得了巨大成功。这座汽车城原本是大众汽车为客户购车建设的新车提货场，现已迅速发展成为欧洲迪斯尼式的汽车主题公园。大众公司希望以此与客户建立长久的联系。

虽然这座主题公园原本并没有打算赚钱，该项目 4 亿美元的投资已经收回。这座汽车城地理位置较偏远，但是很有感召力，沃尔夫斯堡这座只有 12 万人口的小城每天要接待 6000 左右的游客。汽车城的魅力之一是景观，这是一片由废弃的工业用地改造而成的景观园林，园内布置了造型各异的现代建筑、桥梁和绿地（图 21）。大众公司知道，主题公园如果只是展示自己的品牌汽车就会失去回头客，因此开发设计了一系列主题项目和交流沟通活动。汽车公园不仅拥有一流的会展设施，还举办互动性的高科技展览，展示大众品牌汽车和普通汽车的设计艺术、发展历史及其相关信息，公园还包括一个汽车博物馆展示经典车型，七个品牌车型展馆，多家饭店和一家公园自营的宾馆。除了这些设施和项目外，公园还策划了贯穿全年的季节性活动和文化项目为之争辉。称之为 Movimentos Festival weeks 的艺术节以国际性的舞蹈、古典和当代音乐以及研讨会为主要特征，已成为欧洲最重要的舞蹈节之一，每年吸引 3 万多游客。公园与当地政府共同举办的教育项目已吸引 10 万多学者参与研究。所有这些创意不仅使这座小城成为著名的工业中心，而且享有文化精品的美誉。

图 21　位于德国沃尔夫斯堡的汽车主题公园

其他项目包括一个360度剧场，播放驾车安全教育影片；一个虚拟汽车设计工作室，游客可以在此设计自己想要的汽车；模拟驾车设施，游客可以体验各种驾车环境，撞车受力情况。虽然不是每个项目都让人倾心，但是每个人都能在这里找到自己的所爱，这里已成为车迷的必游之地，观众的访问量是预期的两倍。

**2. 经济失败**

汉诺威是一座德国北部的中等城市，算不上旅游目的地，自从汉诺威以一票的优势战胜多伦多获得2000年世博会的主办权以来，在过去的10年中，汉诺威已经花费了30亿美元改造城市面貌，但是，这座城市仍然未能激发起公众对世博会的热情。

与以往世博会重在展示新技术新发明不同，2000年世博会以“人类·自然·技术”为主题设计策划活动，在有的评论家看来，这个意义含糊的主题带有浓厚的教育色彩，不能激发公众的世博激情。在一个信息网络无处不在的全球化时代，电信和网络24小时畅通，国际旅行也已经成为家常便饭，谁还会长途旅行去汉诺威参加大同小异的博览会呢？游客参观世博会不是为了接受教育，完善自我，而是为了体验刺激，感受诱惑，享受乐趣。

美国人似乎已经对国际博览会产生了厌倦，美国举办的最后一届世博会——1984年新奥尔良世博会——完全是一场经济灾难，自从1992年塞维利亚世博会以后，国会决定不再动用纳税人的钱在世博会建造美国馆。因此，在世博筹备后期，美国彻底退出世博会，不举办国家馆，然而美国的存在无处不在——麦当劳餐馆遍及世博园各角落。

2000 年世博会失败的原因之一是缺乏对世博会理念的清晰定位，世博广告宣传未能准确塑造世博形象。2000 年《时代周刊》的一篇文章引述了位于柏林的市场调研机构 Scholz & Friends 的调查结果，“主办方未能准确地向公众传递世博形象，这是一个游乐园，还是一个放大了的博物馆，或者是自然保护区，形象不清。”这篇文章还指出，“长期以来，企业对是否赞助生态主题的展览，或是在展会上展示宣传新产品的效益没有把握。”因此，世博会面临的经济问题之一是缺乏企业赞助，其中，世博产品供应商赞助费，480 万美元，全球合作伙伴，1450 万美元。

由于对世博会的宣传推广不够，外界对正在德国进行的世博会关注甚少，德国的外交机构也没有介入世博宣传，世博筹备工作没有广泛地融入当地居民参与，没有加强公众与世博会的联系。而且，世博宣传未能引起公众的共鸣，产生“非看不可”的冲动与渴望。直到世博会开幕后，组办方才意识到不能达到预期目标，随后启动了针对国内市场的新一轮广告宣传，强调世博会的娱乐性，提出了世博会“只此一次，不会再来”的宣传口号。

与德国 53 个重点主题公园的门票价格相比——平均票价不到世博会的一半（约 30 德国马克），世博会票价显得昂贵，这种高价位（成人票 69 德国马克，即 33 美元，加上昂贵的餐饮费）是让游客望而却步的原因之一。

就世博园的规模而言，交通也是个问题，世博园的公共交通不可靠，游客需要排长队等待，计划从一个展馆到另一个展馆的时间，限制了一天的参观内容。

根据测算，65% 的游客来自德国，30% 来自欧洲国家，5% 来自其他国家和地区。然而，来自主要信息源的统计数据显示，85% ~ 90% 的游客来自德国或讲德语的地区，从 6 月到 9 月，游客中的青少年和年轻人占了大多数，显然，面对观众不足的窘境，主办方采取了多种奖励措施，鼓励青年团体参与世博会。根据组办方的报道，重要人物的访问量很大——包括 65 位国家首脑，400 多名外国政府代表以及 3 万多名嘉宾（包括省市级代表、政府官员、传媒和工商界领袖）。但是总的来说，与上届千禧年世博会（1900 年巴黎世博会）4800 万观众的惊人数字相比，与上届综合类博览会（1992 年塞维利亚世博会）的 4000 万观众相比，2000 年世博会的观众数量显得微不足道。

# Chapter 7

# Expo 2000 Hanover

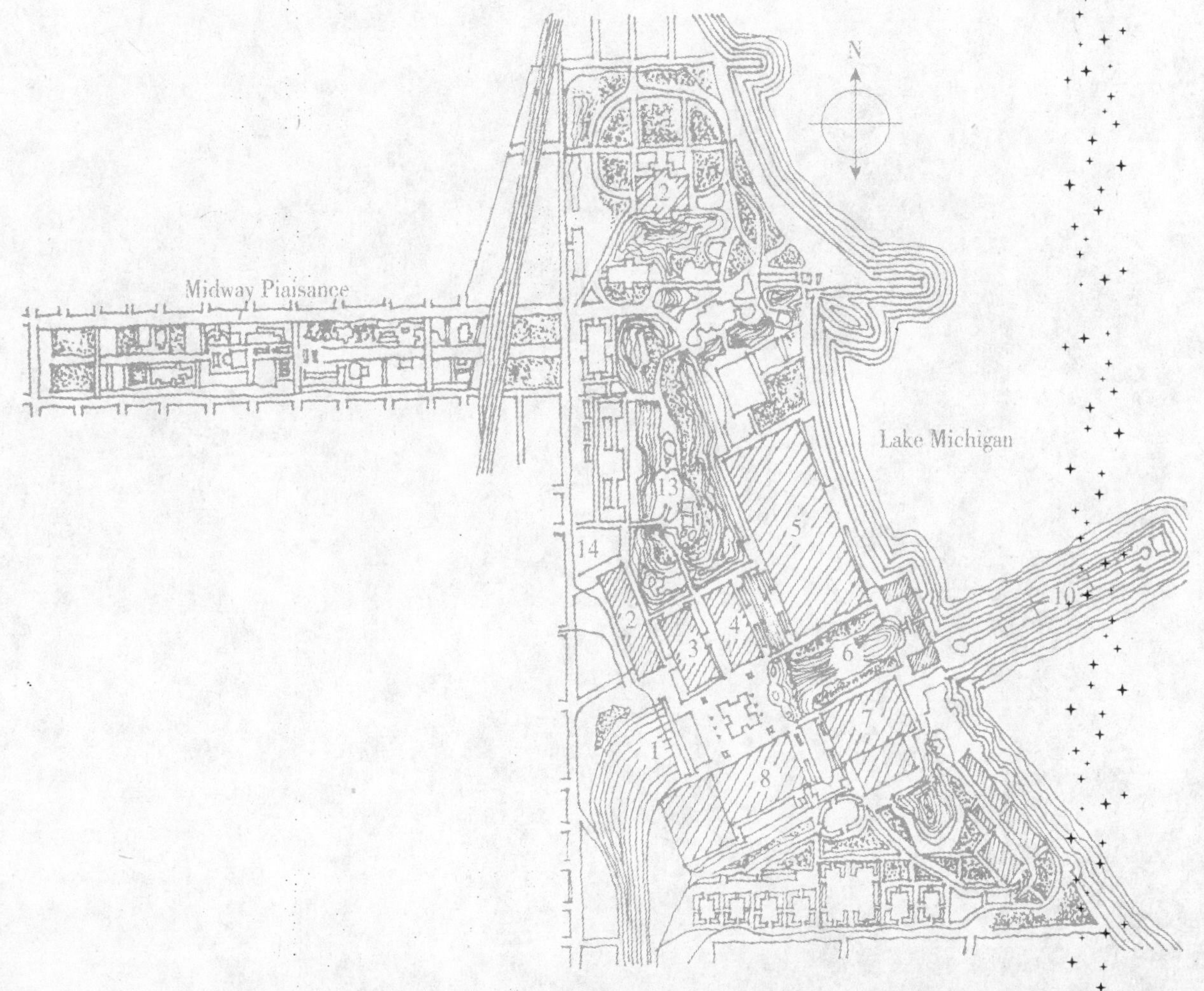

## Background

Eleven years since the Berlin Wall toppled and 55 years after the end of World War II, Germany was being entrusted with the world exposition for the first time in history. Painfully aware of their enduring reputation as the bad guys of the $20^{th}$ century, the Germans were looking to the exposition as a chance to present the world with a completely different image: that of an open-minded, cultured nation of the future. The exposition meant to showcase a united Germany.

Hanover's post-war emergence into a leading trade fair center mirrors how trade fairs in Germany developed after World War II as well as Germany's economic resurrection from the ruins of the War to become one of the world's largest exporting nations.

After the war, Germany was characterized by physical devastation, industrial ruin and chronic food shortages. The victorious Western power decided that the only way for Germany to become economically self-reliant again would be through exporting its own goods. Consequently, Deutsche Messe AG (German Trade Fair and Exhibition Company) was founded, and the first "Hanover Export Fair" was opened in August 1947, which was impressive.

At first, almost everyone was skeptical about Hanover's chances of overtaking Leipzig——the former "exhibition capital" of the defunct German Reich. But in the years that followed, Hanover refashioned itself as a convention town, luring an assortment of events including the world's largest industrial trade fair, the Hanover Messe, and the CeBIT, one of the most important information-technology fairs. Both shows have become the trendsetter for industry and the flagship tradeshows among the many different trade fairs and exhibitions staged by Deutsche Messe AG in Hanover. Other events, which regularly take place at the Hanover Exhibition Grounds, are also recognized as world leaders in their respective fields.

## Humankind-Nature-Technology

Expo 2000, the first fair in the new millennium, offered a perfect opportunity to emphasize humanity's vast potential for shaping its own future in keeping with the principle of sustainable development and for achieving a change of consciousness that would bring about a harmony between humanity, nature and technology.

The overall concept of the Expo 2000 was based on four pillars: Participating Countries (also corporations); Thematic Area; Projects around the world; the Cultural and Events Program.

**1. The Concept of Global Project**

Hanover was selected by the BIE because its proposal was a standout for its progressive, innovative, and environmentally conscious approach. The winning theme, "Humankind, Nature, Technology——A New World Arising," had defined the purpose of the exposition: to create a paradigm in which technology——in harmony with nature——serves humanity. Within this new framework, participating nations had been asked to present local solutions to global problems. In this sense, this world exposition was not just taking place in Hanover, but all over the world where people were developing ideas for the future and putting them into practice. The concept of the global project was to join together model ideas from all over the world in the presentation. About 700 practical projects were presented from around the world, 280 from Germany.

Unlike previous world expositions, which concentrated on presenting advances in technology, Expo 2000 would be concentrating on solutions for the future: solution for current problems in the environment and development. Expo 2000 demonstrated in an attractive, factual and entertaining manner, how the major challenges of the $21^{st}$ century could be met and mastered.

Responses to this question were as varied and individual as the nations giving them. Forty of the African countries were tackling the issues of water conservation and desert usage together in a hall to be opened by Nelson Mandela. The space-conscious Netherlands constructed a dramatic, space-saving pavilion of a multi-tiered structure.

**2. Sustainable Development**

In order to insure that the design and construction related to the fair would represent sustainable development for the city, region, and world, the city of Hanover had commissioned "The Hanover Principles" to inform the international design competitions for Expo 2000. The principles were to be considered by designers, planners, government officials and all involved in setting priorities for the built environment. They would help form the foundations of a new design philosophy.

The ideas of sustainable development and resource conservation had an appreciable impact upon virtually every aspect of the fair planning. Hanover could not be content with merely imitating previous world fairs. There were too many negative aspects of past experience to ignore, especially in the use of Expo site after the fair. The decision to make use of the world's largest trade fair grounds and the existing infrastructure and to adapt them to the development of Expo 2000 was an ambitious attempt in this direction. This new trend found their expression in the Expo architecture as well. New energy-saving concepts had been developed, and natural resources had been used with optimum efficiency. Builders had relied on such renewable materials as wood, paper products and etc. The fair had implemented exemplary solutions, which offered valuable stimulus to architects everywhere and served as an example for participating nations and investors. Many pavilions, dedicated to new purpose after the fair, were planned with almost visionary far-sightedness, and offered exciting insights into unusual structures. Hanover Expo has demonstrated here that the architecture of the $21^{st}$ century can be planned in keeping with both economic and ecological principles while still achieving the highest standard of quality in design.

The Master Plan of the fair was continuously developed and updated every six months, an approach that helped organize and structure the overall planning process. Thus the Master Plan served as a central planning and coordination tool for the fair.

The ambitiousness of the proposal was that Germany had requested that participants submit a detailed after-use plan for their structures both in the name of sustainability and to avoid an "exposition graveyard" like the one left behind from the '92 event in Seville. Most pavilions were designed to provide good service in their next life: Nepal's wooden temple would be reassembled in Hamburg as a tourist information center. The Christian Churches pavilion would be used to reconstruct a monastery in central Germany. Most spectacularly, the Japanese had constructed their elegant, 38000-square-foot pavilion from rolls of paper. At Expo's end, the building would simply be recycled.

The highlight of the nightly performances would be the 80-foot-high water curtains, laser and film projections, and cyclists carrying Bengal flare packs, as an alternative to environmentally unfriendly fireworks.

While these green visions may be awe-inspiring, organizers also planed to wow visitors with a heavy dose of good old-fashioned entertainment. More than a hundred activities and performances were scheduled for each of the Expo's 153 days. The Cultural and Events Program included a Dance Festival, a Theatre Festival, a Film Festival and a Festival of Sports. In addition to the cultural activities around the opening and closing ceremonies, countries were invited to present their own cultural program on their National Day. Other programs included conferences related to the Theme pavilions. Therefore, Expo 2000 fully demonstrated the interaction of the traditional and exotic elements, technology and innovation and visionary-utopian dreams.

Expo 2000 took place from June $1^{st}$ to October $31^{st}$ 2000. Nearly 200 countries and international organizations were presented, but the list did not include the United States, which reversed its decision to take part at a relatively late stage as the organizers failed to come up with enough private money. Therefore, Expo. 2000 is the first world exposition held without the participation of the United States, still it is the most ever for a world's fair.

## Planning of the Fair

In May 1994, a new company, Expo 2000 Hannover GmbH, was created to be responsible for the construction and management of the fair. The company was mostly funded by the German government. Construction began in April 1996.

The Expo site was situated on the original 1, 000, 000 $m^2$ of the Hanover Fair, a measure to reduce the cost of building and removal of the exposition site, and an additional 600, 000 $m^2$ was also made available as a newly opened section to the grounds. The goal of the fair was to present a new type of Expo that would not be merely a passing event but a permanent site, which would take advantage of its infrastructure as a resource and an opportunity, and serve as a motor for urban development in Hanover. Therefore, all planning measures were to be integrated into a feasible and purposeful concept for continued use after the fair.

The Expo site consisted of three main areas (Figure 17):

The Pavilions West Area, comprising 180, 000$m^2$, was used for the construction of temporary structures. It contained exhibits primarily from Latin American, the Near and Far Eastern countries. This area was to be dismantled following the exposition and its pavilions either moved or destroyed.

The Pavilions East Area was a 280, 000$m^2$ area, which contained about 30 newly-built pavilions primarily occupied by European countries. This area, including most of its pavilions, was to be turned into a business park following the exposition. The East and West areas were connected by the cleverly named "Exponale" bridge walkway.

The Expo-Plaza, situated at the north end of the East Area, played a key role in the urban architectural concept for the fair, and formed a link between the two parts of the existing trade fair grounds and the newly developed area around Kronsberg. The form of the square Plaza, which occupied 110, 000 square meters of ground, called to mind a typical southern European city plaza. It served as an important venue for events and receptions, appealing to visitors to stop and spend some time. The Plaza would remain as an attractive urban space after the fair, and be used as elements of a modern entertainment and service center.

The Centre of the Site was an existing fairground owned by the Deutsche Messe AG. A row of five interconnected Thematic Pavilions, called the Theme Park, were located in the east side of this area which had 26 halls with a total exhibition area of 100, 000$m^2$. Although the name brought to mind carnival rides, this theme park was organized around eleven themes such as Humankind, Knowledge, Health, Basic Needs, Nutrition, Energy and other environmentally conscious themes geared toward the future. Objectives of the theme pavilions were to stimulate discussion and to combine education with entertainment.

Many international participants and organizations took advantage of this opportunity and leased presentation areas. In this way, they acquired an attractive setting for their exhibits without the need to erect a much more costly pavilion of their own. About 130 countries had their exhibit area in the trade fair halls at this location.

The spatial integration of architecture and landscape was one of the important approaches to establishing total visual image for the Expo grounds, which were viewed as an organic whole. One of the most striking features was the urban development concept based on an orthogonal system. A broad Avenue, the axial east-west link, formed the backbone of the whole, while the fingers of green area penetrated into the Expo grounds at right angle from it, forming the main structure of the grounds and creating open spaces. These open spaces were settings for encounter, for communication, for dialogue, rest and relaxation. These expansive and clearly structured spaces were functional for the flow of traffic, orientation and operation as well.

The architectural volumes of the halls and pavilions were concentrated in specific areas in order to give Expo the character of a compact and urban setting, easily accessible to visitors. Stretching down the middle of these strange feats of architecture were large stretches of green area, which were turned into parks and gardens, such as Park Wave, Earth Garden, Expo Lake, and etc., each expressing a specific feature. Park Wave featured its undulating topography, rolling along the West Pavilion Site; Earth Garden featured a group of grassy earthen cones, which were topped with caps of polished chromium steal; Expo Lake was the best spot to enjoy the "fireworks show" presented each evening, with a grand stand erected for the event seating approximately 10000 spectators. Broad umbrella-style roof elements forming the Expo Roof provided shelter over large area by the lake. The Roof comprised 10 huge wooden umbrellas, which were covered by a kind of recyclable transparent plastic membrane. It provided shelter against sun and rain, creating a fountain effect with rainwater diverted down along the structures. It is a piece of genuine architectural and aesthetic work.

In addition, the green areas were ornamented with lush gardens of imported plants and flowers from the world over. The idea was to give the visitors the feeling of taking a trip around the world without ever leaving the fairgrounds.

Many of the country pavilions followed the environmental theme, and some were constructed of paper, glass or plain old wood, but in various shapes. Most striking of all was the Dutch Pavilion (Figure 18), winning international acclaim. The theme of the 36 m high building (the fair's tallest structure) was "Holland Creates Space". Six Holland eco-system landscapes were stacked to showcase how a country can make the most out of a small space. Visitors entered on the ground floor and used grand exterior staircases (that wrapped around the building) to move through the exhibit space. The top level contained a small lake surrounded with windmills that generated power for the building.

The Japanese Pavilion (Figure 19) structure was made out of recycled paper tubes, creating a honeycomb like building. The German authorities refused to allow a paper only structure, literally held together at the joints by tape, so a secondary supporting structure made of wood was created to get the needed legal approval. The complete building took 3 weeks to assemble, creating an exhibit space of 72m (long) ×35m (wide) ×15.5m (high).

Building components and methods typical of the participating countries and design concepts of international caliber have created a fascinating sensory experience for the Expo visitors. Most of the exhibition area is still used for major fairs in Germany, though some of the buildings on the Expo site were sold after the fair. The South-Eastern area around Expo Plaza has been turned into Hanover's new center of information technology, design, media and arts. Most of the national pavilion buildings were demolished following the fair.

## Theme Park Failure

However, World-class exhibitions were failing in the year 2000 as the celebration of the millennium went down, with the fun-seeking public apparently rejecting their governments' efforts to keep them entertained. Misfortunes first occurred to Britain's Millennium Dome (Figure 20), an ambitious national project to host a major exhibition and relevant events celebrating the coming of the third millennium. The government spent $ 1 billion to make it a most popular tourist attraction in the year 2000. However, amid a flurry of bad press and lousy attendance reports leading to recurring financial problems, the largest domed structure in the world was sold in the year 2001 to Meridian Delta Ltd, which in turn transformed it into a sports and entertainment venue.

Things hadn't been much better for the organizers of Expo 2000. Being set in the symbolic year of 2000, the fair was also titled Millennium Expo. The organizers were expecting to draw 40 millions visitors to the fair, but only 17.21million people came to see the event. According to Time Europe's reports, organizers at various time projected that 40 million visitors would help generate revenues of US $870 million in admission fees, US $145 million in licenses and US $460 million in sponsorship. However, poor attendance and a lack of key corporate sponsorship led to a financial deficit of more than $200 million.

### 1. Theme Park Approach

But just 80km east of Hanover, in Wolfsburg, a 62-acre theme park opened its gates in July 2000 to coincide with the opening of the World Expo in Hanover, achieving an overwhelming success. The Auto City, built by Volkswagen as a place for VW customers to pick up their new cars, has quickly grown into the EuroDisney of the automobile. Volkswagen wanted to establish long-term relationships with consumers.

Although it was not intended to become profitable, the $ 400 million development cost has been written off. The Auto City has been a surprising success with the audience, given its remote location. The city of Wolfsburg, with a population of 120,000, is drawing an average of 6000 visitors every day. One of its attractions is the landscape, which is an industrial wasteland turned into a magnificent park with shapely modern buildings, bridges and lots of grass (Figure 21). As VW knows a focus on its own brand would soon diminish repeat visitors, themed events and communications have been developed. The park features not only state of the art conference facilities, but high-tech, interactive exhibits showcasing art, history, information, and stories about the specific brands that comprise Volkswagen and about cars in general, a museum filled with classic cars, seven brand pavilions, restaurants and its own on-site hotel. Enhancing this exciting offer are seasonal events and cultural programs spread throughout the year. The Movimentos Festival weeks draws over

30, 000 visitors annually with international dance, classical and contemporary concert, workshops and discussions, known as one of the most significant dance festivals in Europe. An educational program, arranged in collaboration with the local government, has involved more than 100, 000 scholars in the workshops. All these events have given the area the reputation of a center renowned not only for its industrial, but also cultural excellence.

Other attractions include a 360-degree theater showing a safety film by German director Dani Levy, a virtual car design studio where visitors can design their own cars, and simulators that let visitors experience driving a car in various situations, including rides simulating the force of a car crash. Not everything has mass appeal, but there is something for everyone. It has become a must-go destination for auto enthusiasts and is drawing twice as many visitors as expected.

**2. A Financial Failure**

Hanover itself, a mid-sized city in northern Germany hardly known as a tourist destination, failed to capture a broad public imagination, though the city had undergone a $3 billion facelift in the past 10 years since it edged out Toronto by a single vote to gain the honor of hosting Expo 2000.

In contrast with past world's fairs, which tended to showcase remarkable new inventions, this one was developed around the vague theme of "Humankind, Nature, and Technology," which, to some critics, established a curiously pedagogical tone and failed to generate much excitement. In a globalized era of media saturation, when the whole world is available on cable and the Internet 24 hours a day, and when international travel has become commonplace, who needed to venture all the way to Hanover for more of the same? Visitors don't come to be instructed and improved, but instead dazzled, tempted and entertained.

Americans seemed to have soured on world's fairs. The last world's fair held in the United States, Expo'84 in New Orleans, was an unmitigated financial disaster. After the 1992 fair in Seville, Congress decided that it would not use taxpayers' money to fund future U. S. exhibitions at international expositions. Therefore, late in the organizing process, the U. S. dropped out entirely and did not provide a national pavilion, though America was amply represented——via the many McDonald's restaurants scattered throughout the fairgrounds.

Part of the failure of the Expo was a lack of clear perception of what to expect at the fair, as advertising campaign had failed to explain what the Expo was for. In a 2000 Time magazine article a Berlin-based marketing firm Scholz & Friends stated that "the organizers have failed to convey to the public a clear image of what Expo is going to be: an entertainment park, a blown-up museum, or a nature reserve." The same article also stated, "For a long time, companies were unsure if they would be putting money in an eco-show or a showcase for their latest inventions." Hence one of the financial shortfalls came from a lack of corporate sponsorship in which it cost US $4. 8 million to be an official product supplier or US $14. 5 million to become a world partner.

With inadequate marketing, the event went almost unnoticed outside of Germany. German diplomatic services were generally not involved in the process. Preparations for the event did not generally involve local people or encourage local people to identify with the event. The weak advertising efforts failed to appeal to emotions, creating the necessary atmosphere of a "must-see". Only after the fair was open and clearly not meeting expectations was a new advertising campaign created, aimed at the domestic market, stressing the fun side of the Expo, under the slogan: "This only happens once, it's never coming back."

Compared with the entrance fees for Germany's 53 main theme parks, which cost on average less than half the price as the Expo (about 30 DM), the Fair seemed expensive. A steep pricing structure (69 DM, or $33, for an adult entrance ticket, and notoriously expensive refreshments) was one factor keeping the crowds away.

Given the sheer size of the site, transportation was a problem for visitors, as the free transportation was unreliable and there were long line-ups. Visitors had to plan on spending significant amounts of time going from one area to another, limiting the number of pavilions they could visit in a single day.

It was estimated that 65% of visitors would be German origin, 30% European and 5% from other countries. However, key informants suggested that as many as 85% to 90% of visitors were German or German-speaking. From June to September, the large majority of visitors to the fair were reported to be teenagers and young people. Expo organizers had apparently reacted to the low number of visitors by providing various incentives to youth groups to visit the exposition. Organizers reported that VIP participation was strong——65 heads of state, over 400 government representatives and 30000 other VIP (including provincial and municipal representatives, bureaucrats, media and business leaders) visited Expo 2000. As a whole, attendance for the Expo 2000 was seen as poor, considering the astounding visitor's figure of 48 million at the previous Millennium Expo in Paris in 1900, and 40 million at the previous Universal exhibition in Sevilla in 1992.

# 第八章

## 莱比锡博览会——人文的博览会

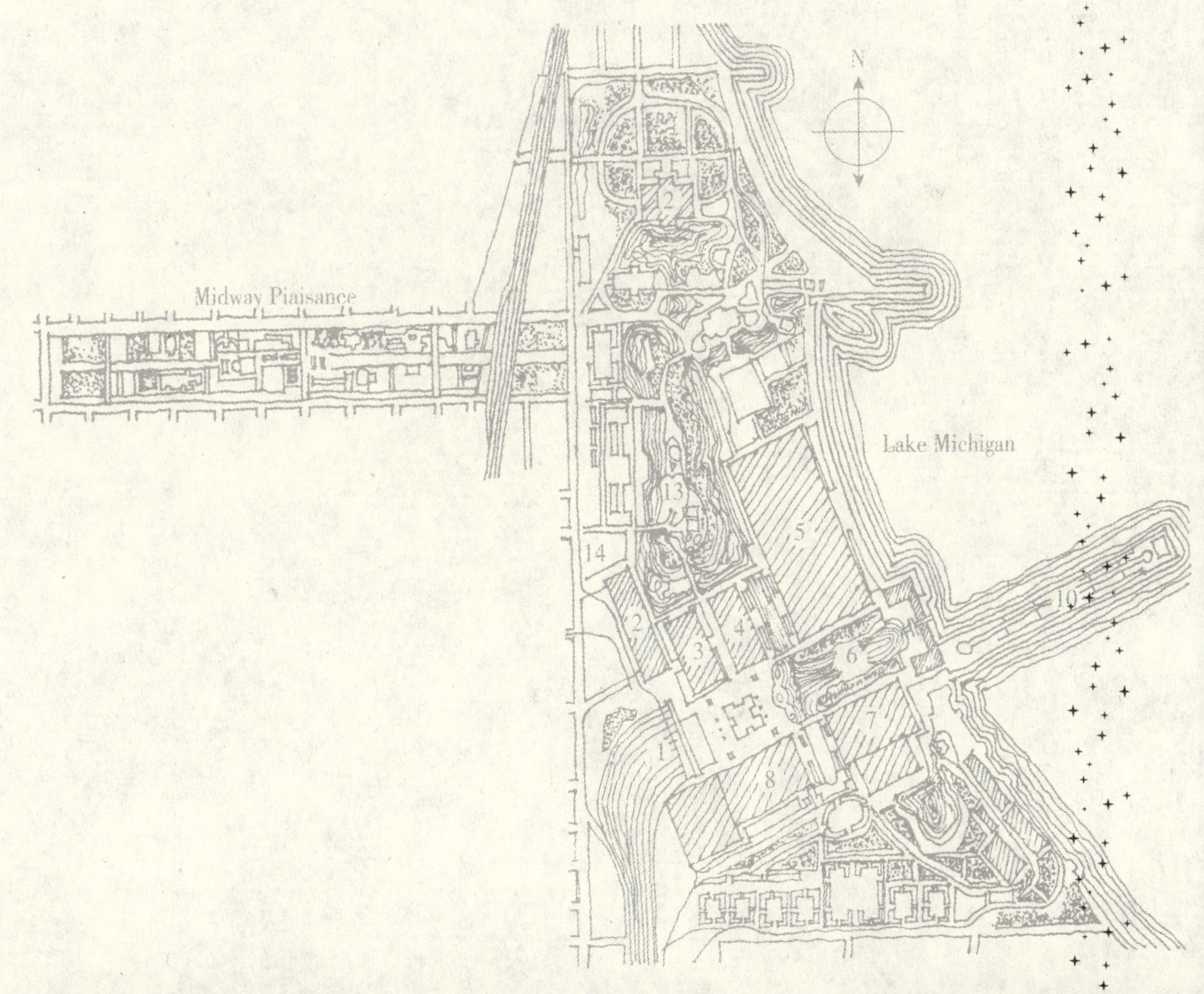

## 莱比锡博览会的早期发展史

博览会对城市历史文化的形成起着重要的推动作用。虽然，莱比锡不是建立在古罗马废墟上的古城，自中世纪末以来，莱比锡一直是泥泞古道上重要的交通枢纽，将罗马帝国的东南与西北联系在一起，这里每年举办三次商品交易会。1507 年，莱比锡交易会被赋予帝国的特权，城市周边 15 英里范围内不允许举办任何交易会，从此，莱比锡的重要地位更加显赫。莱比锡博览会既是世界上最古老的博览会之一，同时也是最年轻最现代化的博览会之一。

大约 1500 年，莱比锡商人和建筑商改进了这里典型的商业建筑的型制。随着城市的发展繁荣，砖结构建筑普及。传统的两层住宅，开间窄，进深长，山墙立面临街。这种建筑形制稍加改造，将建筑的纵轴线转向 90°，形成沿进深走向的内院，平行布置的建筑形成连续的屋檐和围合的内院，出入便捷，构成了莱比锡典型的“廊式建筑”（图 22）。一年三次

图 22 传统住宅开间窄，进深长，山墙立面临街，将建筑的纵轴线转向 90°，形成沿进深走向的内院，平行布置的建筑形成连续的屋檐和围合的内院，构成了莱比锡典型的“廊式建筑”，一年三次的商品交易会就在这些内院中进行

的商品交易会就在这些内院中，在彼此相连的巷道和广场中举办。这种建筑形式使主要街道两侧的临街立面风格统一，醒目的临街立面背后是彼此相连的建筑实体和内院。交易会期间，建筑的一楼是相互沟通的展览区和交易区，各种类型的交易场所共同构筑了一个“贸易世界的序列”。莱比锡城就是一个巨大的市场，享有“全欧洲的交易市场”的美誉。

这些与建筑纵横交错的内院和巷道就是今天所谓的“半公共空间”的雏形，它们在18世纪晚期和19世纪发展成为店铺云集的街廊和拱廊。这种典型的城市布局和专为举办交易会而建的廊式宅邸建筑是交易会在莱比锡迅速发展的产物。过去30年城市规划的必要条件之一——“密度增加导致城市化发展趋势”——在18世纪的莱比锡就已成为现实。但是这种拥挤狭窄的交易场所最终妨碍了交易会的发展。

**1.“样品博览会”的形成**

18世纪中期，商品交易会的形式开始发生变化，英国布料商首先引入了样品订货的交易方式。19世纪70年代晚期，主要的贸易领域不再提供现货交易，而是采用样品订货的方式。

然而，到了1892年，参与交易会的客商从1万人下降到不足4000人，几百年来延续已久的商品交易会传统似乎难以为继。衰落的原因主要有以下四个方面：样品仓库装饰简陋，样品展示效果差；持续增长的货物供应加剧了竞争，就连马背上的流动商人也载着样品，与交易会争夺客商；由于场地的限制，商品展示从一层搬到楼上，给客商出入和货物搬运带来极大不便。

1892年，一个促进博览会发展的专业委员会成立，其主要议程是对莱比锡的交易会进行全面改造：①所有与交易会相关的活动和细节都要经过严格审视和重新考虑，包括为参加交易会的客商举办文化活动，从今往后他们不再受入场费的困扰；②翻新改造原有的展览建筑，创造新的展览建筑，适应新的展览模式——即所谓“样品博览会”的运作需要。1895年，莱比锡博览会成为一个正式机构，这是公众介入原本纯粹的私营经济的重要一步。新型博览会（样品博览会）与传统每年举办三次的商品交易会（专营某类商品）并存，其他形式的集市档期也经历了重组和改进。

这些决定性的，设计严密的措施成效显著，为今天的莱比锡博览会在历史上取得的巨大成功打下了坚实的基础，莱比锡博览会一跃成为世界上最重要的博览会，其辉煌盛事一直持续到1914年。1900年，注册参加春季博览会的客商已超过6.3万人，而且参展人数还在持续增长。

**2. 第二次飞跃**

然而，第一次世界大战以后，备受经济打击的欧洲其他城市开始全力发展经济，德意志帝国出现了一批新的“样品博览会”，位于前列的是法兰克福、科隆、布雷斯劳、柯尼斯堡和柏林，都想挤进这个颇具发展前景的领域。除了柏林博览会以外，其他博览会都以当地为发展目标。莱比锡的优势地位无以匹敌，“品牌产品”的最新发展趋势使莱比锡进一步领先。

为了适应新型博览会的经营运作，莱比锡从19世纪90年代开始对内城进行改造。显然，博览会的发展需求在这座古老的贸易城市具有至高无上的优先地位，老城的中心区全部奉献给了“样品博览会”——这是莱比锡的发明创造。公共空间，如公园和林荫道布置在城市次要的周边地带，城市的宏伟建筑聚集在博览会周围，双环路旁的绿荫丛中，如新建的剧院、学校大楼（莱比锡大学）、高大的市政厅和帝国银行。在这里既可以设计景观，绿化道路，建设重要的公共建筑，又不破坏城市结构。围绕内城环形地带的建设意味着市区面积增加了80%，莱比锡也因此拥有了“迷人的外表”。

博览会设施采用当年时髦的历史建筑风格。内城中的多层办公楼和贸易中心都用于博览会，展位大都出租。新建的大型博览会建筑与传统的商业建筑最大的区别是，方便客商参观展览，从而全面了解所有展品。展览涉及的主要问题得到了根本解决：占据内城最佳位置，方便客商参展和货物运输；创造高品质的室内外展位，这些展位大都布置在楼上，仓储空间设在阁楼和地下室；纵向垂直交通采用电梯，设计保证了楼层空间使用的最大灵活性；现代技术设备，充足的照明，高质量的卫生设施成为标准。为了满足最大的灵活性需求，这种强调功能的建筑必须采用最新的钢筋混凝土技术或框架结构建造。

长期以来，莱比锡一直是德国的工业中心，拥有无与伦比的印刷和出版业：一千多家出版社（有些出版社还很大），一千多家造纸商、印刷商及其相关厂商，在制造领域，只有纽约能与其媲美，此外，机器制造业也很发达，专门制造印刷机械，还有其他大型工业企业。然而，博览会依然是城市地位和声望的重要组成部分，莱比锡博览会的MM标志（Muster Messe——样品博览会）是1917年设计的。

尽管进行了大规模的城市改造，特别是建筑“集合”——建筑密度和容积增大，莱比锡的内城空间再次拥挤不堪，由此，莱比锡进入第二个现代博览会的发展时期。

1918年秋天，第一届技术博览会和第一届建筑专业博览会在莱比锡举办，参展商品不再是便于陈列的货物样品，而是重达数吨的机械、大型设备和材料，为商品交易会而设计的展览建筑不再适用。新型展览需要建设大型地面展厅，并且与铁路连通。因此，在城市东南面“民族之战纪念碑”附近划拨了一块22.5万平方米的土地建设新展馆。最终，技术博览会展览中心在这里落成，包括几十座展馆，占地面积扩大到40万平方米。这里为新型博览会提供了便利的铁路交通条件。技术博览会由一条主轴线与城区连接。

第二次世界大战期间，技术博览会80%的建筑遭到破坏。战争结束后，技术博览会重建，莱比锡博览会对德意志民主共和国同样很重要，因为它展示了社会主义国家所取得的成就。

## 今天的莱比锡博览会

1989年德国统一以后，莱比锡的政治经济地位发生了彻底改变。城市经济遭受双重打击，不仅莱比锡博览会面临激烈的竞争，而且还必须应对和弥补工业遭受的重创。来自西方的博览会竞争势力强劲，西德每座大城市都发展了自己的博览会产业，不必再与昔日强盛的莱比锡博览会竞争。在德国博览会中，汉诺威博览会首屈一指（展厅面积47.5万$m^2$，室外场地22.7万$m^2$；1995年，注册观众达到2300000人，参展商23000），接着是杜塞尔多夫、法兰克福、慕尼黑、柏林、斯图加特、科隆、纽伦堡、汉堡和多特蒙德。排在最后的才是莱比锡。

### 1. 博览会成为经济复苏的动力

随着莱比锡内城功能的衰退，残存的工业潜力成效甚微，博览会必须成为经济复苏的“动力”。与其他博览会先进的后勤服务体系相比，位于市中心的莱比锡博览会运作费用高，缺乏竞争力，这里的场地只适合于举办少数形象宣传活动和与城市氛围直接相关的纯粹的专业展览。因此，需要制定一个全面的解决方案。

尽管万事开头难，尽管众所期盼的德国统一后的“东部崛起”并没有出现，莱比锡别无选择，只能重新开始，将博览会迁往新址。1991年6月，莱比锡博览会公司选择了这条唯一可行的道路，虽然充满了风险。同年10月，市议会以75%的优势投票决定在莱比锡郊区重建博览会，否决了重新启用内城会展中心的议案。原有的展览设施已经落后，重新使用不仅费用高，而且会影响常规运作。考虑到莱比锡博览会公司的实际情况，否定继续使用技术博览会现有展馆的方案是一个大胆，正确的经济决策。杜塞尔多夫和慕尼黑也曾经作出同样的决策，成功地搬迁了展览中心。而且，新的会展中心将规划成一个完整的规模宏大的新城区，而不是由分散的若干会展设施组合而成的联合实体。

将博览会迁至莱比锡郊区的议案引起众多争议。新博览会是否距老城区太远？新博览会是否还是“莱比锡博览会”，或者是一座恰好建在德国中部，交通便利的会展设施？博览会不需要城市环境吗？没有生机勃勃富于传统的老城，新的莱比锡博览会能够生存吗？

大型公共活动，特别是博览会性质的活动，总是与交通状况密切相关，博览会就是市场，市场只有在人流与物流的交会之处才能运作。莱比锡在中世纪就是两条古商道的交会点，独特的地理位置是形成大型博览会的重要因素，其影响力辐射整个德语地区乃至更远。19世纪，莱比锡成为欧洲铁路交通的一个重要枢纽，当时莱比锡已拥有一个“组合式车站”，由位于城北边的三座火车站构成，1915年，世界著名的铁路终点站“宫殿”在这里建成。所有铁路线相互沟通使莱比锡拥有当时最便利的铁路交通，为莱比锡在不到半个世纪的时间里取得的经济成就打下了重要基础。

然而，这类交通方式已不能适应今天的发展需求。工业时代以来，货物及其运输方式发生了变化，道路也发生了改变。商品交易市场已经演变成样品市场，随后又发展成为今天的信息市场，运用现代信息和数据技术。运输方式在途中发生变更，从一种运输方式转换成另一种方式已不经济可行，除非是空运转陆路运输。显然，新的博览会场馆必须建在航空、铁路和公路运输的交会点上，方便运输。

**2. 创造一个会展公园**

但是，新的博览会展馆设计方案的获胜者发现他们面对的不是什么风水宝地，而是一片乱七八糟的工业废墟和废弃的机场，一片缺乏地形变化，毫无生机的平地，距离老城区 7 公里。设计者必须为博览会创造一个崭新的环境，这就是向地下挖掘 5 米，开辟一条 150 米宽，向东逐步凹陷的坡道，形成一个梯形的浅层峡谷景观地带作为博览会的新场址，并且布置了水面和绿地，使之成为一个名副其实的会展公园（图 23）。巨大的中央门厅（80 米宽，穹顶最高处 30 米，长 243 米）布置在这个“人造峡谷”的中轴线上，创造了一个玻璃棚内的人造景观，由树木植物和对称性划分空间的设施构成（图 24）。门厅通向五个既相互沟通，又可灵活使用的多功能“容器式”展厅，它们可以独立使用，但不显得彼此孤立。遵循带状城市的规划理念，交通区环绕建筑布置，这样，同时举办的各种活动互不干扰，即便是几个展览同时布展或撤展，或者是几个区域同时向公众开放也是如此。

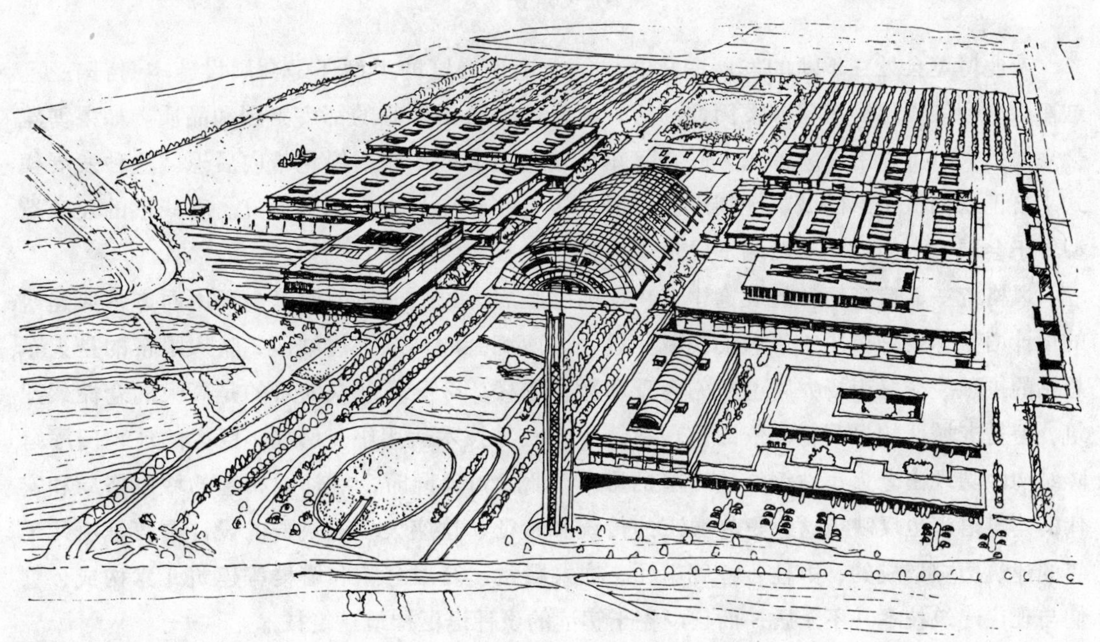

图 23　莱比锡博览会——会展公园平面（1996 年建成）

图 24　玻璃门厅内景

专业博览会处在不断的发展变化之中，无论是展览的类型还是会展设施本身都在变。这座大型会展设施的扩建方案简便易行，不会影响会展中心的都市氛围和品质。如果博览会规模扩大，可以沿着纵轴线方向在停车场建造更多的展馆，绿化带向后退。这种发展模式来自于双面梳子形的城市规划理念，避免留下在建项目未完工的痕迹。直线形的建筑造型便于会展中心向纵深和两侧发展。

风格统一，造型简朴的展览建筑在德国已经成为过去。新的博览会运用西方古典建筑的设计语言体现城市历史悠久的精髓。过去，博览会的观众穿过城区，映入眼帘的是火车总站的拱顶，交易市场大厅上空的穹顶和教堂塔楼。今天，观众面对的是高大的仓储式建筑，但是老城区的景观轮廓依旧体现在新建筑及其技术运用中。例如，巨大的玻璃门厅穹隆结构中隐现出老火车站钢结构穹隆的影子（图 25），同时，沿轴线布置的城市格局和宏伟的建筑语汇也反映了这座贸易城市的传统和特征，这座大型建筑群的设计语言是由几千年的建筑历史形成的，由柱、柱廊、厅、柱式殿堂、筒形穹隆和塔楼等建筑元素构成，它们与现代建筑技术并不矛盾，而且以益于解读的设计语汇构筑建筑技术。

图 25 巨大的玻璃门厅穹隆结构中隐现出老火车站钢结构穹隆的影子

新的莱比锡博览会还必须在与欧洲同行的竞争中建立自己的市场地位，这不是单靠经营几个固定的大型展会可以实现的，还必须经常举办小型专业展览和活动才能生存，这些活动可以同时进行，但互不干扰。例如，高层展厅正在举行拳击比赛，工会大会在会议中心进行，左右两侧的前厅分别在举办包装专业展会和印刷展会，后侧展厅在举办生态专业展会；晚上，玻璃大厅举办音乐会，柱廊厅上演时装秀。所有活动都可以在此进行，既可以举办像建筑展、汽车展或铁道展这样的大型设备展览，也可以将展厅改装成大教堂做礼拜或工会大会堂，一切都安排得恰到好处，为观众提供自然采光，为展品设计人工照明。

**3. 人文的博览会**

在 19 世纪那个技术飞跃发展的时代，博览会带给观众的是奇迹，今天，博览会的目的是搭建人文的舞台让观众去参与，让所有人融入其中，而不是用威严的富丽堂皇征服观众，让他们显得渺小而微不足道。所有与博览会相关的技术，所有用于产品展示和服务的智慧和技巧，都是为了强调人的经历和体验。

这个将城市设计与建筑设计融为一体的创作，其真实目的是将莱比锡博览会的标志 MM 从样品博览会（Mustermesse）演变成人文博览会（Menschliche Messe），让人的需求——而不是展品的需求——成为设计景观空间体验的重点。在这里，观众和参展商就是上帝，展品处于次要地位。每一个细节都经过了仔细考虑，方便观众。观众到达后不必急匆匆地穿过宽阔的停车场，而是像逛会展公园一样体验展览，绿荫、假山、水面、喷泉、露台、柱廊和穿插其间的幽径。通过增加展览区的展览密度，缩短轴线两侧展览项目之间的距离，使新展览中心成为展览空间紧凑，景观空间宽阔的会展公园。

展厅内，客商是设计关注的中心，而不是商品。例如，玻璃大厅中的冬季花园，东入口处的柱廊厅，会议中心的门厅，管理中心的带状玻璃内院，饭店及其所属的购物中心和露台，都布置在阳光下的绿色植物丛中，供游客享用，不受商业展览王国的干扰。设计不仅通过自然采光和绿化满足游客的精神需求，而且通过材料的选择满足他们潜意识中的需求。部分展览区，例如多功能厅和会议中心，在进行教堂活动和政党或工会大会时选用自然采光，在用作展厅时采用人工照明。设计精巧的桥梁、室外楼梯和扶手都采用质地和手感好的木材装饰。

新展馆设计的另一个独到之处是将主要功能区划分成地下与地面两层。就像是在火车站，不同的车次停在不同的站台，便于到达与衔接。地下层的功能只是作为抵达站，候车区，疏导与分流游客。地面层与机场地面平齐，只为展览提供服务，包括博览会的布展、展览与撤展。这种严格的功能区分的好处不只是为了创造环境，更重要的是方便运作。

莱比锡博览会的主题——人文的博览会——定位标准高，这个主题在建筑设计中得以充分体现，使博览会更加人性化。新的博览会中心将布置紧凑的展览区和可以满足各种大小活动同时进行的最大灵活性融入景观设计之中。

今天，“开拓更大的市场”成为莱比锡博览会的座右铭，它意味着定位准确的展览理念和一站式服务方式，为满足展商和观众的需求而量身订制。客户可以利用它的子公司和合作伙伴预定“一揽子”套餐式服务，从展览的主题创意到布展，从餐饮服务到旅行安排，直至展览目标的最终实现。

此外，莱比锡博览会还以多种方式拓展业务领域：进一步拓宽原有的品牌展览的主题内涵，开发新的主题展览，与此同时，发展会议业务。现在，莱比锡博览会的品牌展览涵盖汽车、图书、新媒体、建筑、遗产保护、环境、医药和消费品等多个主题。

莱比锡原有的“老”展览区已经成为一个观光点，基础设施齐全，适合发展“特色旅游”，为莱比锡未来的发展打下了良好基础。

# Chapter 8

## Leipzig World Fair Center——Human Trade Fair

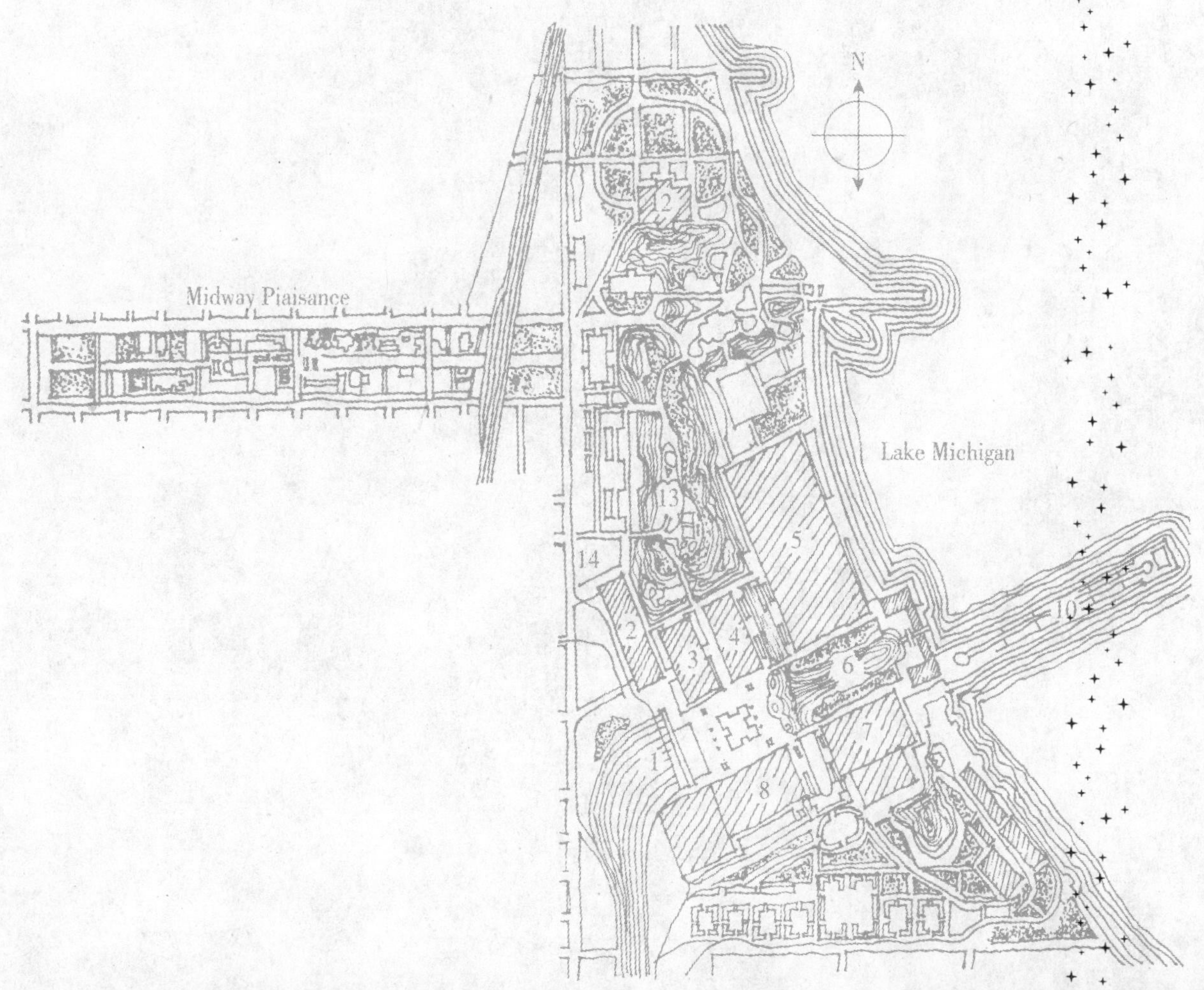

## Early History of Leipzig's Trade Fairs

Trade fairs have had their part in shaping cultural history. Leipzig is not one of those ancient cities built on Roman ruins. However, since the end of the Middle Ages, Leipzig has been an important traffic junction at the intersection of an ancient network of rutted mud-roads, linking the Southeast to the Northwest of the Roman Empire. It was the venue of three annual fairs. In 1507, Leipzig fairs were made imperial fairs, and any fairs in a 15 mile area around the town were banned, which further increased Leipzig's importance. The Leipzig Fair is one of the oldest in the world, and at the same time one of the youngest and most modern.

Around the year 1500, Leipzig's merchants and their builders developed the city's typical business building. As the city became more prosperous, brick construction became standard practice. The traditional one or two-story houses, with narrow plots of considerable depth, their gabled ends facing the streets, were remodeled by turning the buildings' longitudinal axes by 90 degrees, forming inner courtyards along the depth of the plot. Thus, the parallel building volumes with constant eaves levels formed accessible courtyard between them, creating the typical Leipzig 'gallery house' (Figure 22). The three annual goods fairs found their show spaces in these trade-courts and in the adjoining alleys and squares. This type of buildings connected one main street to another in a unified design. Two huge imposing street facades concealed inter-connected slabs of buildings and inner courtyards. During fairs, the ground floor spaces were mainly inter-connected exhibition and sales areas. All the various fair courts put together constitute a 'trade world continuum'. The city of Leipzig was only a big fair, and called 'the marketplace of all Europe'.

The courtyard alleyways intersecting the blocks of buildings are early examples of what, today, is known as 'semi-public spaces' and of what, in the late 18th and in the 19th century, was made into 'gallerias', shopping arcades. The typical city layout and gallery-type fair palace were mainly an outcome of the extraordinary development of the fairs held in Leipzig. 'Urbanity via density' —— one of the major demands for urban planning of the past thirty years——had already been achieved in 18th century Leipzig. But the cramped quarters, in the final resort, harmed the fairs.

### 1. Development of Sample Fairs

As early as the mid-18th century, the goods fairs began to change. English cloth merchants were the first to bring samples of their textiles, from which lengths of fabric could be ordered. Around the late 1870s, key trade sectors no longer offered goods for sale, but mainly kept stores of samples and prototypes of their products.

However, by 1892, visitors had dropped from 10000 to just under 4000, the end for the centuries old trade fair tradition seemed imminent. The reasons for this decline: the bad interior decoration and consequently poor presentation of goods in the sample depots; the steady increase in the amount of goods which led to the competition for the trade fairs from traveling salesmen on horseback showing only samples; accessibility of the sales exhibitions, which for lack of space had moved to the upper levels of the fair courts, was not achieved successfully, neither for customers, nor for transport of material.

In 1892, a trade fair committee was constituted. On its agenda: a general reform was carried out. Everything relevant was critically examined and re-considered, including the cultural events on offer to the fairs' visitors——who from now on were to be no longer intimidated by entrance fees. The old fair buildings were renovated and altered, and the new building structures were created for the new fair organization, the so-called 'sample depot business'. In 1895, the fair was made an official institution of the city, a significant step towards communal intervention in a previously purely private economy. The new type of fair was held in conjunction with the traditional three annual goods fairs, reserved for special goods. The other fair periods were generally re-organized more concisely and fixed anew.

These decisive, almost rigorous measures——a highly effectual achievement——laid the basis of what, with hindsight, was the greatest success in the long history of Leipzig's fairs, and this just in time to turn Leipzig into the most important trade fair internationally until 1914. Already in 1900, over 63000 visitors were registered for the Spring Fair, and numbers grew steadily until 1914.

### 2. The Second Leap

However, following World War I, when communes hit by the depression did their utmost to improve their economic power, a number of new 'sample fairs' established themselves across the Reich (empire) ——Frankfurt, Cologne, Breslau, Konigsberg and Berlin at the forefront, all trying to make their way in this promising business field. Apart from the Berlin Fair, competitors rather geared their shows to their own regions. Leipzig's headstart could not be matched. The new trend towards 'branded articles' rather gave Leipzig a further lead.

The re-development of Leipzig's inner city to make it fit for the new fair operations started in 1890s. It has become clear that the requirements of the fair had precedence over everything else in the old trade city so that the entire old town center had been sacrificed for the 'sample fair', this Leipzig invention. Public spaces like parks and promenade were created in secondary and peripheral locations. The city gathered all its monumental buildings around its Fair-held center——the new Civic Theatre, the new University building, the new huge Town Hall, the new Reichsbank building——in best locations amidst green areas on the double ring road. Here it was possible to landscape and plant the ring and at the same time to place important public buildings in its area without harming the city. Adding the tract of land of the ring to the city center meant that its area increased by 80 percent. And Leipzig got an impressive "external facade".

Trade fair facilities were designed in historic style, fashionable at the time. The inner city multiple-story office and trade centers almost exclusively served trade fairs. Stands were mostly hired. One thing that made the new type of edifice so different from the traditional trade building was that visitors were sent on an inevitable circular tour through the building, offering a complete overview of all available products. Essential to the presentation was a prime location in the inner city with easy access for visitors and deliveries, and a consistently good quality of exhibition spaces in cabins or open stands, which were now situated mostly on the upper floors with ample storage space in basements and attics. Modern vertical access by lifts and maximum flexibility in the use of floor space were designed. Modern technical services and installations, generous lighting and high-quality sanitary facilities became standard. So these highly functional buildings had necessarily to be erected with the latest RC technology, or steel frame construction, in order to fulfill the demand for maximum flexibility.

Although, for a long time, the city had been a huge industrial center, the unique, unequalled location of German printing and publishing industry: it had more than a thousand publishing houses, some of them very large, and over one thousand paper manufacturers, printers and so on. Only New York equaled Leipzig with its manufacturing. Apart from that there were machine-building factories, specialized in printing presses, but also other large industrial plants. However, the fair was a constituent part of the city's significance and reputation. The MM-symbol (Muster-Messe ——Sample Fair) of the fair was designed in 1917.

In spite of this colossal re-development and, above all, "compaction" of buildings, space in Leipzig's inner city became, once again, far too cramped. Consequently, Leipzig's break-through into the second modern trade fair era started.

In the autumn of 1918, when the first Technology and the first Building Trade Fairs were held and the products on show were no longer those relatively manageable prototypes of the consumer goods, but heavy machinery, weighing tons, large installations and materials, the buildings designed for goods fairs were no longer adequate. Ground-floor spaces in large halls, with railway links, were needed for the new exhibits. Consequently, a 225, 000 square meter tract of land was chosen next to the Battle of the Nations Monument, in the southeast of the town. Eventually dozens of halls were built, and the tract of land was extended to 400, 000 square meters. The site was now dedicated to Technology Fairs. The fact that it provided perfect conditions for railway links settled the choice of the new location. The attempt was made to connect fair with the city via a great axis.

During the war, about 80 percent of the Technology Fair was destroyed. After the war, the Technology Fair complex was rebuilt. Leipzig Fair was very important to the German Democratic Republic, since it presented the achievements of the fellow socialist countries.

## The Leipzig Fairs Today

After the political change in Germany in 1989, the political and economic position of Leipzig were radically changed. The city has been doubly damaged, not only is its fair faced with tough competition, but also it has to cope with the loss of its industry and compensate for that. Trade fair competition from the West became almost overwhelming. Every large West-German city now developed its own fair, without having to compete with the one in Leipzig that had formerly reached and attracted the whole nation. Of all German fairs, Hannover is the largest (with 475, 600 square meters of exhibition floor space in halls and a further external area of 227, 700 square meters; in 1995, it registered 2. 3 million visitors and 23000 exhibitors), then followed by Dusseldorf, Frankfurt, Munich, Berlin, Stuttgart, Cologne, Nuremberg, Hamburg and Dortmund. At last, comes Leipzig.

### 1. Fair as the Key Motor for an Economic Recovery

For Leipzig, with its inner city fallen into disuse and its ineffectual remains of industrial potential, the fair has to be the key 'motor' for an economic recovery. When compared to competitive trade fairs with state-of-the-art logistics, the fair in the city center creates such high operating costs that this location can now only be used for just a few image events and highly specialized shows linked to a direct urban situation. Again, a radical solution was required.

In spite of its difficult starting position, and in spite of the well-known fact that the expected so-called 'emergence of the East' did not happen, Leipzig had no other choice but to venture a totally new beginning in moving the fair to another location. So with its decision of June 1991, the Fair Corporation took the risky, but only possible route. In October of that year, the municipal council, with a 75 percent majority of votes, opted for the fair on the outskirts of Leipzig, against reactivating the inner city fair. It was well known that the old site was technically run down and a rejuvenation would have paralyzed normal business apart from being much too expensive. Given the situation of the Fair Corporation, to reject any idea of continuing at the location of the Technology Fair, and using the existing serviceable buildings finally was the right financial decision, though rather bold. Exactly the same decision had been taken by Dusseldorf and Munich before, which very successfully moved their exhibition facilities. It was also right to plan the new fair complex as a unified large landscaped urban development, instead of creating a conglomerate of different exhibition facilities.

Nevertheless, moving the exhibition complex to the periphery of Leipzig is disputable. Is the Fair too far away from the inner city? Is it still the "Leipzig Fair", or is it just any fair facility that happens to be in an easily accessible, prime location in the middle of Germany? Does a fair not need the urban environment? Can the new Leipzig Fair manage without the lively and traditional old town?

Public events, especially the nature of a fair, always have something to do with traffic. Exhibitions are markets and markets best operate where trade routes for goods and people cross. Already in the Middle Ages, Leipzig's location at the intersection of two ancient roads was a constituent element of its large fairs, reaching out to the German speaking areas and beyond. During the $19^{th}$ century, the city became one of the main junctions of European railway traffic. At that time, Leipzig had a kind of 'composite station' made up of three stations well-placed at the north edge of the city where, in 1915, the world-famous 'palace' of a railway terminal was erected. All railway lines were interconnected which meant that the city was served by the most modern means of transport of the time in the best possible way. This essentially contributed to the economic progress in just under half a century.

These means of access would hardly stand the test of today's requirements. Goods and the way they are handled have changed since the industrial age and roads have moved. Sales fairs for consumer goods have become sample markets, and today they are information markets using modern information and data technologies. Transport interruptions on the way, i. e. transferring goods from one mode of transport to another, are no longer economically viable, except for the transfer from aeroplanes to road vehicles. It's clear that the trade fair has to be at the junction between airport, railway, motorway and major road to be best suited to transportation.

## 2. Creating An Exhibition Park

However, the competition winners found no special valuable land to build on, rather a spread-out chaos, rubbish, industrial waste and the leftovers of an abandoned airport——7 km away from the inner city, a rather boring flat landscape. A completely new atmosphere for a new location had to be created. Excavating the ground to a depth of five meters below level, a 150 meter-wide depression in the landscape was made, which gently slopes down towards the east. A kind of shallow valley with water and vegetation has been dug into the trapezium-shaped fair site, which developed into an exhibition park in its real sense (Figure 23). The mighty central entrance hall (80 meters wide, with a height at the apex of 30 meters and a length of 243 meters), stretched along the middle axis of the 'artificial valley', is a glazed artificial landscape full of trees and inbuilt elements that divide up the space in symmetrical fashion (Figure 24). It provides access to five flexibly, variably useable 'container' halls which are interconnected, but can also be used separately for various activities, without appearing to be isolated. In line with the band city concept, traffic zones surround the building islands in such a way that separately staged events do not disturb each other, even when there are several exhibitions mounted or taken down simultaneously or individual areas are open to the public.

What's more, a trade fair is in permanent transition, both for the type of exhibition and also the way the complex itself develops. However, the easy expandability of this large complex does not and will not hamper the urban quality of the fair. If the trade fair grows, halls are erected on the parking area in the longitudinal direction and the trees replanted at the back. This growth pattern in the urban planning concept of a double-sided comb avoids the appearance of unfinished building phases. This is accomplished with a clear linear building shape which caters for the growth in length and width.

Uniformity and simple appearance of exhibition areas in Germany are a thing of the past. The classical design language of western architecture is employed to reflect the old genius of the city. Previously fair visitors crossed an urban landscape, with the vaults of the main station, the domes of the great market hall and tower-like church. Today the fair visitors are confronted with the high warehouse, but the silhouette of the old urban landscape is visible in the new architecture and technology. The steal vaulting of the old main station is discovered again in the vaulting of the large glass entrance hall (Figure 25). At the same time, the axial urban grid of the complex and monumental language also reflect the tradition and the identity of this trading city. The design language of the large-scale architecture is shaped by the thousands of years building history with columns, colonnades, halls, pillared temples, barrel vaults, and towers, which do not stand in dispute with modern building technology, but are rather helpful to structure this with understandable design terms.

The New Leipzig Fair has still to establish its market position amongst its European competitors. This is not achieved with a few seldom large trade fairs, but better through frequent, small specialist events, which take place parallel but separated from another. For instance, a boxing match is being held in the high hall, a union meeting in the congress center, in the front hall to the right is the packaging trade fair, to the left the printing fair, in the back hall an ecology exhibition on various specialist topics, in the glass hall at night a concert, and in the colonnaded hall a fashion show. Everything is possible from the building/car/rail fair to the large church/trade union congress, being correctly accommodated having daylight where necessary for longer occupation by visitors and artificial illumination for exhibition goods.

### 3. Human Fair

In the 19th century, the time of triumphant technological progress, the public was to be confronted with miracles. Today, the aim is participation of visitors on a stage set for humanity, not subjugating and making people small by all its awe-inspiring grandeur, but including everybody. With all its fair-related technology, all the intelligent thought and techniques gone into goods presentations and services, human encounters and human experiences are at the forefront.

The real intention in this urban-architectural new creation is to transform the exhibition symbol 'MM' from a sample fair —— Mustermesse——to a human fair——Menschliche Messe, by relating the requirements of people and not the requirements of products to the center of the spatial experience along the landscaped recess. Here the visitor/exhibitor is king, the product is secondary. Every detail is carefully considered to make things easier for the visitor. He does not have to fight his way through the expanses of car parking on arrival, but experiences the exhibition recess as an exhibition park. Trees, hills, water, fountains, terraces and colonnades skirt the path. As the density of exhibition area is increased into a compact display and events area having short distances on both sides of the artificial landscape, the new trade fair is developed into a spacious parkland with a compact fair.

Inside the rooms of the exhibition, the customer, not the commodity is at the focus. For instance, the winter garden of the glass hall, the colonnaded hall of the east entrance, the atrium of the congress center, the glazed long inner court of the administration center, the restaurants with emporia and terraces, they all lie in sunshine and in greenery for the occupation by visitors and remain free from the commercial world of the exhibitor. The design not only fulfills the psychic requirements of the visitor by natural lighting and vegetation, but also the subconscious demands by the materials it uses. Natural lighting is used in some exhibition areas, such as multi-purpose hall or congress halls, but they can be darkened for shows of goods with artificial light when they are not in use for long sessions containing audiences such as church gatherings, political party congress or trade union meetings. The coverings of the delicate bridges and open stairways and the hand rails are in wood which are pleasing to touch by hand and foot.

One of the specialties of the design was the division of the main functions into two levels. As in a major railway station different trains on different platforms can be easily reached and linked. The lower level section serves only the arrival, the orientation and distribution of the visitor and acts as a waiting area. The upper level at the height of the existing airport site provides only the exhibition services for the trade fair assembly, for the presentation of commodities and for the disassembly. The particular advantage of this strict division of services into two levels is not just atmospheric but also most importantly operational.

The theme——MM, the 'human trade fair' ——demands a high standard, which is reflected in the architectural conception, and contributes to make the fair more human. The design is a synthesis of landscaping, the compactness of the exhibitions and maximum flexibility between large, small and simultaneous events.

Today, the motto of Leipzig Fair is "More Market". This means tailor-made trade fair concepts, precisely devised to meet the needs of exhibitors and visitors, together with an all-in single-source service approach. The customer can use subsidiary and partner companies to book an "all-inclusive" package - from concept to stand installation, catering and travel services and realization at the fair.

The Leipzig Fair expands its business in various ways: well-established themes are broadened, new fairs are developed, and parallel to that, conference business is also encouraged. Successful themes in Leipzig include cars and transport, books and new media, building and heritage conservation, environment, medicine and consumer goods.

The so-called 'old' fair area constitutes a welcome site, suitable for "specialty tourism", with infrastructure already installed for Leipzig's future urban development.

# 第九章

## 1999 年昆明世界园艺博览会

1999 年昆明世界园艺博览会从 5 月 1 日开始，10 月 31 日结束，历时 184 天，是中国政府举办的第一届集国际园艺展览、贸易与技术交流，环境保护专题研讨、艺术表演和生态旅游为一体的世界博览会。

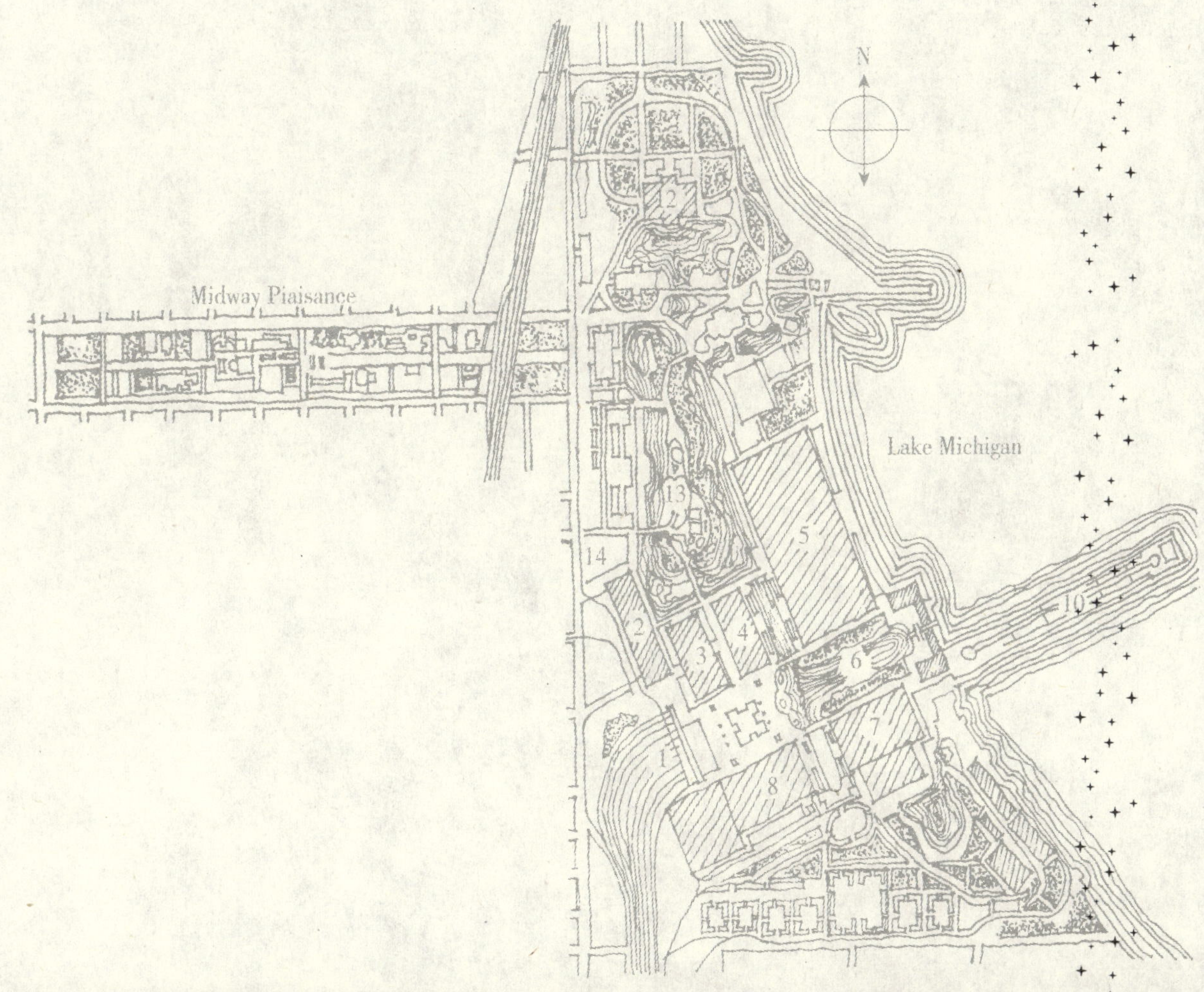

## 背景

自20世纪80年代起，中国国际贸易促进委员会代表国家参加了八届国际博览会，均大获成功，但是，中国当时还不是国际展览局的成员国，国际展览局热切期望接纳中国为国际展览局的正式成员国。1992年9月，双方就中国加入国际展览局，北京在20世纪举办一届国际博览会，以及双方的进一步合作等议题展开了讨论。1993年5月27日，国际展览局接受了中国政府提交的正式申请，中国成为国际展览局的第46个成员国。1994年10月，第46届国际园艺生产者协会大会决定接受中国为正式成员国。同年，中国在1999年举办世界园艺博览会的申请得到国际展览局的批准。

云南具有多样性的气候条件和地形特征，拥有2500多个园艺种类，是中国乃至世界主要的植物基因库之一。“春城”昆明气候宜人，一年四季繁花似锦，独特的自然条件使其成为举办园艺博览会的理想之地。

本届世博会是20世纪的最后一届世博会，以“人与自然：迈向21世纪”为主题，目的是唤起人们在优先考虑自身发展的同时，对21世纪的环境保护和可持续发展问题的思考与关注，这也是中国政府正在为之奋斗的目标。

## 世界园艺大荟萃

世博园位于距昆明市区6公里外的金殿风景区，它不仅是一座具有典型的中国风格和云南地方特色的超大型园林，而且是一场世界级的园艺盛宴。世博园海拔1920~2010米，占地面积218公顷，长2.5公里，宽1.1公里。规划充分利用台地地形，采用组团式布局，功能性建筑相对集中，强调展馆、园林与自然山势、森林和水面景观的和谐与融合，表现了中国造园艺术“源于自然，回归自然”的原则（图26）。

根据世博组委会的创意，以“人与自然”为核心，世博会的主要展览包括：

历史悠久的园林园艺技术，与此相关的成果及其设施；

体现参展国家传统文化与现代文明相结合的庭院建筑；

人类在保护自然环境和保持生态平衡方面取得的成就；

表现各参展国家园林艺术与文化发展密不可分的历史，园艺在人文社会生活中的重要作用；

通过展示人类的科学技术成就表现经济环境与自然环境的完美融合；

举办与世博会相关的经贸大会，促进参展国之间的合作，为园艺产品和先进技术提供市场；

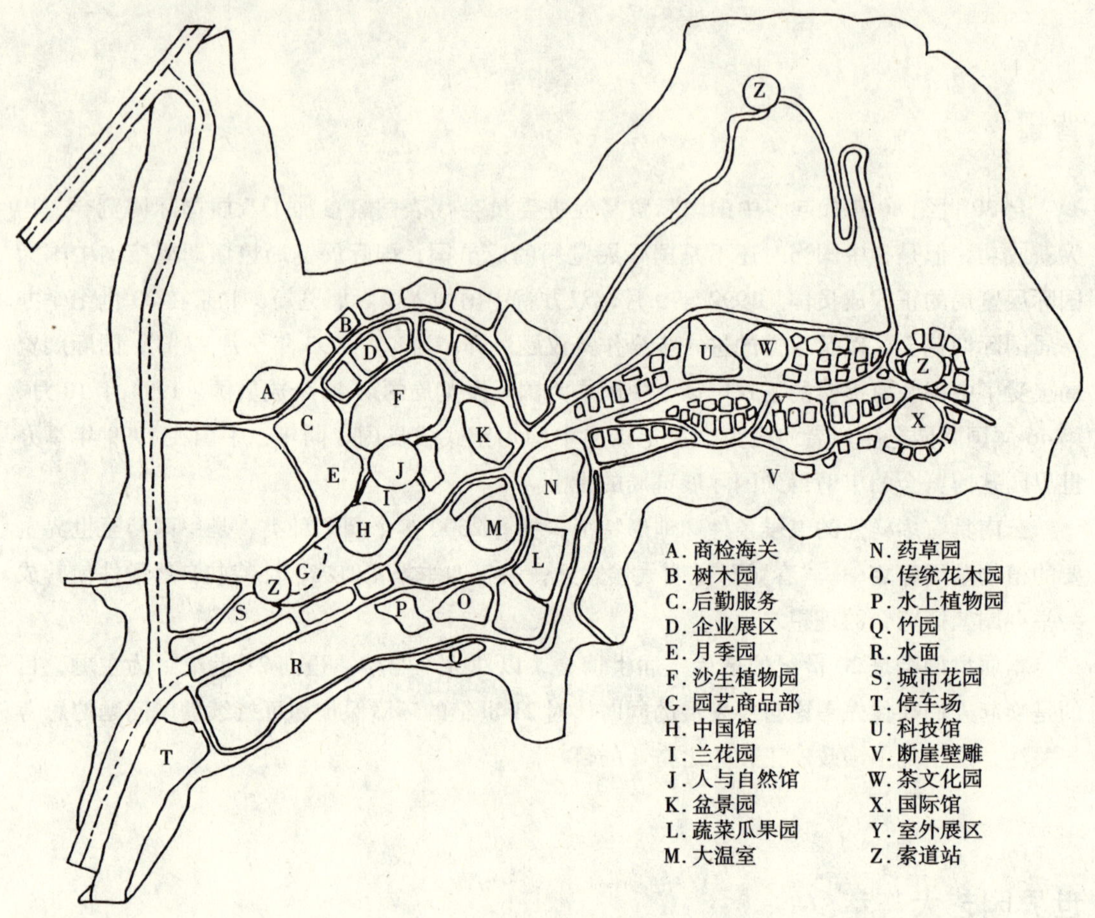


图 26　云南昆明世博园规划

主办各类学术交流活动和专题展览，在园林园艺技术在自然环境保护领域的应用方面，促进各国的相互交流和共同发展。

世博组委会的这些创意完美地体现在世博园的规划布局和艺术化的布置安排之中。世博园主要包括五个室内展区（中国馆、人与自然馆、大温室、科技馆、国际馆），六个专题展区（竹园、果蔬园、草药园、盆景园、树木园、茶园），三个室外展区（中国园区、国际园区、企业园区）和一些公共服务设施。其中，室外展区是世博园展区面积最大，内容最丰富最精彩的园区。

中国园区由 34 座展园构成，主要展示了中国各省、自治区、直辖市以及香港、澳门和台湾地区的自然与人文景观和园艺技术与成就。这里汇集了中国南北各地经典的传统园林，历史悠久，风格迥异，此外，建筑、雕塑、水景（喷泉、水池、小溪、瀑布）和其他小品被用于刻画各省区的自然特征与传统。因此，中国园区被誉为中国园林园艺的“大观园”。

云南“彩云园”位于中国园区的入口处，设计采用开放型的广场形式，环绕一尊巨型铜制孔雀雕塑展开，布置在花园后方两侧的两颗雪松创造出一种围合独立的空间效果。“彩云园”的动人之处在于其波浪形布置的各色花卉所创造的明亮鲜艳和色彩斑斓的景致。

山东“齐鲁园”包含了中国第一山——泰山，第一泉——趵突泉和“至圣先师”——孔子，这种“一山一水一圣人”的展示完美地诠释了人与自然的主题，反映了那里的文化底蕴和独特的园艺风格。

在国际展区，34 个国家和国际组织分别建造了各自的永久性室外展园，展示先进的园艺园林技术，体现各自的文化特征。

作为国际一流的园艺园林精品展示，世博园蕴含了相当的科技含量，通过林木、花卉、园林、园艺、技术和文化展示，体现了人与自然和平共处，和谐发展之美。为了强化世博园的装饰效果与和谐氛围，世博园又增添了许多景观，例如，740 米长的花园大道上布置了“花钟”，“花船”、“花柱”、“花溪”、“花开新世纪”等花雕。其他艺术创作，如主题雕塑、摩崖石刻、水坝等也独具匠心。从这些精致的未来城市景观和园林作品中，景观设计师和城市规划师可以获得灵感，得到启迪。此外，世博园还举办了园艺比赛，旨在提高公众的参与意识，促进园艺事业的发展。

世博会期间，约 940 多万游客参观了世博园，达到了吸引 800 ~ 1000 万游客的目标。95 个国家和国际组织参与了本届世博会——创造了世界园艺博览会的纪录。

1999 年世界园艺博览会为昆明留下了一座世界级的永久性大型园林，如此规模和品质的世博会有助于打造云南省的整体形象，进一步促进开放，实施可持续发展战略，发展支柱产业，刺激省内经济发展，改善城市基础设施，提高社会道德。

## Chapter 9

# The Horti-Expo Kunming 1999

The '99 Kunming World Horticulture Exposition scheduled to run for 184 days from May 1 to October 31 is the only one the Chinese government has ever hosted that features an international horticultural exhibition, trade and technology exchanges, academic seminars on environmental protection, art performances and an eco-tourism program.

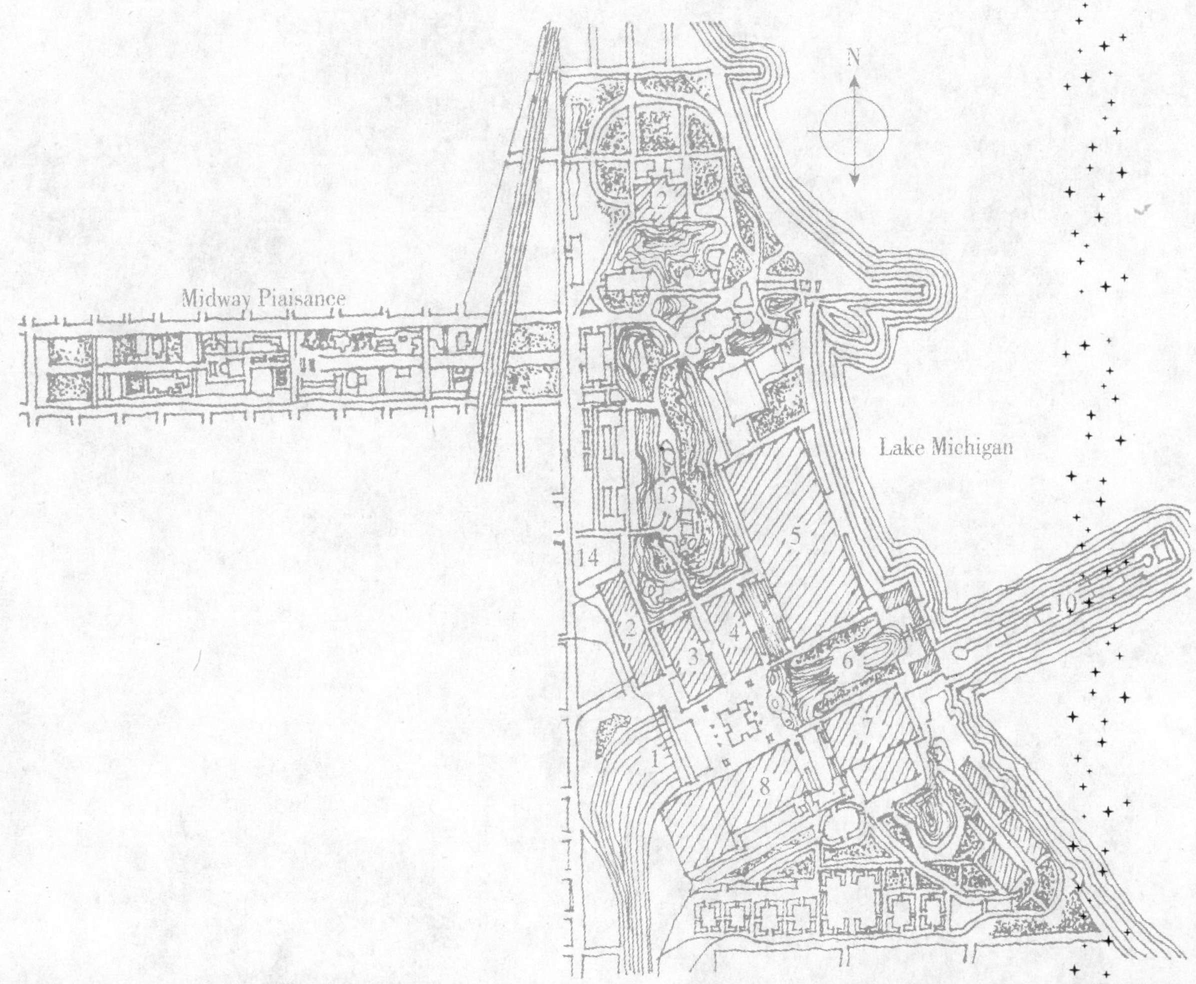

## Background

Since the 1980s, China Council for the Promotion of International Trade (CCPIT), in the name of the state, has taken part in 8 international expositions and won out every time. But China was not a state member of BIE then and BIE earnestly hoped to accept China as its formal state member. In September 1992, the two parties had a discussion with regard to such issues as China's joining the BIE; Beijing's holding an expo within the 20th century, and cooperation between the two parties. On May 27 1993, the BIE confirmed that China had been accepted as the 46th formal state member of the BIE after China submitted the official statement. At the 46th members' conference of the AIPH (the Association of International Horticultural Producers) in October 1994, a resolution was made that China was accepted as a member of the AIPH. In the same year, the application that China would hold an international horticultural exposition in 1999 was ratified by the BIE.

With highly diversified climate and topography, Yunnan Province is home to more than 2500 horticultural species, and is one of the major botanical gene banks for China and the world. Known as "City of Eternal Spring" with agreeable climate and blossoming flowers all the year round, Kunming is richly endowed with unique natural conditions for holding the horticultural exposition.

The exposition is the last of its kind in the 20th century, which centers round the theme of "Man and Nature: Marching into the 21st Century". The exposition aims at appealing for attention to be given to environment protection and for efforts to be made for sustainable development in the next century when man is giving priority to development, which is also an objective the Chinese government is striving for.

## A Grand World Exhibition of Horticulture

The exposition site is located in the "Golden Temple Scenic Area", 6 km away from the downtown of Kunming. It is a first class garden with typical Chinese and Yunnan characteristics, and a grand exhibition of horticulture from everywhere in the world as well. It sits at an elevation of 1920—2010 meters above sea level, with 218 hectares in area, 2. 5 km in length, and 1, 1 km in width. Taking advantage of the terracing topography, the planning adopts clustered pattern, with relative concentration of functional structures, emphasizing the harmonious integration of pavilions and gardens with the natural environment of mountain, forests and lakes, reflecting the principle of Chinese gardening "originating from nature and returning to nature" (Figure 26).

According to the Organizing Committee of the Expo, on the theme of "Man and Nature", the main exhibits are:

Long-standing gardening and horticultural techniques and achievements as well as relevant facilities;

Courtyard architecture integrating the traditional culture and modern civilization of participating countries;

Achievements portraying human's efforts to protect the natural environment and maintain ecological balance;

History indicating the inseparable relations between horticultural arts and cultural development of respective nations, and the important role of horticulture in social life of humanity.

To portray the perfect integration of the economic and natural environment by displaying the achievements yielded in the scientific and technological development of the mankind;

To convene economic and trade conferences related to the Expo so as to promote cooperation among participating countries and offer markets for horticultural products and advanced horticultural technology;

To sponsor conferences for all kinds of academic exchanges and specialized exhibitions to promote exchanges and mutual development of gardening and horticultural art technologies used in natural environmental protection in different countries.

The conception developed by the Organizing Committee of the Expo is presented in the layout and esthetic arrangement of the Expo Garden. The Expo Garden mainly consists of five Indoor Exhibition Areas (China Hall, Man and Nature Hall, Large Green House, Science and Technology Hall and The International Hall), six Theme Exhibition Areas (the Bamboo Garden, the Vegetable and Fruit Garden, the Herbal Plants Garden, the Potted Landscape Garden, the Tree Garden and the Tea Garden) and three Outdoor Exhibition Areas (The National / Chinese Exposition Area, The International Exposition Area and The Exposition Area for Enterprises), as well as some public service facilities. The Outdoor Exhibition Areas occupy the largest exhibiting area, with the largest collection of exhibits and overwhelming beauty.

The National Exposition Area, comprising of 34 domestic gardens, mainly showcases the natural landscape and cultural scenic spots as well as scientific and technical achievements and techniques in horticulture in all the Chinese provinces, municipalities directly under the Central Government and regions including Hong Kong, Macao and Taiwan. It is a distinguished gathering of Chinese traditional gardening from the south to north, with long-standing history, distinct features and different styles scored in China. In addition, architecture, sculptures, water displays (fountains, ponds, streams, waterfalls) and other items are used to describe each province's natural character and heritage. Therefore, the National Exposition Area is complimented as a "Grand View Garden" of Chinese gardening and horticulture.

The "Caiyun Garden" of Yunnan Province, located at the entrance of the Zone, is conceived as an open plaza, built around a large bronze statue of a peacock. The two large cedar trees at the back corners of the garden create a sense of enclosure and independence. The most impressive of the garden is a myriad of flowers, planted in a wavy pattern, giving this garden a bright, colorful feature.

The "Qilu Garden" of Shandong Province includes a representation of the first mountain in China——the Taishan Mountain, the first spring——the Baotuquan Spring, and the great Saint——Confucius. This "one mountain, one spring, one saint" display best interprets the theme of man and nature, reflecting the connotation of culture and the unique horticultural style there.

In the International Exposition Area, there are permanent outdoor gardens built by 34 countries and international organizations respectively, reflecting the advanced horticultural and gardening technology of those countries and their cultural features.

As a display area of the world top-class horticultural and gardening masterpieces, the Expo Garden boasts the considerable technical and scientific elements, which embody overwhelming beauty of peaceful co-existence and harmonious development of man and nature, with its trees, flowers, gardens, horticulture, technology and culture display. To improve the ornamental function of the Expo Garden and the harmony in it, a lot of scenery has been added in the Garden, for example, the 740m-long Flowery Boulevard consisting of such flower statues as "Flower Clock", "Flower Boat", "Flower Pillar", "Flower Creek" and "Flowery Bloom in New Century". Other esthetic creations such as theme-oriented sculptures, cliff carve, dam are unique in their design. Landscapers and city planners may have great inspiration and ideas from this fine prospect in future city and garden works. In addition, competitions have been organized aiming to mobilize the public participation and promote the horticultural development.

In the course of the Expo, more than 9.4 million Chinese and foreigners visited the Garden, successfully fulfilling the goal of 8 million to 10 million tourists. 95 countries and international organizations have participated in the exposition——a record for this kind of world exposition.

The '99 World Horticulture Exposition has left Kunming a huge world class garden meant to be permanent. An exposition of this quality and size has helped build up its image and facilitate further opening-up of Yunnan province. It is conductive to implementing the sustainable development strategy, fostering pillar industries, propelling provincial economy, improving city infrastructure, and upgrading social moral.

# 参考文献/Reference

[1] Hermione Hobhouse. The Crystal Palace and the Great Exhibition [M]. New York: Athlone Press, 2002.

[2] Stanley Appelbaum. The Chicago World's Fair Of 1893 [M]. New York: Dover Publications, Inc, 1980.

[3] History of Columbian Exposition, The Exposition in American Culture [EB/OL]. The Free Dictionary. Com.

[4] John E. Findling. Chicago's Great World's Fairs [M]. Manchester and New York: Manchester University Press, 1994.

[5] The World Of Tomorrow, The 1939 New York World's Fair [M]. New York: Harper & Row, Publishers.

[6] Richard Warts and Stanley Appelbaum. New York's 1939—1940 World's Fair [M]. Original Dover (1977) Publication.

[7] Remembering The Future, The New York World's Fair From 1939 to 1964 [M]. New York: Rizzoli, 1989.

[8] Robert W. Rydell. Fair America: World's Fairs in the United States [M]. Smithsonian Institution Press, 2000.

[9] Bill Cotter. The 1964—1965 New York World's Fair (Images of America) [M]. Arcadia Publishing, 2004.

[10] Exploring America's Space Age World's Fair [EB/OL]. nywf 64. com.

[11] 1964 New York World's Fair [EB/OL]. The Free Dictionary. Com.

[12] Showcasing Technology of the 1964—1965 New York World's Fair [EB/OL]. westland. net. November 11, 2006.

[13] The Hannover Principles: Design for Sustainability [M]. William McDonough & Partners, 410 East Water Street, Charlottesville VA 22902.

[14] Evaluation of Canada's Participation in Expo 2000 in Hannover. Germany [EB/OL], Corporate Review Branch, 2003. 3. 24, Canadian Heritage.

[15] EXPO 2000 Hannover GmbH. Architecture Hannover [M]. //汉诺威建筑艺术展. 陈潇潇，葛诗利译. 大连理工大学出版社，2004.

[16] Theme Park Debacle [EB/OL]. Time Europe, August 28, 2000, Vol. 156, No. 9.

[17] Kristina Malsberger. A Fair to Remember [EB/OL]. VIA AAA Traveler's Companion, May/June 2007.

[18] Hannover Set for "Biggest World's Fair" [EB/OL]. CNN. com. Travelguide News.

[19] Volkwin Marq. Hallen/Expo Halls 8 +9: Expo 2000 Hannover Gmbh [M]. Prestel Pub, Germany, 2000.

[20] Leipzig Messe More Market! [EB/OL]. leipziger-messe. de.

[21] 江三戈，吴采薇. 世界园艺博览园景观规划设计 [M]. 北京：中国建筑工业出版社，2002.

[22] The Organizing Committee of 1999 Kunming International Horticultural Exposition. A Brief Introduction to 1999 Kunming International Horticultural Exposition China [EB/OL].

[23] 丁衡祁，李欣，白静. 会展英语 [M]. 北京：对外经济贸易大学出版社，2006.

[24] BIE-Paris [EB/OL] . org.